KITCHEN HERBS

KITCHEN HERBS

*The Art and Enjoyment of Growing Herbs
and Cooking with Them*

SAL GILBERTIE

PHOTOGRAPHS BY JOSEPH KUGIELSKY

CULINARY TEXT AND RECIPES BY
FRANCES TOWNER GIEDT

BANTAM BOOKS
TORONTO · NEW YORK · LONDON · SYDNEY · AUCKLAND

For Marie

KITCHEN HERBS
A Bantam Book / May 1988

All rights reserved.
Copyright © 1988 by Sal Gilbertie.
Photographs copyright © 1988 by Joseph Kugielsky.
Illustrations by Lauren Jarrett.

Book design by Barbara N. Cohen and Debby Jay.

Library of Congress Cataloging-in-Publication Data

Gilbertie, Sal.
  Kitchen herbs.

  Includes index.
  1. Cookery (Herbs) 2. Herb gardening. I. Giedt,
Frances Towner. II. Title.
TX819.H4G55 1988   641.6'57   87-47911
ISBN 0-553-05265-9

Published simultaneously in the United States and Canada

Bantam Books are published by Bantam Books, a division of Bantam Doubleday Dell Publishing Group, Inc. Its trademark, consisting of the words "Bantam Books" and the portrayal of a rooster, is Registered in U.S. Patent and Trademark Office and in other countries. Marca Registrada. Bantam Books, 666 Fifth Avenue, New York, New York 10103.

PRINTED IN THE UNITED STATES OF AMERICA

KP 0 9 8 7 6 5

ACKNOWLEDGMENTS

Producing a book of this kind is like creating an herb farm. It is the product of many hands. If you are as lucky as I am, you surround yourself with a lot of talented people, and through all the sweat and shared frustration you finally reap the joys of a job well done.

My thanks to:

Fran Giedt, for originally approaching me with the concept for this book, and for the delicious recipes that she developed and styled for these pages.

Joseph Kugielsky, for his professionalism and creativity, and his near-saintly patience and charming personality, which carried us through many long and difficult photo sessions.

The fine people at Bantam, particularly my editor, Coleen O'Shea, who offered me the chance to do the book, and who stuck by us with encouraging words throughout the project; Becky Cabaza, Coleen's assistant, who pulled all the details together for us with friendly and unflagging patience; and Fran McCullough, who guided us with her diligent attention to detail and always with a pleasant and charming manner.

Dawn Totora, my delightful and beautiful daughter-in-law, whose discerning eye and artistic talent helped us in so many photo sessions, and whose car transported bushels of fresh herbs to the many shootings.

The entire staff at Gilbertie's Herb Gardens, who held the fort while I was out working on the book. Special thanks go to Nancy Cook, for keeping the greenhouses going and growing, as well as for her research on the histories and proper Latin botanicals of the herbs featured in this book; Laura Szeligowski, for keeping the office running and the orders rolling; my son, Tom, for overseeing the work at the farm during the dog days of summer; my mother, "Nana," for keeping our gardens looking so beautiful, often working in them from sunrise to sunset; and my daughter Celeste, for typing from my awful handwriting and for gently nudging me to keep writing whenever I wanted to quit.

Bob Weiss, my dear friend who has helped me to value the really important things in life, and who was always there for encouragement and support.

Larry Sheehan, whose writing talent always finds a way to make my words sound good, for the unselfish gift of his time and support, and most of all, for his warm friendship.

Thank you, Lord, for making my life so full.

CONTENTS

INTRODUCTION

My family has been involved in gardening, both personally and professionally, for three generations.

My grandfather, Antonio Gilbertie, worked for a commercial grower in Fairfield County, Connecticut, for some thirty years, when, at the age of 56, he built a range of greenhouses and went into business on his own. Subsequently my father, Sal, and two uncles, Ed and Tony, joined him, and eventually expanded the business with greenhouse ranges in both Norwalk and Westport.

In the 1930s, there was a tremendous market for cut flowers in New York City, and basically my grandfather grew just about anything that could be cut, bunched, and shipped and sold into that market. Principally he grew pansies, chrysanthemums, carnations, and the most popular bulb flowers such as daffodils, tulips, and irises. He pioneered with some species, for example forcing wedgewood irises for delivery in the winter months. He also grew flowers that were considered unusual in florist shops in those days, among them anemones, ranunculases, freesia, calendula, sweet peas, and dianthus.

During World War II, virtually every family with a back yard (or front yard) of any size grew a victory garden, and the Gilbertie greenhouses began raising vegetable seedlings to meet this new demand. Garden centers as we know them today did not exist and it was to the greenhouses that people turned for their tomato and pepper seedlings and their flats of lettuces and other crops. The gardens were an expression of patriotism and also a very practical solution to at least some of the scarcities experienced in American households in the war years.

After the war, the demand for vegetable plants continued but the bottom dropped out of the flower market as far as growers in the Northeast were concerned. The advent of commercial aviation made it possible for Southern growers to reach the New York metropolitan market with cut flowers at cut-rate prices, labor and fuel costs being much lower in the South. Air freight put many commercial growers in our area out of business.

The Gilberties survived by diversifying. My father tapped a brand-new market when he began growing potted plant crops for the major holidays of the year: poinsettias for Christmas, lilies, tulips, daffodils, and hyacinths for Easter, and azaleas, cinerarias, and calceolarias for Mother's Day. He also grew bedding plants such as geraniums, petunias, fuchsia, and lantana for which there was a huge market with the new homeowners of the postwar building boom, all of whom had new yards and gardens to be planted and landscaped.

Our family had always grown herbs in our own gardens for use in the kitchen, with a distinct partiality for Italian favorites like basil and oregano. But we had never considered raising herbs to sell to the public. Then one day, early in the 1950s, my father received a special order for plants from the superintendent of one of the many great estates located in the county. It was common for these private grounds superintendents to stop by a greenhouse in the fall and place an order for the plants that would be needed for the following spring. Over the winter the grower would take the necessary steps, whether starting the desired plants from seed or bulb, or propagating them from cuttings or root division, to fill the order.

In any case, this superintendent came by and showed my father the plans he had drawn for a large formal culinary herb garden on the estate. It was circular, about sixty feet in diameter, and divided into twelve pielike wedges. The wedges would be separated by small brick walkways leading to a central urn designed to contain a bay tree. To fill this garden, the superintendent figured he needed sixty plants each of twelve culinary herbs including rosemary, thyme, oregano, tarragon, marjoram, chives, and sage.

That winter, to be on the safe side, my father planted a hundred pots of each variety. He had excellent results. In fact, after he delivered the order to the estate in April, there were still hundreds of young, healthy herb plants left over. So he set them out for sale in front of one of the greenhouses, under a small hand-lettered sign: HERBS FOR SALE, 3 for $1.00.

When the plants sold out, practically overnight, a light went on in my father's head, and he turned to me and said,

"Quick, Sal, learn about herbs!"

At this time I was fresh out of college and full of enthusiasm and ambition. In the weeks to come, I gathered and read over fifty books about herbs. My father had sensed a new market and wanted to explore it. He certainly knew how to grow the more common varieties of herbs, backed up by his extensive experience in growing dozens of other types of flowers and plants, but he wanted us to be familiar with all the techniques and procedures that might come in handy if we made a serious commitment to growing herbs commercially.

Thus my herbal education began. I was impressed to discover the tremendous variety of herbs and the myriad uses to which they have been put in every culture, seemingly, since time immemorial. I was fascinated by the rich lore and legend associated with herbal plants. I was beguiled by the mystique surrounding herbs and herbalists generally.

But there was one major disappointment in my six-month-long research project. I found little valuable practical information for actually growing the herbs. There was no hands-on information to advise gardeners on such critical matters as soil condition, irrigation, propagation techniques, season-by-season care, harvesting methods, and long-term maintenance of the herb garden.

Even the Department of Agriculture, through its Cooperative Extension Service, had little solid information on growing herbs at the time. And so I learned on my own. It was extremely slow going in the beginning. Reliable sources of seeds and cuttings were hard to find, and there was confusion

KITCHEN HERBS

4

among growers about the best way to gather, store, package, and ship seed. It was even difficult to get the correct identification for many plants.

Slowly but surely I sorted out fact from fancy and began to get better results in propagating herbs both indoors and out. By a lucky coincidence, one of my customers turned out to be president of the Herb Society of America. She was Mrs. Percy Cashmore and lived in nearby Weston, Connecticut. Her personal knowledge of herbs was a great help to me, and through all her contacts in the Herb Society, I also built up a network of reliable sources of information on herb culture. Our herb business started to grow.

In 1969 we suffered what I thought at the time was a major setback. As it turned out, the event provided me with an invaluable crash course in mass production and marketing techniques that our business is still benefiting from today. That year Simon and Garfunkel's hit recording, "Scarborough Fair," with its lyrics, "parsley, sage, rosemary, and thyme . . ." had put

kitchen herbs in the hearts and minds of most Americans. Coincidentally, the Great Danbury State Fair was celebrating its 100th anniversary that summer, at a site about 20 miles north of us in Connecticut. I decided the time had come to introduce our herbs to the public in a big way.

I prepared by raising 70,000 individual plants of parsley, sage, rosemary, and thyme in our greenhouses. When the week of the fair arrived, I took a large booth in the middle of the main tent. I hired a welder to build a special rack that would hold 3,500 plants. I hired two other men to drive between our greenhouses in Westport and the fair site twice a day, in order to replenish the rack, for I was counting on selling a minimum of 7,000 plants a day.

Well, 710,000 fairgoers passed by our booth that week, and many stopped to smell and admire the herbs, but we sold a grand total of 412 plants. I had made one major miscalculation: people carrying cotton candy, cups of beer, babies, and balloons don't have free hands for herb plants.

On the positive side, in preparing for this debacle I had learned methods for growing healthy herb plants in large quantities. This allowed me to greatly expand my wholesale business in subsequent years and to serve wholesale customers better. Also, in anticipation that the general public would have problems identifying herbs correctly, I developed a system (which I eventually trademarked) of printed labels that show both the Latin botanical and common names for each herb and also give growing and usage instructions. This allowed me to reach my retail customers more effectively as well.

Though my father did not live to see the growth in popularity of herbs in the last decade, he did witness the first tremors of interest and, of course, he was entirely responsible for my plunge into the subject. Today we grow more than 350 varieties of herbs and add new varieties each year. Culinary herbs remain the highest in demand, as I suspect they always will, and it is the thirty-four most popular and useful varieties of these that are covered in *Kitchen Herbs*. I hope they will bring you as much contentment as they have brought me.

GUIDELINES FOR

GARDENING WITH KITCHEN HERBS

Herb plants vary from each other so much, often even within the same botanical family, that it is hard to offer useful generalized information on their culture. That is why I have treated each of the thirty-four varieties featured in this book individually. Under each herb you will find cultural advice to help you grow that specific herb successfully. The easiest way to create a kitchen herb garden is to acquire the herbs as established plants and simply transplant them to your prepared soil bed, but where practical I have also provided advice for starting the plants from seed, cuttings, or root division. You will also find information on when to harvest each herb, methods for extending the season of many herbs, and other ways to get the most productivity out of your plants.

Some fundamental gardening principles do apply to virtually all herbs, and these are discussed here. I hope even experienced gardeners may benefit or get some new ideas. The guidelines have evolved through nearly three decades of growing literally millions of herb plants, observing how they perform in all seasons and in all kinds of weather, and experimenting with numerous techniques and procedures for growing the finest plants.

Here then are some basics to follow to ensure the success of your own garden.

GARDEN LOCATION

While some herbs, like mint, tolerate shade, and others, like sweet woodruff or angelica, positively thrive in it, the vast majority of herbs grow best in a sunny location. The Mediterranean countries, where many herb varieties originated, have the hot and dry summers that cause these plants to grow abundantly and fully. Long hours of sunlight force the herbs to produce the oils that give them their unique aroma and flavor.

Pick the site in your yard that receives the most sunlight during the growing season. Fruit-producing crops like tomatoes do best when they receive eight to twelve hours of sun daily in midsummer. Most kitchen herbs will grow with as little as six hours of sunlight a day, but, like tomatoes, they will grow better and stronger, and therefore be more productive for your kitchen, in as much sun as you can provide them.

Similarly, if you are growing herbs in containers in a window or on a balcony, patio, or deck, choose the most southerly location, and you'll get the most out of your plants.

Also, pick a site that receives good air circulation. Most herbs are susceptible to fungus. A breezy location helps to keep moisture from lingering on plants too long. Avoid planting too close to buildings, walls, and fences or shrubs that block the air. The single most important piece of equipment in my greenhouse operation is the fan. In the absence of Mother Nature's winds, we use electric fans to generate the air movement that keeps plants dry.

People sometimes complain to me that their herb garden has deteriorated rapidly after the second or third year. In most cases it's because they planted the herbs too close together in the first place. When plants are overcrowded, air circulation is stifled and problems begin.

Even professional gardeners sometimes make the mistake of overplanting. On a visit to Colonial Williamsburg a few summers ago, I noticed that several of the model herb gardens were doing poorly. The gardens were in full sun, beautifully laid out, and seemed to be getting the proper attention, but many of the plants looked unhealthy. The reason was that boxwood hedges had been planted on the perimeter of the gardens and now had grown so thick that they were blocking out both light and air.

Incidentally, if your herb garden is set in the middle of a lawn that is cut by one of the new lawn-service companies now widely franchised, be aware of a possible danger from herbicides. Most of these companies routinely spray clients' lawns with herbicides from time to time, to keep out weeds. But if the treatment is scheduled for a windy day, or if the operator of the equipment happens to be careless that day, it's possible the spray will drift into your herb garden. Ask your lawn service for assurance this will not occur.

GARDEN SIZE AND DESIGN

There are six different garden plans included in *Kitchen Herbs* (page 76): the Salad Herb Garden; the Italian Herb Garden; the Edible Flower Garden; the Fish-Herb Garden; the Salt-Substitute Herb Garden; and the Dessert Herb Garden. The designs vary in shape and pattern but each occupies about 75 square feet—plenty of space for growing all thirty-four kitchen herb varieties—but use your own imagination to create the shape and size garden best suited to you. The plans are offered as a stimulus for your own

creativity. No two gardeners are alike, and I would never expect to find two herb gardens that are identical. The needs and desires of the individual gardener, and the special features and requirements of the site selected for the plantings, practically guarantee that every herb garden will be a unique place with a look all its own.

Several factors should be taken into account in planning your own garden, however. Knowing the size, shape, and spreading pattern of each kitchen herb is indispensable. I compare herb gardening to landscape architecture practiced on a small scale. Each plant should be located to complement its neighbor and not get in the other's way.

Taller-growing plants should be put on the north side of the garden so they don't shade the other plants or block your view of them. Low-lying prostrate or creeping varieties of kitchen herbs belong in front of the taller varieties, often making attractive accent plants near edges. Some kitchen herbs, like parsley or chives, grow effectively in rows and you may want to use them for your borders.

Generally, perennials must be given more room than annuals or biennials, because they are permanent residents that will get bigger every year. Some perennials grow on single stems and remain quite manageable even after several years. Others produce many stems and grow in a wide bush form. Still others spread through an underground network of roots and new shoots and need to be dug up and reduced periodically. A single mint plant left unchecked in good growing conditions will spread five feet in every direction within three years.

Unlike vegetables, most herbs do not require a rich, well-fertilized soil to grow in. They do, however, require a well-drained soil. They don't like "wet feet," as we say in the trade, and in low-lying land where water fails to pass through the ground quickly, the roots of the plants grow poorly and may even rot. In a properly drained soil bed, herbs grow lush and complex root systems.

If your garden site is marginal in this respect, there are two ways to correct it. Rebuild the soil bed. Or elevate the garden. Or do both.

Rebuilding the soil bed of a 75-square-foot garden is not a particularly daunting task, though it does take some effort and manual strength. The idea is to dig out your moisture-retaining sod and replace it with soil that has been conditioned for fast drainage. If you dig out the entire site to a depth of one foot, you'll need 2 to 3 cubic yards of the conditioned soil to refill it. The following mix of ingredients will provide an ideal medium for the new garden (I use the same proportioned mix for potting plants at Gilbertie's Herb Gardens):

6 cubic feet of sterilized topsoil

3 cubic feet of perlite (crushed volcanic ash) or pumice (*not* vermiculite, a corklike mica substance that retains moisture)

6 cubic feet of peat moss

6 cubic feet of sand or fine gravel

The topsoil serves as the basic source of nourishment for the herbs. The perlite lightens the soil and the peat moss conditions it. The sand allows the entire mix to drain rapidly.

Raising the garden is another effective way to improve drainage. I use railroad ties or wood (treated with a preservative like Cuprinol; avoid creosote, which can be toxic to plants) to create the garden perimeter. Unless the existing soil is already well-drained, fill in the newly created space with the mix described above. If you're building such a garden on top of an existing lawn area, first break up the turf with a spade or grub ax and turn it grass-side down. Then fill in the area with your well-mixed growing medium of topsoil, perlite, peat moss, and sand.

An elevated garden, standing apart from its surroundings, can be quite pleasing esthetically. It's easier to tend and cultivate a raised bed because you don't have to bend as far to reach it. You can even do your harvesting from a comfortably seated position on the border material.

But improving drainage is by far the most important reason for raising your garden level.

Be sure to have your soil analyzed chemically to determine the degree of its acidity or alkalinity. The soil test can be arranged through the Cooperative Extension Service (see the U. S. Government listings in your telephone book). Or you can test it yourself using kits that are on the market, generally selling for under twenty dollars in garden centers and hardware stores.

As a rule, most herbs do best in slightly acid soil with a 6.5 pH reading. Basil, parsley, and dill produce more foliage in a slightly sweeter soil.

Soil conditions vary throughout the country. There are dark, humus-rich soils; light, sandy soils; and hardpan or gumbo soils; and they all can produce a wide range of pH readings.

Soils that are too sweet—high on the pH scale—are acidified by adding small amounts of sulphur, or by incorporating peat moss, pine needles, or oak leaves into the bed. Soils that are too sour—low on the pH scale—need liming. For the 75-square-foot garden described earlier, about 10 pounds of ground dolomitic lime would raise the pH in the soil one full point.

I try to keep my gardens between 6.2 and 6.8 on the pH range.

FERTILIZING THE GARDEN

Unlike fruit-producing vegetable crops, herbs are not heavy feeders, but some fertilization is desirable for many of them. To a 75-square-foot garden in the spring should be added 15 to 20 pounds of dried manure. Worked into the soil, the manure will give the new plants an excellent organic feed for the first six to eight weeks of the growing season. Or enrich the soil bed with a commercial fertilizer. One I have had success with is Electra, a highly organic 5-10-3 powdered plant food.

During the growing season, some kitchen herbs benefit from additional side dressings of fertilizer, and I have indicated under the individual herbs when that is called for. A side dressing consists of a trowel full of dried manure, or a handful of commercial fertilizer, scratched into the soil immediately surrounding the plant.

Generally, all the annual growers, like basil, dill, and fennel, produce much better when they receive some additional fertilization. Well-established perennials, like thyme, sage, and rosemary, are not heavy feeders, although large growers, like lovage, can use the extra dressing from time to time.

Keeping a small herb garden free of weeds is a modest and satisfying task. With kitchen herbs, you're in the garden frequently anyway, to gather ingredients for your soups and salads and flavors for your entrees. Keeping the ground free of weeds is the work of a minute, if you do it on a regular basis, yet it yields important results. Weeds harbor insects, cut down on air circulation, and blur the esthetic effect of the garden. Left to go to seed themselves, weeds beget more weeds.

If you are too busy to perform the cultivating duty, or perhaps, if you are not near your herb garden except on weekends, Dupont has come up with a new product you might want to consider buying. It's a "landscaping fabric" that can be used as a kind of permanent mulch just beneath the surface of your soil bed. The material is porous, permitting water to drain through, yet sufficiently dense to keep undesirable grass and weeds from taking root. It comes in wide rolls, like wallpaper, sells for about ten dollars a yard, and can be cut and trimmed to suit the dimensions of your garden and the locations of your plants. It's easiest to incorporate into a brand-new garden, but it can also be adapted for existing gardens.

Speaking of mulch, I don't recommend the use of conventional mulch in herb gardens for several reasons. Most mulch materials keep the soil too wet too long. Mulch gives slugs and other pests a place to hide. Pine-bark mulch drains nitrogen from the soil and makes the garden too sour for herbs. Grass clippings cause the same change, and if they come from a lawn that has been treated with herbicides, so much the worse.

WATERING THE GARDEN

Improper watering is one of the most common gardening mistakes I've observed over the years. It runs a close third to locating the garden under insufficient sun, and putting plants too close together. Follow these five simple rules for properly irrigating your kitchen herbs and your plants' will stay vigorous and productive.

1. Wait until plants have just begun to wilt before you water. If the soil is dry for the first 2 to 4 inches but damp at 4 to 6 inches, it means there's still enough moisture in the soil bed for healthy plants to reach and use. By waiting another day or two, you'll encourage the plants' roots to dig a little deeper.

temptation to turn on your garden hose. Wait until early the following morning. They won't perish overnight, and by keeping the garden dry after dark, you'll discourage fungus.

3. Water only when the garden needs it. Frequent short waterings do plants more harm than good by making the surface of the soil too wet and discouraging deep root development.

4. Water thoroughly when you do water. To insure soaking the soil bed to a depth of 6 to 8 inches, do the job in two stages. Go through the garden once with your hose or watering can, then repeat the process.

5. Water at soil level. To keep kitchen herbs dry and free of fungus problems, use gentle streams of water at the base of the plants, rather than spraying the entire garden from above with a hose or sprinkler.

These rules apply to container gardening, as well, but with one important difference. Kitchen herbs in clay pots or other containers dry out much faster than plants in the ground. During hot spells I would recommend that container gardeners check their herbs once a day, and water them as needed.

2. Water in the morning. If you come home one summer evening and find your herb garden looks dry and the plants have begun to wilt, resist the

SCREENING THE GARDEN FOR INSECTS

A mixed, outdoor kitchen herb garden as featured in our plans is virtually insect-free. To start with, herbs like garlic, chive, and thyme are natural pest repellents. When the garden receives proper air circulation and is kept free of weeds, and the plants themselves are well-spaced and properly watered, unfriendly insects rarely will be drawn into it.

If you raise kitchen herbs indoors, or bring some of the herbs in from the garden for the winter, you may have problems with whitefly, spider mites, or other insects. Here are some preventive steps:

• Make sure the plants are in a sunny, dry, well-ventilated location. Maintain a mixture of plants— grow six or seven different herbs in the window, not just a patch of parsley. Expose your plants to warm, breezy days by opening windows or taking them outside temporarily.

• Examine the herbs daily—if you're using them in your cooking you will have occasion to do this anyway. Make sure you check under leaves, because most insects feed upside down. If you discover a major infestation, it may be better to destroy the plant and start all over. But if the problem is limited, I recommend spraying the plant with a safe insecticide.

Safer's Insecticidal Soap is a commercial spray that deters insects yet leaves the herb safe for culinary use. Spray the affected plant with this solution every third morning, for six or seven applications.

Nana's Bug Juice is a homemade alternative created by Nana Gilbertie. I make it by combining a couple of cloves of garlic and a teaspoon of cayenne pepper with a half cup of water or cider vinegar. Then I mix it well in the blender, filter it through cheesecloth, and pour it into a mister for spraying the plants. Even if the herbs appear insect-free, I'd recommend spraying once a week with this solution for any culinary herb kept indoors.

I have indicated the best or most practical method of propagation for each kitchen herb in the individual sections. It's impractical to start some kitchen herbs from seed, because reliable seed is unavailable, because germination is so slow, or simply because, when only one or two plants are desired for the garden, it's probably no more costly to buy an established plant than a packet of seeds, and far less trouble.

The charts below show which herbs may be sown directly into the garden and which should be sown indoors, for later transplant into the garden. I also suggest that some herbs be grown in rows, more or less like a vegetable crop raised from seed, and that some be grown in clusters—a small circle spot-sown with several seeds. For maximum leaf production, I prefer to row-sow chives, dill, fennel, sorrel, savory, arugula, parsley, and garden cress. More for esthetic reasons than anything else, I prefer to cluster-sow watercress, nasturtium, borage, caraway, chervil, basil, and coriander. I just think these herbs grow more attractively in bunches.

However, both sowing methods work equally well for all these herbs, and if, for example, you are very involved with French cuisine with its reliance on chervil as a basic herb, you might prefer to grow chervil in rows so you get more chervil to harvest.

And, if your garden design doesn't permit a long border row of parsley, you can just as easily grow that herb in a single cluster.

For starting seed indoors, use a sterilized feed mix containing peat moss, potting soil, and perlite. Avoid mixes with moisture-retaining vermiculite in them as roots tend to rot in this medium. Without packing it down, fill small trays or 4-inch clay or plastic pots with the feed mix, then roll the surface smooth with a pencil or dowel. (Use peat pots when herbs are started indoors for later transplant outside into the garden.)

Sow the seed to the depth and intervals specified on the chart, then cover with fine sand. Keep the soil moist until germination. If you cover the sowing vessel with plastic wrap, you'll create a warm, humid condition for the seeds. It's a good trick to use with the slower-germinating seeds, such as parsley, but be sure to uncover sprouts the first day they appear.

Once seed has sprouted, move the seedlings to a sunny window in a room where the temperature does not exceed 60 to 65 degrees Fahrenheit. Water only in the morning hours. If seedlings become stringy, it could mean the location isn't sunny enough, as will happen even in a window with a sunny exposure when there are five or more overcast days. Keep the seedlings trimmed until sunny weather returns.

KITCHEN HERBS

STARTING FROM SEED OUTDOORS

	Seed Size	Space Seed	Depth of Seed	When to Plant	Time to Germinate at 70°	When to Thin	Thin to Space	Harvest
Arugula (Roquette)		row	¼"	When ground warms	5 days	3 weeks	1"	6 weeks
Borage		2 seeds spot	½"	After last spring frost	10 days	3 weeks	—	7 to 10 weeks
Caraway		3 seeds spot	½"	"	14 days	"	—	7 to 10 weeks
Chervil		"	¼"	"	7 days	—	—	6 to 8 weeks
Chives		50 seeds in cluster	¼"	When ground thaws	10 days	—	—	10 to 12 weeks
Coriander		6 seeds spot	½"	After last spring frost	8 days	—	—	8 weeks
Cress (Garden)		row	¼"	When ground warms	5–7 days	3 weeks	3"	6 weeks
Dill		6 seeds spot	½"	After last spring frost	7 days	—	—	8 weeks
Fennel		6 seeds spot	½"	"	7 days	3 weeks	4"	8 to 10 weeks
Nasturtium		3 seeds spot	1"	"	7 days	—	—	leaves-3 weeks flowers-10 weeks
Parsley		row	½"	When ground warms	3 weeks	6 weeks	1"	8 weeks
Savory (Summer)		row	¼"	After last spring frost	7 days	3 weeks	6"	6 weeks
Sorrel		row	¼"	When ground warms	8 days	4 weeks	4"	8 weeks

STARTING FROM SEED INDOORS

	Seed Size	Space Seed	Depth of Seed	Time to Germinate at 70°	Transplant Out or Begin to Harvest Indoors
Arugula (Roquette)		1/8"	1/4"	3 days	4 weeks
Basil		1/2"	1/4"	4 to 5 days	6 weeks
Burnet		1/2"	1/4"	8 days	6 weeks
Chervil		1/2"	1/4"	6 to 7 days	6 weeks
Chives		1/8"	1/4"	6 to 7 days	8 weeks
Coriander		1/2"	1/2"	7 to 9 days	8 weeks
Cress (Garden)		1/8"	1/4"	5 days	6 weeks
Cress (Water)		1/4"	1/8"	5 to 7 days	6 weeks
Dill		1/4"	1/4"	5 days	6 weeks
Fennel		1/4"	1/4"	5 to 7 days	7 to 8 weeks
Leek		1/4"	1/4"	5 to 6 days	6 to 7 weeks
Nasturtium		1"	1"	5 days	3 weeks
Parsley		1/4"	1/4"	14 to 18 days	6 to 8 weeks
Savory (Summer)		1/8"	1/4"	5 days	4 to 5 weeks
Sorrel		1/8"	1/4"	5 days	6 weeks

Container gardening can be great fun, but it requires more time and expense than the typical in-ground herb garden. Its great advantage is that you can move your containers to the area that best provides for the needs of the plants. When no other means are available, city dwellers as well as suburbanites happily turn to container gardening as an effective way to bring fresh kitchen herbs into their daily lives.

There is an endless variety of containers suitable for planting herbs—barrels, terra-cotta pots, old copper buckets, just about anything that will hold soil and drain well. Flea markets and secondhand shops are a great source of interesting containers if you have a collector's eye. Clay strawberry jars, with deep pockets that will hold enough soil and moisture for the plants, are especially pleasing. Window boxes spruce up a house or apartment as well as offering a handy source of kitchen herbs for summer seasoning. If the window box is on a southern exposure, as it should be ideally, you will find that the herbs keep on growing in the box well into the cooler fall months: the reflected heat from the building gives the plants an extra shot of warmth and prolongs their season.

More important than the type of container you select is the size of the container. Very small pots are impractical because the limited amount of soil in them dries out too quickly. In hot weather small pots may need to be watered several times daily, an inconvenience even for the gardener who's at home all day.

Wood containers hold moisture better than clay containers, but a large clay pot will grow kitchen herbs just as well. To keep the clay from drying out as quickly, splash water on the outside of clay pots whenever you are watering the herbs.

Container gardens require more frequent watering than in-ground gardens, and the more a potted plant is watered, the more nutrients are leeched from the soil. That's why potted herbs need fertilization more often than garden herbs. I have used the powdered organic fertilizer Electra with success on my potted herbs. Unlike all-chemical fertilizers, which tend to jolt plants into growth, Electra remains in the soil and is taken up as the herbs need it. A dosage early in the season should keep the herbs supplied with nutrients for four to six weeks. Thereafter scratch a handful of the powder directly into the soil around the plants about once a month.

What can be more satisfying than to throw a midsummer cookout on your patio or deck, surrounded by containers filled with your favorite herbs? Reach out and snip a piece of rosemary for that sizzling lamb chop. Sprinkle some fresh tarragon into the barbecue sauce. Rub the rim of your iced tea glass with some mint or lemon verbena. Or just nibble on some fresh parsley as you flip the burgers. And all the while the fragrance of the herbs complements the aroma of the grill. That's the life, and herbs make it possible.

HERBS IN
THE GARDEN

ARUGULA (ROQUETTE)

ERUCA VESICARIA SATIVA

An annual herb growing in loose-leaf form to 10 inches with strong-tasting spinach-green leaves.

Roquette has come a long way. The early English herbalist John Gerard dubbed it "a good sallet herbe." My father grew arugula, the Italian name for roquette, along with *broccoli di rapa* and *chicoria catalone*, as a staple salad ingredient that was good for us because "it gives you iron." And now roquette is listed as arugula in the "gourmet vegetable" sections of seed catalogs. It has truly arrived.

The harsh, almost bitter flavor of the herb has been described as a combination of peanut and horseradish. For me the pungent taste is a welcome counterpoint to the more bland-tasting lettuces. Like burnet, cress, or sorrel, it's an herb that can give a salad piquancy, but I also enjoy arugula all on its own.

Arugula can be started from seed directly in the garden, as early in the spring as the soil can be worked, for this herb thrives in cool weather. In fact it will perform better in the middle of the summer if it is planted in a location that receives partial shade.

Grow the herb in rows, as you would a crop of spinach. Sow the seed in shallow furrows, thinly (at ½-inch intervals) and evenly, in a single row or two or three rows that are 12 inches apart. Sprouts appear within four to six days.

In three weeks, thin each row to leave plants at 1-inch intervals. Use those thinnings for your first salads. When leaves reach 4 inches high, begin harvesting and keep at it all summer long. Continual cutting will keep arugula fresh and tender. If you let the plant go into flower, the leaves become too bitter. Should this occur, simply pull the entire crop up and sow a second crop. We sow arugula throughout the growing season in our garden. Our final sowing in October gives us fresh greens for our salad on Thanksgiving Day.

Arugula grows well in small pots or containers. Use the approach described above and, as always with container gardening, be sure to check the plants for watering every day in hot weather. The seed from a single package will fill a windowbox on a sunny sill with arugula for your kitchen all summer long.

Arugula is also known as rocket but don't confuse it with a completely different plant called sweet rocket (*Hesperis matronalis*). It too can be used as a salad green but it doesn't have the distinctive arugula taste. It is best known for the sweet aroma it releases in the evening hours.

BASIL

OCIMUM BASILICUM

*A tender annual that grows in an erect bush
to 24 inches, producing oval green leaves
with a strong, sweet, minty-clove taste and aroma.*

Basil is the most tender of kitchen herbs, with no resistance whatsoever to cold weather, and also one of the most popular. With its special affinity for tomatoes, it has long been a mainstay of Italian cooking. My grandmother had a wonderful idea; she always alternated basil plants with her tomato vines for the convenience of picking basil leaves each time she harvested a tomato. She knew that there's nothing quite like the taste of a newly plucked and sliced sun-ripened tomato enhanced by some coarsely chopped basil, topped with a drizzle of olive oil and freshly ground black pepper. Grandmother Garofalo also knew that the powerful basil scent that was released when she snipped the herb would chase whiteflies and gnats, two common tomato pests, from her garden.

But there's more to basil than this. At a 1986 national conference on herbs at Purdue University, I saw dozens of varieties of basil in one of the demonstration gardens. Some of the varieties had surprising and unorthodox basil flavors such as clove, camphor, and cinnamon, but what really impressed me was the ready availability of so many types of basil today,

compared with just a few years ago. This versatile herb has definitely entered the American culinary mainstream and can be an exciting challenge to the person who likes to experiment in the garden and kitchen.

Although I grow and sell about a dozen varieties, I recommend that you choose one or two from among the following types of basil for your kitchen herb garden. They are the most productive varieties offering the characteristic and popular basil flavor.

Bush basil (*Ocimum Basilicum*) grows to 24 inches in height, with oval leaves 1 to 2 inches long, dark green, smooth, and glossy. This is a vigorous grower that needs plenty of space in the garden—leave 18 to 24 inches on all sides. Like all the varieties described here, it produces a tubular spike of white or lavender flowers.

Fine-leaf basil (*Ocimum Basilicum 'Finum'*) is the basil of choice among the French chefs I know, who claim the flavor of the leaf is more delicate. The plant grows 18 to 20 inches tall and is an attractively compact bush with pointy ½- to ¾-inch-long leaves.

Dwarf basil (*Ocimum Basilicum 'Minimum'*) grows

in a neat globe-shaped bush to 8 to 10 inches. It's an excellent choice for pots or windows where space is limited. Trimmed as it grows, it can be shaped into a perfect ball, as I've seen it proudly displayed in terra-cotta pots on sunny doorsteps in the streets of Rome. For both ornamental and culinary use, the best seed in this variety is called Spicy Globe. It was originally developed by Northrup King but is carried by most seed companies.

Lettuce leaf, or Italian, basil (*Ocimum Basilicum 'Crispum'*) is the most productive of all the basils. It can grow up to 3 feet tall and I've seen bushes that have filled out to the sides almost that much as well. The leaves are correspondingly large, about 3 to 5 inches. That translates into a lot of pesto, but I don't recommend it for a small herb garden because it takes up too much space. It really belongs in a large vegetable garden, but if you're interested in a big basil harvest, this is the variety for you.

Purple, or dark opal, basil (*Ocimum Basilicum 'Purpurascens'*) is often promoted as an "ornamental basil" because of its striking purple-bronze foliage, and it does make an attractive accent plant in flower gardens and borders, growing 18 to 20 inches tall. But it also has that characteristic basil fragrance so it's just as useful in the kitchen as the green varieties. In fact I think it makes the best basil vinegar of all; the leaves bring a magenta color to white vinegar that is quite attractive.

Lemon basil (*Ocimum Basilicum 'Citriodorum'*) adds a lemony tang to the sweetness of the basil. It's been relegated to use in tea in this country but I've found that it is excellent on many types of fish. Some of the cuisines of Southeast Asia also feature it. The lemon basil plant grows to 18 to 20 inches tall and has pointy leaves that are much lighter in color than those of the other green basils.

As the most tender of all the herbs (and vegetables), basil is introduced into the garden last, and, in the fall, is fully harvested from the garden first.

Unless you live in a southern climate with a long growing season, it's not advisable to sow basil directly into the herb garden. The seeds would germinate but the plants would take so long to put on growth that you would lose a lot of harvest time. These days, most nurseries and garden centers offer young basil plants for sale in the late spring. Alternatively, you can start plants from seed indoors. Sowing should take place about four to six weeks from the date of your last expected frost in spring. Wait until night temperatures stay above 50 degrees before moving the seedlings into the garden. In four to six weeks, the plants should be large enough for you to begin harvesting leaves. Fertilize the plants at this time and at three- to four-week intervals thereafter.

To encourage basil to grow in a bush, periodically pinch the center stem 1 inch from the top. This will also prevent the plant from flowering and going to seed, thus reducing leaf production.

As cold weather approaches in the fall, be alert to the possibility of a premature freeze or near-freeze in your area. If a windy night in the low 40s is expected, harvest your entire crop of basil beforehand. You can also dig up and pot any of the more compact varieties of basil and bring this indoors to a sunny window. The plant won't last all winter but it will give you several more weeks in which to harvest fresh sprigs.

After you've harvested the crop, strip the leaves from the stems, cleaning them if necessary, and freeze in plastic bags in recipe-size portions, Or, to dry, hang in small bunches in a dark place. Once the leaves becomes brittle—usually in a week or two—strip them and store them in an opaque jar.

BORAGE

BORAGO OFFICINALIS

*A sturdy annual growing to 30 inches,
with bristly oval gray-green leaves, cucumber-flavored,
and clusters of blue and rose star-shaped flowers.*

English gardeners pronounce this herb to rhyme with "courage," perhaps because of its long association with that virtue. Pliny recorded that borage leaves and flowers, mixed in a cup of ruby wine, would drive away all sorrows and bring courage to those who drank of the mixture.

Like many annual herbs, borage does not take kindly to transplanting, so I recommend starting this herb directly from seed in the garden after the soil has warmed in the late spring. Locate in a place that receives full sun. Sow to a depth of about ½ inch, in clusters of two to three seeds at 18- to 24-inch intervals. Germination occurs in about ten days. Growth will continue slowly but steadily until the nights turn warm. Fertilize the seedlings at this time. Presently borage will shoot up quickly, producing an abundance of leaves and lovely flowers. At maturity, the flower clusters may become so

heavy that staking is necessary to keep the plants erect.

Harvest borage as soon as possible, beginning eight weeks from sprouting, as the tender young leaves of this herb are the most desirable for salads. Mature leaves become too bristly and coarse to eat raw, but they can be cooked up with vegetables or meats, or used for making a delicious and uniquely flavored iced tea.

Borage loses its distinctive flavor when it is dried. Flowers can be preserved in ice cubes for later use in teas, dessert toppings, or candied cake decorations.

Some gardeners like to plant a succession crop of borage to carry them through the fall, sowing this seed in late July. This technique works well if space is available. I simply keep my original borage planting well fed and cultivated for a more than adequate season-long yield of leaves and flowers.

BURNET

SANGUISORBA MINOR
(OR)
POTERIUM SANGUISORBA

*A perennial herb growing in loose-leaf form
to a height of 8 inches in the first year,
yielding greens with a nutty cucumberlike flavor.*

Along with cress, arugula, and sorrel, burnet (also known as salad burnet) is a tried-and-true performer in the gardens of salad lovers. These plants produce generous amounts of leaves that add not only volume to a fresh salad but unusual piquant tastes as well. And they come back year after year with relatively little care.

Burnet is a particularly strong grower in the early spring, so you can enjoy the taste of fresh cucumbers in your salad long before the cucumber season begins. Incidentally, burnet does not upset the stomach, as do cucumbers for some people. In fact, chewing fresh burnet leaves has long been considered a digestive aid. It is also commonly added to facial creams to improve skin condition.

Oddly enough, though it eventually becomes a rapid grower, this herb is very slow to germinate and establish itself when it is sown directly into the garden, so I recommend starting burnet from seed indoors or acquiring young plants from a garden center in the spring.

The plant grows in a leafy manner, similar to loose-leaf lettuce, and reaches a height of 6 to 8 inches in the first year. Leaves can be harvested when they are 4 inches high, within a month of being transplanted into the garden in the first year. Keep cutting back the plant as younger leaves are the most tender and flavorful.

Burnet will tolerate semishade—a location that gets only six hours of sun a day. It is fairly hardy, and in areas with mild winters burnet will keep producing foliage for you well into December. And, after it finally dies down, it reappears in no time, pushing up new growth in the spring not long after the chives show up again. The new leaves should be taken early as well; allowed to reach full growth (up to 18 inches), burnet becomes tough and chewy.

I suggest digging up burnet at the end of the second year or the beginning of the third year, dividing the plant with a spade, and replacing only half of it in the garden. This will ensure more tender growth.

Although burnet is unsuitable for bringing indoors, it does lend itself to container gardening if the soil bed is large enough—at least 2 cubic feet. But to take full advantage of burnet's productivity into the early winter months, avoid terra-cotta containers, which are damaged by freezing temperatures.

In the world of herbs, there's always something new to learn. Not long ago, Rene and Lee Chewning, owners of the Chick Cove Herb Farm in Deltaville, Virginia, introduced me to burnet vinegar. I'm famil-iar with dozens of herb-flavored vinegars but this was a new one on me. It had the same nutty cucumber flavor of the burnet leaves and, I was informed, it's as easy to make as any of the more familiar herbal vinegars.

In any case, burnet now grows in my garden for two reasons: for salads, and to make my new favorite salad dressing.

CARAWAY

CARUM CARVI

A hardy biennial growing in an erect bush to 24 inches, with feathery, fernlike leaves, producing seeds in the second year that possess a pungent, nutty, carrotlike flavor.

Along with parsley, caraway is a biennial, so both these kitchen herbs call for a different approach to their culture than do perennials or annuals. A biennial takes two years to mature: its root system survives the first winter in the garden, then grows rapidly to seed early in the second growing season, and is finished.

Making a place for caraway in your kitchen herb garden is well worth the effort as this plant brings a delicate, fernlike texture into the garden. Its membership in the carrot family is evident in its feathery foliage, which looks so much like carrot tops, in its deep tap root, and in the carroty taste of its leaves and seeds.

Although it is slow to germinate, about two weeks, caraway can be sown directly into the garden. It does not transplant well, so if you start the seeds indoors, do so in peat pots, which can be planted in the ground, and move into the garden after a good root system has formed.

In its first year of growth, caraway reaches a height of 6 to 8 inches. Its leaves, which are smoother and darker green than carrot leaves, may be harvested for salads or other uses throughout the first year.

The plant dies down to the ground in late fall and begins new growth the following spring. By midsummer it reaches a height of 24 inches with two stalks topped with clusters of white flowers. The flower clusters develop rapidly into the aromatic seeds that lend that distinctive flavor to Old World cabbage dishes such as cole slaw and sauerkraut and, of course, to caraway-seeded rye bread.

It's important to harvest caraway seeds, once they have begun to dry, by snipping the clusters with your fingers or with scissors. If you leave the plant to mature, the seeds will eventually fall and scatter throughout the garden. The seeds will germinate the following season in places you had planned for other purposes.

Place these seed clusters on a fine screen or inside a cheesecloth sack and hang them in a dark, dry, and well-ventilated room until the seeds are thoroughly dried. This will take about one to two weeks. Separate the seeds from the chaff by rubbing them between the palms of your hands, then store the seeds in an opaque jar with a tight-fitting lid.

Early in the second year, while your original crop begins its last stage of growth, sow a new crop of caraway elsewhere in the garden, and repeat this procedure every year thereafter. In this way, in spite of the herb's biennial timetable, you can harvest caraway seeds on an annual basis.

CHERVIL

ANTHRISCUS CEREFOLIUM

An annual growing on slender stems to 8 to 10 inches with feathery leaves possessing a subtle anise-tarragon flavor.

The subtle flavor of chervil has made it popular in French cooking for centuries, but only in recent years have we seen it widely accepted as a kitchen herb in this country. In part that's because chervil seed has not been readily available here. Also, people who've tried the herb in dried form have probably been disappointed with it. In the drying process, chervil loses most of its fragile savor. You really must use it fresh to enjoy its taste in your soups, salads, or vegetable dishes.

There is a curly-leafed variant of chervil (*Anthriscus Cerefolium 'Crispum'*). It grows and tastes exactly like the flat-leafed herb and is slightly harder to find.

When you assign a place for chervil in your garden, pick one that gets some shade during the day, perhaps from a taller-growing neighboring plant. Chervil needs only six hours of direct sunlight in the growing season to thrive. It will literally burn up under daylong hot summer sun.

Even in semishade, chervil tends to go to seed in midsummer. So, to ensure a steady supply of fresh chervil from May through September, I suggest grow-ing the herb as a succession crop in the following manner.

Start from seed directly in the garden early in the season—around the date of your last expected frost. Mark a short row of 1 to 2 feet about ¼ inch deep. Sow the seeds about ½ inch apart and cover with sand. Water gently every morning until germi-nation, which should occur within a week. In about six weeks, you can begin harvesting the leaves.

At this point, start a second row of seeds in a row parallel to the original row, about 6 inches away, and proceed as before. When you begin harvesting this crop, pull up the first crop completely and use that row to sow a third crop. Continue this sowing/harvesting/sowing cycle, using only the two short rows, and you'll never run out of chervil.

Alternatively, sow a cluster of three to four chervil seeds no deeper than ½ inch, water gently each morning, and in about six or seven days sprouts will appear. Even if all the seeds germinate, no thinning will be necessary. The slender-stemmed plants will tolerate each other in a group, and this style of cluster planting is very attractive.

As a small herb chervil is suitable for container gardening and it may also be grown indoors in a sunny window during the winter. Using two pots, the same succession-crop method described above can work indoors as well as out.

Remember to harvest chervil from the outside, picking the older stems and leaves and allowing the newer center shoots to continue to put on growth.

Since chervil does not dry with decent flavor, and since it is so easy to grow indoors in pots, keep your supply coming all winter on the windowsill.

CHIVES

ALLIUM SCHOENOPRASUM

A perennial herb with a mild onion flavor growing in slender green shoots to a height of 10 to 12 inches.

Herb gardeners have a special affection for chives. Every year in early spring, chives are the first sign that the garden is full of energy. Chives are our harbinger of spring.

Sprouting from ebony-colored seeds that could easily be mistaken for chunks of freshly ground black pepper, chives grow somewhat like ordinary grass, in slender green shoots to a height of 6 to 8 inches in the first season. Left to mature into the spring of a second season, parent shoots explode in a spherical lavender blossom, an edible touch of beauty for a summer salad.

Like misery, chives love company, and I strongly recommend planting them in clusters in the corners or elsewhere in the garden. Alone or in rows, chives are neither impressive nor practical. If your garden design *depends* on chives in rows, narrowly bracket each row with cardboard or some other material before sowing, to confine the germination to the desired area.

Whether you want clumps or rows of chives, wait until the ground begins to warm, following the last killing frost, before sowing directly into the garden. Fresh seeds germinate easily in eight to ten days. Until sprouts appear, cover the planting area with burlap to prevent heavy rains from redistributing the seed all over the garden.

A more weatherproof approach is to sow your seeds in pots indoors eight weeks earlier in the year—I use 4-inch pots and sow about fifty seeds in each pot—then transplant the chives into the garden when they are about 4 inches tall. This method lets me position the plants exactly where and how I want them.

Like tarragon and lavender, chives prefer a relatively sweet soil with a pH factor of at least 6.5. When they are not grown in well-drained soil in this range, production is too sparse.

Don't be reluctant to cut chives way back throughout the growing season. The more they are harvested, the better they will grow, especially in the second and subsequent years when, left unchecked, they would rapidly become heavy and thick-stemmed.

Some chefs insist on "fine-leaf chives" for their kitchens and seed companies have begun to offer the herb under that name. I've grown it only to find that by the second year it looks exactly like standard chives. "Fine-leaf," I suspect, simply refers to the slender shoots of any first-year crop of chives.

In late fall, extend the productivity of your own crop of chives by cutting them all to ground level and bringing the harvest in to freeze or dry. Simply freeze them whole in plastic freezer bags then chop them up as you use them, straight from the freezer. Or, lay the herb on paper towels in a dry, airy place. In a week, the crop will be ready to store in a container for use in winter soups and salads. The container must be opaque or light will bleach the chives and they'll lose both color and flavor very quickly. Home-dried chives are not as flavorful as fresh, but they are more savory than commercially available brands (all of which come from one source, incidentally, a megafarm in California).

Most of the more than a hundred varieties of chives are cultivated primarily for their blossoms. They have some onion flavor, but not to the degree we enjoy in the basic culinary variety. When found in the kitchen, these flowering chives are used chiefly as garnishes or salad decorations. The two most popular with my customers are Moly chives (*Allium Moly*), which produces a lovely daffodil-yellow blossom, and Roseum chives (*Allium roseum*), which has a rose-colored flower. Seeds are not available for these species, so they must be started from bulbs in the fall. They will come into blossom the following spring at about the same time as tulips. In fact, Holland is the principal supplier of these allium bulbs as well as the flowers it is more famous for.

Another popular nonculinary variety is Gigantium chives (*Allium gigantium*). As the name implies, it is the Godzilla of the chive family, with a bulb the size of a large apple. It produces a spectacular 6- to 8-inch purple blossom on a stem that measures 3 feet high.

For the borders of your kitchen garden, there are two other varieties of chives well worth considering: garlic chives (*Allium tuberosum*) and curled chives (*Allium senescens glaucum*).

Garlic chives, also known as Chinese chives or *nira* in Japan, combine the taste of garlic and chives and are flavorful additions in salads or any dish where just a hint of garlic is desired. The leaves are flat and grow thickly to a length of 6 to 8 inches. In Connecticut, delicate white blossoms appear on the garlic chives in July and August. We add the blossoms to salads, too. Or we harvest stem, flower, and several leaves together and insert them in a bottle of wine vinegar. It looks pretty, and in a few days the vinegar is imbued with a subtle garlic flavor.

This herb produces a typical chive bulb cluster that may be dug up and used in soups or salads, but we prefer to leave it in place to produce more leaves. Like chives, it can and should be cut back regularly.

In the fall, dig up the bulbs and divide them. One cluster of three bulbs will produce twelve to fourteen bulbs the following year. These can be divided again, and within two or three years, your entire garden can have a perimeter of garlic chives, a proven deterrent to bugs and garden pests.

An unrelated species that looks as though it belongs in the *Allium* family is Society garlic (*Tulbaghia violacea*). It has lavender blossoms, an attractive blue-green variegated leaf with a white stripe running through it, and a flavor similar to that of garlic chives. It grows profusely in Southern California but it will not survive in areas where temperatures drop below 20 degrees. It can, however, be grown in the Northeast if treated as a tender perennial.

Curly chives have small, gray-green leaves that spiral as they grow, hence the name *curly*, and lavender blossoms. The chive flavor is rather mild. They don't grow as tall or as erect as garlic chives but otherwise their culture is the same.

All chives are high in vitamins A and C, and all chive flowers attract bees to the garden, so this popular and versatile herb is healthful for gardener and garden alike.

CORIANDER

CORIANDRUM SATIVUM

A tender annual herb growing to 18 inches high, resembling parsley in its foliage and color, the leaves possessing a bittersweet orange-sage flavor.

Coriander is truly an international herb, used widely in Asian, Indian, Mexican, and Caribbean cooking. The growth in interest in Tex-Mex cuisine in recent years is primarily responsible for its spreading popularity in the United States. My customers ask for it by various names—Indian parsley, Chinese parsley, cilantro, or coriander—depending on their own culinary roots.

The word *coriander* comes from the Greek *korios*, meaning bedbug, a rather derogatory term for such a useful kitchen herb. Apparently the pungent odor of the plant's leaves was offensive to whoever gave it that name. In spite of its name, coriander has been embraced by cooks and amateur healers (it is reputed to soothe aching stomachs and relieve nausea) for about 3,000 years—not bad for a bedbug.

The flavor, incidentally, is not as pronounced in market bunches of coriander as it is in the home-grown herb. That's because commercial crops are heavily fertilized, which increases leafy growth but takes away some of the essential oils and flavor.

The herb grows readily from seed but transplants poorly, so it is best to sow it directly into the garden. Wait until all danger of frost is past as coriander is a heat-loving herb. It needs full sunlight to grow erect and strong.

The seeds are relatively large—about the size of peppercorns. For a small cluster of plants, sow a half-dozen seeds within a 6-inch circle, cover with ½ inch sand, and water every morning until germination, about six to eight days. Harvest the leaves as needed, beginning eight weeks after plants appear. Frequent harvests will help prevent the herb from going into flower, which would slow leaf production.

For greater productivity, sow coriander in succession crops. Mark a short row of 1 to 2 feet about ½ inch deep. Sow the seeds about 1 inch apart and proceed as above. At the time you begin your harvest, plant a second row parallel to the original row, about 1 foot away, and repeat the process. When you begin harvesting this row, pull up the first crop completely and use that row to sow a third crop. Continue in this pattern for as long as your warm weather permits and you'll be amply supplied with the herb.

Most gardeners grow coriander primarily for its leaves, but if you wish to harvest seeds, which are milder in flavor, then let your plants mature (harvesting leaves sparingly if you wish). In late summer, collect the seedheads after the first seeds have turned brown. Hang them upside down in a dry, well-ventilated room and let the remainder of the seeds ripen. Place a tray or paper bag under the seedheads to catch any seed. In about two weeks remove all the dried seeds and store.

In Hispanic countries there is an herb called *cilantro de punta,* or pointed cilantro (*Eryngium foetidum*), which is interchangeable with coriander in recipes, because it has the same distinctive flavor. In fact, it is offered along with coriander as a kind of bouquet garni in Caribbean markets. The *recao,* or mix, consists of a fresh bunch of pointed cilantro, a fresh bunch of coriander, and a small sweet pepper plant. These are among the essential ingredients for a sauce called *sofrito,* which is commonly used in stewed beef dishes and rice and bean casseroles.

Although it tastes like coriander, pointed cilantro is unrelated botanically, belonging to the sea holly family. The seeds are minute—maybe 1/50 the size of coriander seeds—and much slower to germinate. The leaves are broader, stiffer, and pointier, and the seed cluster is tubular rather than umbrellalike. Pointed cilantro grows moderately well for me here in Connecticut but it grows much better in tropical conditions.

CRESS (WATER)

NASTURTIUM OFFICINALE

*A perennial salad herb growing
in shallow streams in compact loose-leaf form to
6 to 8 inches with piquantly flavored foliage.*

CRESS (UPLAND)

BARBAREA VERNA

*An annual salad herb growing in compact loose-
leaf form to 4 inches, its foliage imbued with a
mild peppery taste.*

Watercress is the third biggest crop of commercially grown herbs for the American market, behind only parsley and chives. As its tangy, crunchy leaves are widely used for salads, soups, and garnishes, as well as the indispensable ingredient in the classic watercress sandwich, it's no surprise large farming operations have evolved to satisfy the demand.

But how does one grow a plant that requires such special conditions—it grows naturally in the beds of clear, shallow streams with a gentle current.

B & G Growers is a major supplier of this unique herb. The firm moves with the seasons, spending winter in the South and summer in the North, to harvest huge quantities of watercress in Pennsylvania, Georgia, and Florida. It creates huge sunken beds, plants the cress seedlings, and then floods the area, using equipment that also keeps the water circulating as it would in a brook. Using this method, the company produces six full trailer loads of watercress a week.

If you are one of the lucky few to have access to your own stream, you may be able to grow this herb yourself, but make sure the stream is free of pollution before you put in the effort required. The technique is quite simple. About six weeks before the last frost date, sow the plant from seed in 3- to 4-inch pots, using a sandy well-drained soil mix that is kept moistened until germination, about five to seven days. When the seedlings are well established, with a strong root ball, transplant into a level, calm-water area of your stream bed, making sure a large rock or other barrier is positioned upstream of the young plants.

The cress will reach its full height in another three to four weeks and you can begin harvesting. As a perennial, it will reappear in the spring of every succeeding year, provided stream conditions remain favorable, and it will gradually spread if it has room to do so without encountering too fast a current.

If you, like most of us, are without a country stream running through your land, you can create an artificial body of water to raise cress, just as the commercial growers do. Dig a trench 10 inches deep in your garden and frame it with boards on either side, about 8 inches apart. Layer the trench with sand to 1 inch deep, then transplant your watercress

seedlings into the area 18 inches apart, placing flat stones in between the plants. Run water from the hose into the trench every morning until it floods. In about three weeks, you can start harvesting. If your spring days stay cool, the harvest will continue into early summer, when it will peter out. In the fall, as the weather cools again, you can repeat the procedure and enjoy harvests up to the second or third hard frost.

Upland cress, you may be glad to learn, is much less demanding than watercress. Its flavor is slightly sharper. Sow the seed in a ¼-inch deep row in the garden as soon as the ground begins to warm. It will germinate quickly—within a week—and harvesting can begin within six weeks. You can also easily grow this type of cress indoors in pots for salads and sandwiches in the winter.

Two other varieties of cress, curled cress (*Lepidium sativum* 'Crispum') and garden cress (*Lepidium sativum*) are easy-to-grow annuals that must be resown every two weeks in warm weather as they bolt quickly. The effort would be worth it if the flavor of the leaves were anything like watercress or upland cress. So, if you're limited to growing cress on land, I recommend the upland cress variety.

DILL

ANETHUM GRAVEOLENS

An annual herb growing to 48 inches, producing lacy blue-green leaves, yellow flowers, and numerous umbrella-shaped seedheads; the characteristic dill flavor is more pungent in seeds than in leaves.

This stately plant with its elegant, spidery foliage has figured prominently in herb gardens since classical times. The Greeks and Romans wove garlands of dill stems into crowns for their heroes, and used its yellow flower clusters to decorate wreaths and freshen the air of their banquet halls. Today its versatility in the kitchen is well known; the famous dill pickle is only one minor example of the use of this herb, which seems to taste good in almost anything, including bread, eggs, cheese, fish, meat, salad, and soup.

Since the standard variety of dill grows 3 or 4 feet high, gardeners with limited space may prefer Dill Bouquet (*Anethum graveolens* var.), which reaches only about 2 feet in height. The smaller plant has the same aromatic leaves and seeds, so it's an excellent choice for growing in containers. Another variety, Indian dill (*Anethum sowa*), is grown widely in Japan and India as an essential ingredient in curry powder, but it has a slightly bitter tang that probably would not please most American palates.

Start dill from seed in well-prepared soil, and if you are planting the tall standard variety, locate it on the north side of the garden so it won't put other plants in shade later in the season. Sowing can be done in late spring, around the date of the last expected frost in your area. Mark six to eight circles, with 4-inch diameters, in a row, with about 18 inches between each circle. Then sow six to eight seeds within each circle, cover with sand, and water gently each morning until germination, in about five days.

Dill grows rapidly in its early stages, so, contrary to my recommendations for most herbs, it should be watered and fed regularly. From the time it is 2 inches high, gently water around the base of the plants in the morning every two days, and fertilize once a month. When dill is not fertilized, it begins to turn yellow. Once the plants reach a height of 6 inches, about six weeks after sprouting, you may begin to harvest some of the foliage. Don't cut too deeply, however, or you will retard development of the umbrellalike seedheads, which in my region mature about twelve weeks after the sprouting.

Cut the seedheads after the first seeds have turned brown (as in harvesting coriander). Hang them upside-down in a dry, well-ventilated space and let the seed drop on a tray or in a bag. Dill seed may also be dried in a slow oven. Use the seed to make dill vinegar or for other uses, or store in an airtight, opaque jar. The dried seed will keep its flavor for several years.

Dill foliage also can be saved. At the end of the season, after taking the seedheads and before the leaves turn brown, harvest, wash, pat dry, and store the leaves in plastic bags in the freezer. Or dry them in bunches and then strip the leaves for storage. Or chop them first and then dry them on trays or in the oven.

Even the stems can be put to good use. We cut down our dill near ground level, leaving the clusters of seedheads intact as a kind of spray. After drying them, we use the seedheads as decorations or garnishes, and we weave the stems into rustic baskets and wreaths.

If any of the dill seed scatters in the garden, don't be surprised to see new young dill seedlings show up as "volunteers" the following spring.

FENNEL

FOENICULUM VULGARE DULCE

A very tender perennial growing in stalks to 4 to 6 feet with lacy green foliage possessing a delicate anise flavor.

Sweet fennel and two closely related varieties, bronze fennel (*Foeniculum vulgare dulce 'Rubrum'*) and Florence fennel (*Foeniculum vulgare azoricum*) all produce leaves and seeds with a licorice flavor that goes well with oily fish and in soups, stews, and salads.

Both the sweet and bronze fennel grow almost exactly like dill and will reach 6 feet in height in areas with mild winters. In gardens where winter temperatures drop below 20 degrees Fahrenheit, however, the herb does not reach its full height, even when started very early in the spring, so it really must be treated as an annual, with a fresh sowing every year. Nevertheless I like to grow both varieties in alternating rows toward the back of the herb garden. The effect of the bright green leaves of the sweet fennel, interwoven with the feathery red foliage of the bronze fennel, is striking.

Fennel may be started from seed directly in the garden after all danger of frost is past. Sow six to eight seeds in clusters of 4-inch diameter, cover lightly with sand or soil, and keep moistened until germination, about seven days. When plants are 4 inches high, thin out to two plants per cluster. Fertilize six

weeks from sprouting. When plants reach 8 inches, begin harvesting the fresh leaves and tender stems. Avoid chopping plants back severely. Cut alternate stems so that each plant continues to enjoy full growth, and you'll be able to enjoy fresh-cut fennel all season.

In mild climates, fennel will have time to grow to its maximum size and will form clusters of yellow flowers late in the season. When the seedheads begin to turn brown, cut them off the plant, bring them inside, and dry them on a screen or in a cheesecloth bag in a dark, dry, and warm room. When fully dried, in about two weeks, separate the seeds from the stems by rubbing them between your palms, then store them in an opaque jar.

The slender stalks of fennel, pliable when harvested, can be shaped into wreaths, baskets, placemats, and numerous other decorative items for the home.

Florence fennel is the variety I grew up with as a boy, and this finocchio remains my favorite kind. A dwarf variety growing only to 20 to 24 inches, it resembles celery, with its large bulbous base and short stalks, and can be found in most Italian markets in the fall. It too is easily started from seed sown directly into the garden. It has more tolerance for cold than its larger cousins, and so can be left in a northern garden through several frosts, as late as Thanksgiving.

My father grew several hundred Florence fennel plants in our family garden every year. We munched on fresh white stalks of fennel before and during meals most of the winter. He would harvest the plants and store them in a giant trench he used as a root cellar. Here he also stored kale, cabbage, carrots, rutabaga, potatoes, and parsnips, protecting the vegetables with layers of salt hay and leaves. My main winter after-school chore was to uncover the vegetables my mother needed for supper each night. Most kids were sent to the store. I was sent to the trench. But the reward of sipping wine at a special holiday meal through a hollow stem of Florence fennel made it all worth it.

GARLIC

ALLIUM SATIVUM

*A very hardy flat-leafed onion-family herb
that grows to 18 inches
and produces a cluster of edible cloves as its root.*

My grandfather was a small man, barely five feet tall, and he never talked much, but we always knew when he was around. He chewed garlic cloves for his health and the garlic aroma preceded him wherever he went.

Probably more has been written about garlic as a healing agent than any other herb. My grandfather used it as an aid for blood circulation. Civilizations ancient, medieval, and modern have also found it to be invaluable for giving extra strength in battle, curing the bite of the viper, expelling worms, and numerous other properties. Its high sulphur content accounts for its proven success as an antibiotic.

Most gardeners value garlic for its wide range of uses in cooking. It is one of the easiest kitchen herbs to grow, so there's no reason to exclude it from your garden plan. As garlic is a natural insect repellent, I plant it at 4- to 6-inch intervals all along the perimeter of my vegetable gardens. With its flat, shiny green leaves, it makes an attractive border in addition to providing guard duty and giving me an abundant crop.

You can get a reasonably good harvest out of garlic by planting it in the early spring, but a fall planting will yield bigger sets, or heads, of garlic cloves the following fall. That's because at least six months of growing time are required for a good-size head to develop. When garlic is planted in the fall, about a month before the expected date of first frost, the ground is still warm, allowing the roots of the plant to become established. Thanks to the roots, when the plant emerges from dormancy in the spring, it has a six- to eight-week head start on spring-planted garlic.

If you are starting from scratch in a spring garden, by all means plant garlic at this time. The head of cloves that you harvest in the fall will be small—about the size of a 50-cent piece—but the flavor will be excellent, far superior to that of supermarket fare.

Garlic heads suitable for planting may be obtained from seed companies or garden centers. Heads should be large and pure white in color; veins of purple or green may indicate immaturity, in which case poor germination will result. Separate the cloves (about ten to fourteen per head) and plant at 6-inch intervals. Poke a hole in the soil to a depth of about 2 inches: bury your first two fingers to the second knuckle for exactly the right depth. Set each clove in the ground root end down (the root end is blunt, the stem end is pointy), then cover with soil, pack lightly, and water well.

Fall-planted garlic may not produce shoots until early in the following spring. Sprouts appear at about the same time as chives and by midsummer the leaves should reach their full 18-inch height. Cut back flower stalks to promote bulb production. The leaves may be snipped for salad greens or seasonings without hurting the plant if you limit your harvest to alternate leaves and cut no more than 6 inches.

In late fall of the second year, when the leaves turn yellow and die down, the bulbs are ready to be dug up and harvested. I use some of the fresh sets to immediately replant my garden borders for next spring.

Elephant garlic (*Allium Scorodoprasum*) is grown like regular garlic, but allow more room between plants—12 inches—to accommodate the enormous bulbs produced by this variety, sometimes weighing over a pound. Also, this variety benefits from richer soil and occasional fertilization. Spade manure into the planting area, and fertilize in the spring, when shoots appear, and once again in midsummer. The sweeter, milder flavor of elephant garlic has won it many adherents. People who have found regular garlic hard to digest may tolerate elephant garlic. Its cloves being larger, it is easier to handle in the kitchen than regular garlic; it does not keep as well, however.

HYSSOP

HYSSOPUS OFFICINALIS

*A hardy perennial growing to 24 inches,
producing narrow dark green leaves,
mint-spicy in fragrance and taste,
with spikes of blue, pink, or white flowers.*

The Bible frequently cites hyssop for its medicinal values, and early cultures used it as a principal herb in purification ceremonies. Its literal Greek translation is "aromatic herb," and it has long been used as such for flavoring fruit cups, fish dishes, and meat pies. Its pungent aroma also happens to repel insects, particularly whitefly, and on that score alone, hyssop, like santolina, belongs in every kitchen herb garden.

Hyssop varieties are usually identified according to the color of blossoms they produce—blue, pink, or white. For many years, we tried and failed to track down seed for genuine white-flowering hyssop plants. Seed merchants advertised "white" but the blooms usually came out blue; by the time they flowered—in mid-August—it was too late to sow another variety. Finally we acquired the desired variety from a private herb grower in California, and ever since we have collected our own true white hyssop seed from descendants of plants of that variety. Incidentally, if you intend to collect your own seed of any herb that produces a range of color in its flowers, be sure to

segregate the hues. Otherwise bees will cause the plants to cross-pollinate and, in the case of hyssop, you'll probably end up with an in-between lavender color.

Hyssop is easy to grow from seed. Sow the seeds indoors about six weeks before the last frost date in spring, then transplant them into the garden when sprouts are 2 to 3 inches high. Plant two or three seedlings in a cluster. In the first year, hyssop will grow to about 12 to 15 inches and produce just a few flowers, but the growth pattern will be much stronger and bushier in the second season. In fact, after the second year, it's a good idea to keep the bush trimmed and shaped or it will become somewhat shabby.

Hyssop grows so vigorously in Southern climates that gardeners frequently train it as an attractive hedge border. It is so hardy that even in the North it lasts well into the winter with its almost evergreen foliage, permitting harvest of leaves and sprigs often through Christmas. However, since it adapts poorly to indoor conditions, it is best left in the garden.

When trimmed to create a hedge, hyssop does not produce flowers. If you allow this plant to blossom, be sure to harvest the blooms before they have opened fully. Use the stalks in fresh bouquets, or hang them upside down in bunches to dry. Once the hyssop has dried, store it in a dark glass container until you are ready to sprinkle the hyssop flowers on a fruit cup or salad.

LAVENDER

LAVANDULA ANGUSTIFOLIA

A hardy perennial growing in a compact bush to 30 inches, with slender blue-green leaves and fragrant spikes of lavender-blue flowers.

English lavender has been a favorite perfume herb for centuries, treasured by emperors and kings. Originally collected for its oils from plants growing wild, the sweet scent became affordable for common folk only after the plant began to be cultivated widely by gardeners. Today, lavender is used as a kitchen herb with increasing frequency, as innovative cooks find new uses for the bittersweet pungency of its leaves and flowers in fish dishes, vinegars, jellies, and desserts. But even if it has only limited culinary appeal for you, chances are you'll want lavender in your kitchen garden for its fragrance and beauty—and for its insect repellent properties.

There are dozens of varieties of lavender. For practical purposes, I divide them into two groups: hardy and tender.

The original English lavender, known to veteran gardeners as lavender 'vera,' and its various subspecies, all of which grow somewhat more compactly than the plant from which they are derived, are winter-hardy. Lavender 'Munstead' (*Lavandula angustifolia 'Munstead'*) grows to 15 inches but is similar to English lavender in leaf and flower. Lavender 'Hidcote' (*Lavandula angustifolia 'Hidcote'* var.) grows to 12 inches with brilliant purple flowers. This variety has the deepest color blossom of all the lavenders. Lavender 'Rosea' or 'Jean Davis' (*Lavandula angustifolia 'Rosea'*) grows to 12 inches and produces pale pink blossoms.

The group of lavenders that do not bear up well in cold climates are, however, excellent indoor plants. Provided they are not overwatered, they perform well in a bright southern exposure that enjoys cool night temperatures. Generally, these tender perennials will be killed off if left outside in areas where winter temperatures drop below 20 degrees Fahrenheit. So, if raised outside in the summer, they should be kept in pots for later transfer to the house. Spanish lavender (*Lavandula Stoechas*) grows to 24 inches, has narrow gray leaves, dark violet flowers, and a camphor-rosemary scent. French or fringed lavender (*Lavandula dentata*) grows to 24 inches, has fernlike leaves, light blue flowers, and a strong resinlike aroma. Spike lavender (*Lavandula latifolia*) grows to 30 inches and has broad leaves that yield generous amounts of the camphor-scented oil that is often used in soaps. Wooly lavender (*Lavandula lanata*) grows to 20 inches and has dense wooly-white leaves of fragrant bright violet blossoms.

Lavender is slow to start from seed and difficult to start from cuttings, so I recommend that you buy your lavender plants from a reliable garden center in the spring. Plants may be set out after all danger of frost is past. Add limestone to the planting site, if necessary, to bring the pH to 6.5 or higher. Unless you purchase large, one-year-old plants, not many blossoms will appear in the first season. Indeed, I recommend trimming the plant from time to time to keep it from flowering; you'll get more uniform and compact growth that way. In the second season, after about six weeks of growth, the plant will flower profusely. Subsequently, trim the bush every year after flowers have been harvested.

Cut flower spikes well before blossoms begin to fade, or they will not dry attractively. Leave the spikes on a screen in a dry, dark room for three to four days. Then store in a sturdy container (like a cigar box) from which you can draw for garnishes for the dining table or aromatic decorative flourishes elsewhere in the house.

LEEKS

ALLIUM PORRUM

A hardy biennial herb with a sweet, mild onion flavor, growing in a stalk of flat, broad, gray-green leaves to 24 inches.

Leeks are known in France as "the poor man's asparagus," but they are appreciated by all for their wonderful flavor, the sweetest and mildest in the onion family. Like most herbs, the leek's history is long and varied. The slaves who built the pyramids in Egypt practically subsisted on leeks. The Roman emperor Nero drank leek soup daily to improve his voice. For all we know, while he fiddled and Rome burned, there was a pot of leek soup simmering away in his kitchen. And today the leek has acquired the high status of national emblem of Wales.

I grow several rows of leeks every year for a friend who lived in France for a time and fell in love with leek soup. Because I always harvested them for her by early winter, I had never seen leeks develop their distinctive seedhead in the second year. I did so for the first time during a visit to Colonial Williamsburg in Virginia. I had to ask the tour guide to identify the onionlike plants with their large seed pods. No one in our group knew I was a professional grower, but I was embarrassed not to have been able to identify the plants as leeks myself.

For maximum production, leeks should be grown in rows, but you can plant them singly or in clusters of three or four for an interesting effect. They cannot be grown in containers successfully.

Start leeks from seed indoors, about six weeks before the spring gardening season begins. There are several varieties of leeks available. I've had good results from American Flag, a variety offered by most seed companies. Sow the seed in rows in a tray or pot, cover with about ¼ inch of sand, and keep the seedbed moist until germination. This herb germinates fairly quickly, in five to seven days, but the sprouts grow slowly. Water in the early morning hours only when the soil looks dry to the eye.

In about six weeks, the seedlings should be about 6 inches high, about as thin as pencil lead and closely resembling young chives. When the garden is warm enough—about one month following the last frost—transplant the seedlings to the garden at 6-inch intervals in straight rows about 12 inches apart. The site should be enriched with topsoil and manure, since leeks require more nutrients than most herbs. Some gardeners plant leeks in a 6-inch-deep trench, then gradually fill the trench with soil as the plants mature. I prefer to plant leeks at soil level and then hill them up after they begin to put on vigorous growth, ten to twelve weeks after transplanting. Both methods cause the base of the stalk to blanch, increasing the usable part of the leeks for cooking.

The first time people grow leeks they are often dismayed by the slow rate of growth. Early in the season, most of the growth occurs in the root system, so progress is invisible to the anxious gardener. After about two months, when the roots are finally well established, the leaves practically explode into growth.

Harvesting can begin after the stalk reaches a thickness of at least ¾ inch at the base. The longer leeks remain in the ground into the fall, the wider the base will become until it reaches full maturity at

about 2 inches in thickness. Incidentally, the 3-inch-wide leeks sometimes seen in the marketplace are not necessarily ideal for kitchen use, for these larger stalks often contain hard, inedible cores.

Leeks have such a tenacious root system that it requires a spade fork to dig them up—you can't pull them up with your hand as you would onions, shallots, or garlic. Remove them from the garden only as needed. Leeks don't store well, but they will stay healthy in the garden all winter long. However, when the ground freezes, they are almost impossible to harvest without damaging them. Mulch them with salt hay early in the winter and you can easily dig them as needed all through the winter months.

LEMON BALM

MELISSA OFFICINALIS

A very hardy spreading perennial bush growing to 24 inches, with serrated, lemon-flavored leaves growing in pairs on sturdy stems, producing white flowers in midsummer.

Lemon balm is the preeminent tea herb, its lemony flavorful leaves producing infusions, hot or cold, that stimulate the heart yet calm the nerves. It can also be used in soups and salads or any other dish requiring a touch of lemon. Try it in place of mint, with which it is sometimes confused, in recipes. It's one of the easiest and most reliable kitchen herbs to grow. Virtually indestructible in the garden, it tolerates both sunny and partial shade conditions and comes back year after year.

Lemon balm may be started from seed, but the seed is so minute and the growth pattern of the seedling so slow, that the procedure must begin some three months before setting it into the garden. Most gardeners will prefer starting with a healthy plant acquired from a nursery or garden center in the spring. Alternatively, the plant can be propagated by root division if you have a friend or neighbor willing to let you dig up a portion of a mature plant, preferably in the late fall.

Some gardeners like to locate several plants of lemon balm in a row, but I think it grows too vigorously to serve as a manageable border, and I prefer to locate it by itself somewhere in the middle of the kitchen garden. Like mint, it performs well in moister, shadier conditions than do most of the kitchen herbs, but will also do well in full sun when kept well watered. A young lemon balm planted in late April will have 6-inch stems ready to harvest by mid-June. By the end of the first growing season, it will reach a height of about 18 inches. After dying down in the late fall or early winter, it will reappear the following spring, just a week or two after the chives show up. In the second growing season, you could take as many as six to eight substantial harvests, so fully does the herb grow at this time.

If you wish to confine its growth, don't hesitate to cut into the plant to within a 6-inch diameter in late fall of the second year, and every two years thereafter. Use the same procedure to bring lemon balm into the house for the winter. Separate a clump of the bush with a spade in October or November and bring it inside in a 6- to 8-inch pot. Although it will not grow as vigorously indoors, it should provide you with plenty of fresh lemon balm throughout the winter months.

Tea lovers recommend using dried lemon balm leaves for making their favorite beverage. The harvested stems can be hung in bundles in a dark, dry, well-ventilated room for seven to ten days, then stripped and stored in an opaque container for later use.

Golden lemon balm (*Melissa officinalis aurea*) is a decorative subspecies that produces lovely variegated gold and green leaves in the cooler early spring and late fall phases of the growing season. It doesn't grow as tall as lemon balm, nor is it as hardy, but it makes a compact and attractive selection for your kitchen herb garden.

LEMONGRASS

CYMBOPOGON CITRATUS

*A very tender perennial
growing in dense broad-bladed form to 3 feet
like an ornamental grass,
and possessing a strong lemon flavor.*

Lemongrass has long been grown in commercial fields in Florida for its essential oils and as a base for citrus-flavored potpourris. With the increased interest in oriental cooking, the tropical aromatic lemongrass has become a popular kitchen herb in this country for the first time. Its intense lemon flavor enhances fish dishes and gives tea brewed with the herb a delightful flavor. In southern India and Ceylon, where it originated, lemongrass is known as "fever grass" because of the curative properties of infusions made with it.

Because it is so tender, lemongrass is best treated as an annual in northern gardens. It turns brown and dies in cold weather. If dug up in clumps and brought inside to a protected location, the herb will winter over successfully, without, however, producing fresh growth in the meantime. In Southern gardens, where the plant does survive throughout the year, clumps should be divided every second year to keep growth fresh and tender.

Lemongrass can only be grown from root division, so purchase plants from a nursery or herb farm. Sometimes, you may find it for sale, complete with roots, in an ethnic produce market, in which case you can attempt propagation from this source. Cut the blades down and plant the base in a moderately rich, moist soil area. Within a few weeks, you should have a well-established clump of lemongrass.

Harvesting may begin when the grass reaches 12 to 15 inches in height. Harvest at regular intervals thereafter, especially after heavy growth begins in midsummer. If you have a surplus of lemongrass, you can chop it into ½-inch pieces and dry it between paper towels. Then add the dried herb to dried orange and lime rinds for a delicately scented textured potpourri.

LEMON VERBENA

ALOYSIA TRIPHYLLA
(FORMERLY LIPPIA CITRIODORA)

*A tender perennial shrub growing to 8 to 10 feet
with pale green, spear-shaped leaves with
a powerful citrus aroma and the truest lemon flavor.*

Most herb historians claim that Spanish explorers carried lemon verbena to Europe in ships from its native habitat in Chile and Argentina. If so, they must have made the voyage during the summer months. Had they crossed the ocean in winter, they would have tossed the plant overboard as dead, because it always sheds its leaves in January and February.

Lemon verbena thrives in the hot sun and in warm southern climates will reach its full height of 10 feet and produce delicate spires of tiny pale lavender blossoms. In a short but hot summer, it can reach 4 to 5 feet. When grown in a planter, tended over the winter months, it can be maintained at a height of 6 feet or more.

It can be grown as an annual, planted in the spring and allowed to be killed by the first fall frost. It has the most authentic lemon scent of all the lemon-flavored herbs and is superb in potpourris, fruit cups, fish recipes, and beverages from iced teas to straight-up martinis. I know a man who rubs his mustache with its leaves—he calls lemon verbena his after-shave.

The only viable means of propagation for this herb is by cutting, a tedious procedure. I recommend buying a young plant and placing it in the garden after the last frost. Locate it where it can enjoy full sunshine. Fertilize the planting site.

If you bring the plant indoors at the end of the first season, plant it in a 6- to 8-inch clay pot and bury the pot in the garden. Otherwise, removal of the plant in the fall would be difficult owing to its deep tap root. Make sure the edges of the pot are beneath the soil line so the plant doesn't dry out. With the first cool nights of fall, dig out the pot and bring the plant inside to a sunny window. (When it loses its leaves, don't lose heart; in proper conditions it will begin putting forth new leaves in March.)

You can begin to harvest lemon verbena once a week by mid-summer. Growth occurs rapidly during the hottest weather, so take advantage of it. Cut long stems—8 to 10 inches—and strip the leaves for fresh use or, if you have a surplus, hang the stems upside-down to dry in a dark, dry, well-ventilated area; in five to seven days, strip the leaves and store them in airtight, opaque containers. Dried lemon verbena holds its flavor and scent for years, which is one reason it's so popular with potpourri makers.

LOVAGE

LEVISTICUM OFFICINALE

*A very hardy perennial growing in upright bush
form to 72 inches,
with broad, serrated, pale green leaves
that possess an anise-celery flavor.*

In the Middle Ages in Europe, lovage was known as "love parsley" for its reputed aphrodisiac qualities. When the Pilgrims came to America, they brought the herb with them as a digestive aid. Today in this country lovage is enjoying renewed popularity because of the growing interest in vegetarian cooking. Its foliage has the properties of a yeast extract and can replace meat and bones in giving body to homemade soups. The unique lovage flavor, a sweet combination of anise and celery, also gives a lift to stews and casseroles with or without meat in them.

Lovage is easy to cultivate but, as the biggest of all kitchen herbs—growing up to 6 feet tall after the first year—it needs plenty of space in the garden. Like dill and fennel, it belongs on the north side of the garden where it won't shade smaller plants. Lovage itself will tolerate partial shade. Because of its great size it is unsuitable for growing in containers.

The plant can be started from seed directly in the garden in areas with long growing seasons, but Northern gardeners are better off starting it indoors, then transplanting outside when the weather warms.

Sow the seed in a pot about six weeks before the expected date of the last spring frost in your area.

Lovage seed is flat, dark brown, and about half the size of a pea. Incidentally, germination rate on old lovage seed is quite poor, so order your seed in the fall or winter immediately preceding the year you intend to sow it. Sow three or four of the seeds to ensure at least one healthy seedling. Sprouting occurs in ten to twelve days.

By the time of transplant, the seedling will be about 4 inches high. When you move it into the garden, fertilize, then keep well-watered for the first week or two. Fertilize again once every four to six weeks during the summer. In the first year the plant will grow vigorously but it will only attain a height of 24 inches. You can begin to harvest when it is about 12 inches high—pick side stems and use both stems and leaves in lovage recipes.

The plant will die down to the ground about six weeks after the first frost, then resume growth in the early spring, reappearing about a month after chives show up again. In the second year, growth is rapid, and the lovage plant will reach 4 feet by June and 6 feet by the end of the season. As during the first year, the plant should be fertilized at four- to six-week intervals.

A seedstalk will form among the stems in early summer. If allowed to mature, this stalk would produce a large seedhead. Unless you are planning to harvest the lovage seed, which has a sweeter and more aniselike flavor than the foliage, remove the seedstalk when it appears. This will promote greater leaf production in the plant. It also prevents the possibility of the herb self-sowing throughout the garden.

Should you desire the fresh seed for herb butter or other uses, then allow the seedstalk to form and harvest the cluster when the first seeds have begun to turn brown, about midsummer.

In the spring of the third year, before new growth starts, dig up the lovage and split the root system in two. Replant one of the roots, and discard the other (or make a present of it to another gardener). This procedure will revitalize the plant and encourage maximum growth. Left undivided, lovage roots tend to knot up and become less and less productive.

Lovage leaves can be harvested from early spring to late fall, but the foliage yellows rapidly when kept long after picking, and does not lend itself to freezing or drying.

MARJORAM (SWEET)

ORIGANUM MAJORANA

A tender soft-stemmed perennial growing to 12 inches in a loose bush, producing oval leaves and tiny pink-lavender flowers imbued with a pungent, sweet, sagelike aroma.

The ancient Greeks and Romans crowned newly married couples with this herb as a symbol of happiness, and sweet marjoram has grown so profusely in Sicily that it remains to this day on the coat of arms of the ancient city of Marjora (from which it gets its name).

There are three other varieties of marjoram that gardeners may be familiar with: wild marjoram (*Origanum vulgare*), pot marjoram (*Origanum Onites*), and

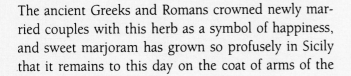

showy marjoram (*Origanum pulchellum*), but none of these has the distinctive taste of sweet marjoram. In fact, recipes that vaguely call for "marjoram" instead of "sweet marjoram" as an ingredient sometimes mislead cooks into using one of the other varieties, which impregnate a dish with a much more pungent seasoning than expected or desired.

Properly identified and used, sweet marjoram is one of the most versatile of kitchen herbs, complementing eggs, sausages, soups and stews, chicken, lamb and pork, salads, and all the Brassica and legume vegetables. It's also well-suited for container gardening since its root system doesn't mind confined spaces. Brought inside for the winter, it will fill your kitchen with its fragrance every time you snip from it.

Sweet marjoram requires a great deal of time and patience to start from seed, so I suggest acquiring healthy young plants from a garden center in the spring. Transplant to the garden when the soil is warm, making sure it receives plenty of sunlight and air circulation.

Harvest leaves beginning four to six weeks after transplant; some people like to wait for the tiny flowers to form, then harvest sprigs of leaves and blossoms together. Regular harvesting will keep the bush growing neatly. Uncut, stems eventually fall over and take root in the soil, producing a more untidy plant than you may care for.

After the first frost in the fall, cut the plant down to 1 inch from the ground. Hang the harvested stems in a warm, dark, dry room for five to seven days, then strip the leaves from the stems and store in a tightly lidded opaque container.

Meanwhile, dig out your plant and transfer to a 6-inch pot. Bring it indoors to a sunny window. Do not overwater and give it plenty of breathing room—sweet marjoram does not grow well when it is crowded in with other plants, so you may have to find it a sill of its own.

A new hybrid of this herb, called hardy sweet marjoram (*Origanum × majoricum*), was recently developed; it promises to perform better in cold-winter climates. It grows taller and more erect than sweet marjoram, to about 24 inches, but has the same tiny gray-green leaves. It is supposed to be hardy only as far north as the Mid-Atlantic states, but I've grown it in Connecticut for the past three years and it has come back following each winter. Hardy sweet marjoram tastes as good as sweet marjoram, so if my plants continue to survive, I will start recommending it to my customers for their outdoor gardens.

MINT (PEPPERMINT)

MENTHA × PIPERITA

A very hardy spreading perennial growing to 24 inches, with dark green oval leaves, purplish underneath, and a sharp, spicy fragrance.

MINT (SPEARMINT)

MENTHA SPICATA

A very hardy spreading perennial growing to 18 inches, with pointed, serrated green leaves and a mild fragrance.

Mints are like some teenagers—easy to grow, but difficult to control. I no longer plant mint in the herb garden. I have tried wood, metal, mortar, and asphalt walls and by the second or third growing season, the mint manages to grow in, around, under, or through the walls. For this reason I recommend growing mint by itself at the edge of a property—it will tolerate partial shade—or in containers at least 12 inches in diameter. It's a joy to have this piquant herb handy on a patio or balcony for snipping leaves to garnish an evening cocktail or sprinkle in a fresh salad.

According to Greek mythology, mint was created when Proserpine, envious of a beautiful nymph named Mentha, changed her into a creeping plant to be trampled on forever by mortals. Today, it is the leading commercially grown herb in this country, with over 50,000 acres under cultivation, mostly in California, Oregon, and Indiana. Both peppermint and spearmint are raised to extract the strong oils from their leaves, principally for use in toothpaste, chewing gum, and perfumes. A lesser known commercial application for mint farming occurs in Lexington, Kentucky, every year. During the first week of May, some 300,000 sprigs of Kentucky mint (*Mentha spicata spp.*) are harvested to make all the mint juleps consumed at the Kentucky Derby.

There are over four hundred mints, many of which are useful as kitchen herbs. The more peppery peppermint is the basis for an excellent herbal tea or as an accent in iced drinks or salads. Spearmint is generally preferred as a cooking mint, enlivening the taste of peas, carrots, and potatoes in particular.

For a less penetrating but still refreshing flavor, there are a number of mints with fruit flavors for use in fruit salads, desserts, and beverages. You might want to grow at least one of these for the excitement of incorporating its special flavor in your recipes. They include apple mint (*Mentha suaveolens*), orange mint (*Mentha × piperita citrata*), grapefruit mint (*Mentha suaveolens × piperita*), pineapple mint (*Mentha suaveolens 'Variegata'*), ginger mint (*Mentha × arversis 'Variegata'*) and Crisped Scotch mint or Bergamot mint (*Mentha × gracilis 'crispa'*). The last named, possessing a delightful lemon flavor, should not be confused with bee balm, which is sometimes called bergamot.

Although not considered as desirable as culinary herbs, two creeping varieties of mint may be suitable for planting in smaller niches. Pennyroyal mint (*Mentha Pulegium*) is a small-leafed plant growing to 3 inches high, so strongly flavored that it is the base for a kind of "organic" flea collar for pets. It is one of the few mints that can be started from seed. Corsican mint (*Mentha Requienii*), which is the variety used to produce the famous liqueur crème de menthe, is the lowest creeper with the tiniest pale green leaves. It

hugs the ground and spreads quite slowly compared to most mints, and is not hardy in cold climates.

The best way to start most mints is from cuttings or root division. In the early spring, when established plants push up their sprouts with remarkable vigor, you can easily dig up a few runners from the mint patch of a friend or neighbor. Remove 2- to 3-inch-high stems with roots intact and set them in a container filled with a good soil mix or in a moist but well-drained location in your yard. Other than making sure the transplant receives water if needed for the first week, there really is no other care required, and by the end of summer you'll have a healthy patch of mint yourself.

Mint can be harvested ruthlessly without affecting its growth. However, the leaves bruise easily, like tarragon, so handle your harvest with care. If you allow flowers to form beginning in midsummer, leaf production will slow down. For maximum production, harvest at the onset of flowering and you'll get many harvests in one growing season. Although all mints die down to the ground in late fall, some varieties may be brought inside for the winter. I've had particular success with growing both peppermint and orange mint indoors. In the fall, dig a few shoots with their roots intact and plant in a 6-inch pot for your sunniest windowsill, and you'll have fresh mint most of the winter. Don't attempt this procedure with spearmint varieties, however, since they require a period of dormancy in the winter and will not perform indoors during the winter months.

To dry mint, harvest entire stems of the plant and hang the stems in a dry, airy, dark room for at least a week. Mint takes a bit longer to dry than most herbs because of its high oil and water content. When dry to the touch, strip leaves from the stems and store in an airtight, opaque container. Spearmint can be crushed before storing but peppermint, preferred for tea, is better left in leaf form and used that way in making infusions. Mint leaves can also be easily frozen into ice cubes for future use in drinks or recipes.

NASTURTIUM

TROPAEOLUM MAJUS/MINES

A tender annual growing in a trailing stem to 8 inches, with rounded, heart-shaped leaves, peppery in flavor, and yellow, orange, or red flowers, also edible.

Whenever children from the neighborhood school come in for a class visit, I arrange for them to plant nasturtium seeds in pots to take home. The pea-sized seed is easy to handle and germinates quickly, in five to seven days, so it's perfect for introducing kids to herb gardening.

Besides being simple to grow, nasturtium adds welcome color to an herb garden. I like to interspace it with chives, thymes, or garlic along borders. Or, after planting up a new garden, I will sow nasturtium at random in groups of three or four. Within three weeks the plants will be large enough for leaves to be harvested from them. Flowers appear about eight weeks after germination.

Nasturtium is native to South America, where it is often called "Indian cress." In fact the spicy, peppery flavor of both its leaves and flowers is similar to that of watercress, and is used abundantly in the traditional salads of Mexico, Chile, and Argentina.

There are several varieties of nasturtium, includ-ing a "tall" variety with stems growing 18 to 30 inches long, and a type that produces a variegated leaf. I recommend the variety usually labeled "dwarf" as this is the most compact grower, producing stems about 8 inches long. With its less unruly growth pattern, it's more suitable for use both in the garden and in containers.

Avoid using old nasturtium seed; only fresh seeds germinate well. Sow when the soil is warm. Push each seed into the ground to a depth of 1 inch. If left closer to the surface, the seed might "float" to the top when it is watered, then dry out before germination occurs. Plant seeds in groups of three or four, leaving 6 to 8 inches between groups of seeds. Sprouts appear in about a week and harvesting may begin about three weeks after that. For maximum leaf and flower production, fertilize the plants every three to four weeks. When flowers are allowed to go to seed, the green pods that form may be harvested, pickled, and used interchangeably with capers.

OREGANO

ORIGANUM

*A perennial herb growing in a spreading bush pattern,
to a height of 15 inches, producing spade-shaped leaves
of sharp, spicy flavor, and white flowers.*

Oregano is something of a mystery herb, at least to the major seed companies. They insist on selling the variety *Origanum vulgare* as true oregano, although it is, in fact, wild marjoram. Marjoram, though quite similar in appearance, lacks the flavor we expect of oregano—what I call the pizza-quality aftertaste. It has a strong, peppery, minty tang all its own, and no self-respecting pizza is made without it.

So before buying a plant labeled oregano, break off a leaf and taste it. If it reminds you of pizza, you know it's the real thing. If the taste is mild and innocuous, it is probably wild marjoram. If you already have a plant in the garden and are not sure of it, wait until it flowers. If the blossoms are pink or lavender, the plant is wild marjoram.

Incidentally, the dried oregano sold on the spice racks in supermarkets is usually not made from oregano plants but from a variety of coleus. This annual, also known as Mexican oregano, is a large and rapid grower, thus commercially attractive, and has the unique oregano taste even though it is not in the botanical family of oreganos. To complicate things a bit more, another unrelated species with the pizza flavor is an upright growing thyme called, not surprisingly, thyme oregano.

We grow four different oregano varieties that have the oregano flavor to varying degrees and are suitable for culinary purposes. All of them are white-flowering plants.

The first and most popular variety is called true oregano on the labels we use to identify plants; other growers sometimes call it "dark leaved" or just "plain" oregano. This is a hardy perennial with dark green spadelike foliage. It grows in a compact bush up to 6 or 8 inches tall. Milo Miloradovich, a delightful woman who wrote extensively on herbs in the 1950s, once stopped by our gardens to chat about oregano. She believed that botanically, it probably belonged in the mint family. Though she has since passed away, a recent study by botanists at Cornell University tentatively confirms her original claim.

The second variety is called Greek oregano and actually grows in several forms, all also flowering white. It tastes like true oregano except that after chewing it for a few seconds your tongue begins to sting. For that reason we describe it to customers as the oregano with the bite. Italian markets carry packaged whole dried oregano marked "Made in Greece." I've experimented with this seed source on several occasions and discovered a wide range in growing habits. Some plants grow erect and have very pale green leaves. Others grow close to the ground, almost like a creeping variety, and have a large ovate leaf structure, dark green in color. And still others come up as a bush with tiny, gray-green leaves.

The reason for all these variations in Greek oregano, I suspect, is simply that the herb, as it grows wild on the hillsides of Greece, is allowed to go to seed, and cross-pollination occurs.

Oregano Maru, our third variety, has the strongest oregano flavor of all. It grows erect and very tall—about 2 to 3 feet—but does not spread as readily as the other oreganos. Though hardy, it is not a vigorous grower so it may not be as productive for your kitchen.

The fourth and final species is golden oregano, and I include it in the general grouping mainly because it produces white blossoms. However, this variety is not strongly flavored and is probably more suited as a garnish for the eye than an accent for the tongue. It grows in a bushy mound about 4 inches high and 12 to 15 inches wide. The striking gold of its leaf adds an unexpected color to the garden. In early spring and late fall, the cool weather seems to make the gold even more radiant and it is noticeable from a long distance.

Except for the Greek variety, oreganos should be propagated from cutting or root division because they tend not to grow true to taste from seed. Make your division in early spring, before new growth starts, or late fall. The plant may be dug up, potted, and brought inside at season's end, or left in the ground to winter over, resuming its growth in the spring.

Give new oregano plants plenty of room in your garden—about 18 inches on all sides—as they spread rapidly. To prevent the kind of cross-pollination that occurs on the Greek hillsides, be sure also to harvest your oregano just as it begins to flower. This will prevent the bees from crossing your pizza-quality oregano with some drab marjoram from down the street. Should that occur, you may find that next season you have a plant that is flavorless and produces rose-pink flowers.

Even if you can't use large quantities of oregano in your cooking at harvest time, cut it in bunches and hang it from beams in your kitchen or family room. That's what my wife, Marie, likes to do, drawing on the decorative supply for her sauces all through the fall and winter months, and enjoying its aroma in the house as it dries.

PARSLEY (CURLY)

PETROSELINUM CRISPUM CRISPUM

*A hardy biennial herb producing tightly curled,
finely cut rosettes on long stems, growing
to 8 to 10 inches.*

PARSLEY (FLAT-LEAF)

PETROSELINUM CRISPUM NEAPOLITANUM

*A hardy biennial herb producing flat, larger,
and more strongly flavored leaves than the curly,
growing to 8 to 10 inches.*

© WALTER CHANDOHA

A man telephoned me one warm afternoon in mid-April and asked in a puzzled voice if there was any professional secret to sowing parsley seed.

"Not really," I assured him.

"Well, do you wear a special glove, or spray your fingers with silicon?" he went on, and then gave me a good-humored account of his efforts to sow parsley in his garden that morning, after soaking the seed overnight per the instructions on the seed package. In fact, parsley seed becomes adhesive when wet and will stick to the fingers like glue. But the seed is very slow to germinate, and wetting it first speeds up the process; hence the commonly heard advice to soak the seed overnight before sowing. "Well," the frustrated gardener concluded, "it's probably easier to wet them in your mouth and then spit them into the ground!"

Parsley "for festivity" was used by the ancient Greeks and Romans to absorb the fumes of wine in their banquet rooms, thinking it would allow them to drink more without becoming intoxicated. We all know parsley as a seasoning agent and garnish of the first order, so widely available in markets year-round, that we tend to take it for granted. Its versatility in cooking is unparalleled among kitchen herbs. It modifies the very strong flavors of the *Allium* family and helps to blend the flavors of other herbs. Virtually every meat, soup, or salad is improved by its addition. But it has other uses, too. It's rich in vitamin C, aids digestion, and freshens the breath—chew that parsley garnish following a meal, don't leave it on the plate!

Both curly and flat-leaf parsley grow the same way, but many people prefer the flat-leaf varieties because they are more strongly flavored. Parsley can be grown from seed sown directly in the garden but, as indicated, special care is required. As the seed takes twenty to twenty-five days to germinate (as long as carrot seed), the trick is to keep the seedbed evenly moistened until the sprouts finally appear. Here's how to do that.

Plan your sowing for about two weeks before the last expected date of a killing frost in your area. Fertilize the seed row where you intend to raise the parsley. Mark the row to a depth of ½ inch and sow the seed (without presoaking) at ½-inch intervals. Cover the furrow with sand, then moisten thoroughly. Now cut a 1-inch × 6-inch wood plank to the length of the row and thoroughly soak the board. Cover the row with the wet board, which will keep the seed moist and in place (in the likely event of spring showers), at the same time preventing weeds from taking hold and keeping the ground from cooling too much at night.

After the first two weeks, lift up the board every day to water, if necessary. As soon as seedlings appear, remove the board. Within two to three weeks of germination, the plants will be well established, but still small, so weed the row every three to four days. In another two to three weeks, the parsley will be 4 inches high and you can begin to harvest leaves.

Your parsley will continue to provide plenty of foliage throughout the first growing season and well into the winter months. I've harvested it from under snow on Valentine's Day. In the second spring, as a biennial, it will grow rapidly, producing broad flower clusters similar to the umbels of dill, caraway, or Queen Anne's Lace. Cut these umbels, pretty as they may look, as soon as they begin to form and you'll get more leaf production out of the second-year plant. Meanwhile, you should sow a fresh crop of parsley for the new season, which should be ready for you to pick by the time the old plants expire.

If you want parsley in the kitchen in winter, don't try digging the plant out of the garden, because its long tap root does not lend itself to transplant. Instead, start a fresh crop by sowing seed in August or September in a container that you can bring inside. Cover the sowing pot or tray with plastic wrap to help keep the soil moist during this herb's germination period. Parsley makes an attractive hanging basket in the winter in a sunny foyer or by the window over the kitchen sink.

With fresh parsley available in food markets all winter, few cooks still dry their own, but my mother does. She dries it on cookie trays in her oven, replacing her oven light with a 100-watt bulb for the purpose. The drying process takes most of the day, then she stores it in opaque bottles. The taste is much superior to store-bought dried parsley since this herb won't hold its flavor more than three to four months in dried form.

PURSLANE

PORTULACA OLERACEA

A low-spreading annual with round red/purple
stems and fleshy, oval leaves up to 1 inch long,
possessing a sharp, fresh taste.

When we were growing up, our unofficial "god-mother" was a wonderful family friend from New Jersey named Antoinette DeFeo. Antoinette was a well-loved but somewhat eccentric woman. On her frequent visits in the summer, she would wander through our yard and garden gathering wild-growing purslane to mix with the salad of the day. That's how I learned to appreciate purslane as a salad herb. I especially like it in combination with chervil. But most gardeners still classify it as a pesty weed, like dandelion: purslane does grow and spread rapidly in any sunny location.

While it's possible to gather purslane in the wild, à l'Antoinette, I prefer to cultivate it in a row in the salad garden. Sow the seed directly in the soil following the last frost. Thin the seedlings to 6 inches and begin to harvest in about six weeks, when the shoots are 4 to 6 inches. If the plants get ahead of you during the growing season, cut them back to 3 to 4 inches and they will send out tender new shoots within seven to ten days. Old stems may be stripped of their leaves and pickled.

I prefer the yellow or golden purslane, *Portulaca oleracea sativa,* to the standard variety as it is more attractive and grows somewhat more erect. Both varieties have the same fresh taste.

ROSEMARY

ROSMARINUS OFFICINALIS

*A tender single-stem perennial growing
as a compact shrub to 1 to 4 feet, with needlelike
leaves, imbued with a strong, pinelike aroma,
and pale blue flowers.*

Rosemary is the queen of kitchen herbs. Its powerful fragrance makes it desirable for many uses, in the kitchen and elsewhere. Its compact beauty lends itself to display indoors or out, in containers or in the ground. It can be trained as topiary. It is seen so often in Christmas wreaths and other decorations that it has a special association with that holiday for many people. Traditionally, it is given "for remembrance" and in fact very few gardeners ever forget to include it somewhere in their plans.

Some varieties of rosemary lend themselves to particular uses. Prostrate rosemary (*Rosemarinus officinalis prostratus*) grows only 3 to 4 inches high, but its curving stems stretch and cascade on all sides. It is most attractive in hanging baskets or window boxes, or planted at the edge of gardens or atop garden walls. Pine-scented rosemary (*Rosemarinus officinalis* 'Benendan Blue' var.) makes a decorative miniature Christmas tree; it can be gradually trained to a tree shape while providing cuttings and fragrance in the garden all summer, then brought indoors for the holiday. Foresteri rosemary (*Rosemarinus foresteri*) is a more vigorous grower than the standard rosemary, with denser foliage that some people find more desirable. There are also subspecies that produce pink or white flowers instead of the more common blue blossoms, all of which, incidentally, are tiny sparkles of color on the foliage.

All varieties of rosemary are easy to grow provided they receive plenty of sun and air circulation. If rosemary is located in a stuffy corner, inside the house or out in the garden, it begins to lose its leaves and soon develops a mildewlike fungus that makes the plant unsightly and eventually kills it.

Rosemary is difficult to propagate from seed so we start our plants from cuttings. This is not a complicated procedure but it requires a lot of attention over a period of six to eight weeks. Most people will prefer to buy already established young plants in the spring from a nursery or garden center. Wait until after the last frost to put the plant into the garden. To facilitate bringing the rosemary indoors in the fall, transfer the young plant into a 8-inch clay pot at this time. Then plant it, pot and all, in the garden in your desired location. Make sure the rim of the pot is below the soil line, otherwise the clay will conduct heat into the ground and dry out the soil too rapidly.

If you planted the rosemary directly into the garden, you could dig it up in the fall, then pot it and bring it inside. But you would damage some of the roots in the process and set the plant back at a time when it needs all its vigor to become acclimatized to indoor living conditions.

Leaving it in the pot, however, means it should be checked more often to see if it needs water. In this respect, treat it just as you would if you planted rosemary in a hanging basket or window box. Fertilize three times during the growing season: once in the spring, in midsummer, and finally in late summer or early fall.

Rosemary is not a rapid grower. In the first year, wait until new growth has formed before harvesting sprigs, or about six weeks after transplant. You'll recognize the new growth by its fresh green look. In the second year, the stem will start becoming woody.

Avoid cutting into woody parts as this will hinder development of the plant.

If you bring your rosemary indoors, you'll be able to harvest from it throughout the winter, the quantity depending on the age and size of the plant. I can't overemphasize the importance of locating your rosemary plant properly for its indoor season. A sunny window with a southern exposure is essential. In the Northeast most homes get plenty of air movement in the fall and early spring, when windows and doors are opened with some frequency. But the air becomes fairly stagnant in the months of December, January, and February, and that's when some people begin to have trouble with their plants. I've noticed that homes with forced hot air heating systems have less trouble than others. That extra air movement helps to keep the rosemary healthy.

Sprigs of rosemary can be dried on a tray or screen, then chopped coarsely in a blender or coffee grinder and stored. But if you have a live rosemary plant with you year-round, chances are you'll prefer to enjoy the queen of herbs fresh.

SAGE

*A hardy perennial shrub growing to 36 inches with
long, oval, gray-green leaves of strong aroma,
and spikes of lavender-blue flowers.*

"Why should a man die when sage flourishes in his garden?" goes the old proverb. But which sage? There are at least five hundred varieties of this most populous of all the herb families. They offer a multitude of subtle differences in flavor, color, or growing and flowering habit. Many, though technically perennial, are too tender to survive cold winters, however. That's why I usually recommend common gray or garden sage or its smaller version, dwarf sage (*Salvia officinalis* 'Nana'), for kitchen gardens. Both plants are hardy and produce leaves full of the volatile oil that impregnates fowl, game, and fatty meats like pork with the familiar sage flavor.

The dwarf sage grows only to a height of about 8 inches, so it is ideal for very small gardens and patio planters or windowboxes. It's also a good variety to pick for a winter house plant, because it is manageably small yet has the desired flavor for cooking.

Sage is difficult to propagate so I recommend acquiring young plants in the spring from a garden center or reputable grower. Sage is related to the popular garden flower salvia, and you'll see a resemblance between them in leaf configuration and growth pattern. In fact some of my customers insist on asking for sage as *salvia,* its Italian name, and they sometimes get sent to the red salvia in our flower section rather than to the herb department.

Transplant the young sage to the garden after all danger of frost is past in the spring. If the plant has been hardened off in a cold frame or porchway, it can be moved into the garden two to three weeks earlier. Cut leaves and sprigs as needed once the plant begins to grow vigorously in the garden. In its first year, this may not occur until early summer or later, but in succeeding years, you can begin the harvest as soon as new tender growth appears on the shrub. Cut flowers as they form to promote leaf production.

Sage becomes mushy when thawed after freezing and it loses its pungency when dried, but it can be saved. Cut 6 to 8 inches of top growth from the plant two or three times a year (after the first growing season), then dry the bunches in thin layers. Sage leaves are heavy so drying may take a bit longer than most other herbs, about seven to ten days.

In addition to the basic culinary sages, there are two other groups worth considering, as they have the sage flavor in addition to other features. They are the fruit-flavored sages and the colorful sages.

Pineapple sage (*Salvia elegans*) grows to 30 inches, producing a bright red flower and fragrant pineapple aroma. It won't tolerate cold weather, so it must be grown as an annual in the North. It's attractive in the garden and brings a fresh bite to fruit salads and cold summer drinks. Fruity sage (*Salvia Dorisiana*) has a mixed-fruit flavor that works well in potpourris. It also is too tender for northern winters but, with its velvety leaves and pink flowers, it makes a handsome plant.

Three colorfully leafed sages are especially use-ful as decorative accent plants. Tricolor sage (*Salvia officinalis 'Tricolor'*), as the name suggests, boasts variegated leaves of gray, white, and purple. Golden sage (*Salvia officinalis aurea*) has a mixed yellow-and-gray leaf, and purple sage (*Salvia officinalis 'Purpurea'*) comes in various shades of purple. All three are medium-size hardy plants, growing in an attractive moundlike fashion to about 15 inches, with leaves somewhat milder in flavor than those of common sage but still pungent enough for culinary purposes. A mixed planting of these sages produces an excellent decorative effect. I fill a long windowbox outside our dining room with all three along with several colorful thyme plants. We harvest directly from it while enjoying its beauty all summer.

SANTOLINA

SANTOLINA CHAMAECYPARISSUS

*A very hardy perennial growing to 15 inches,
with silver-gray or green foliage
and golden floral buttons.*

Sometimes called "lavender cotton," santolina is tra-ditionally used as a border around formal herb gar-dens. It has no culinary properties, but I always include it in a kitchen garden because it repels in-sects and other pests with its harsh, bitter aroma. It is the best herb bug repellent I know. Placed in the center and the corners of a small garden, santolina helps to keep its neighbors healthy and adds beauty with its lacy foliage and yellow flowers. It can even be trained, as topiary, to grow in a variety of forms from square to sphere (though pruning prevents blossoming).

Santolina is difficult to start from seed, so the only viable means of propagation is by cutting. Better yet, start with young healthy transplants from your nurseryman or garden center. Once in the garden, santolina will be with you for many seasons to come, and with relatively little care.

SAVORY

SATUREJA HORTENSIS

A very tender soft-stemmed annual growing to 18 inches in a loose bush form with narrow, piquant leaves and tiny white flowers.

An elderly German woman speaking limited English came into our garden center one day looking for an herb she called *Bonnerkraut*. She walked with a cane and seemed a bit frail, so I invited her to sit down while I tried to satisfy her order. I spent about fifteen minutes bringing out pots of different herbs for her to inspect, but none measured up. Finally in frustration she asked to see my gardens and I accompanied her as she hobbled to the first garden. When she came to a row of summer savory, she whacked it with the tip of her cane, as if to scold it for hiding from her, and declared, *"Das ist Bonnerkraut!"*

Bonnerkraut, I learned later, is German for "bean herb," and, indeed, summer savory is well known for its affinity for dishes with beans, lentils, or peas. In fact, the old woman interplanted summer savory with bush beans in her own garden in the same way my grandmother always grew basil in between her tomato plants. Some herbs and vegetables simply deserve each other.

Some health-minded cooks value summer savory because it can be used as a salt substitute in their recipes. The herb acts on a dish as a seasoning agent in much the way salt does.

Summer savory is easily grown from seed. After all danger of frost is past, sow directly in the garden, either in several clusters 8 to 10 inches apart, about three seeds to a cluster or in a row, seeding about ½ inch apart. Cover with fine sand and keep moist until germination, which is fast: often within four to five days. Thin plants to 1 inch after three weeks.

Make your first picking of tender new shoots about six weeks after plants first appear, when they are 4 to 6 inches high. Then they will begin to grow more vigorously and within four to five weeks you should be able to harvest regularly as needed.

Cut the plant down to the ground before the first frost in the fall. Hang in small bunches or dry on trays, then strip the leaves for storage.

Winter savory (*Satureja montana*) has a bit more pungent taste than summer savory. Some gardeners prefer it because it is a perennial, requiring little care after the first year. It germinates extremely slowly and must be started indoors from seed at least four months before setting out. Many garden centers sell winter savory seedlings in the spring. This is a much easier way to get the plant started in your garden.

This plant can be put out anytime around the

last frost date. Sprigs can be harvested in six to eight weeks. Reaching 12 inches in height, it has a compact, shrublike growing habit. It's normally hardy, but it may suffer winterkill in very wet conditions. It becomes overly woody with age and should be replaced with a young plant every three to four years.

Creeping winter savory (*Satureja repandra*) is a perennial but it grows much lower to the ground than its cousin. It has the same strong flavor. Its prostrate growth pattern makes it ideal for hanging baskets, pots, or the edges of a garden. Rock and herb gardeners often fancy this variety.

SHALLOTS

ALLIUM ASCALONICUM

A hollow-stemmed onion-family herb that grows from a bulb to 8 inches, producing clusters of bulbs coveted for their delicate onion-scallion-garlic flavor.

Raymond Saufroy of West Danville, Vermont, is the shallot king of the Western world. Before retiring in 1963, he owned an haute cuisine French restaurant in New York City. Then he started another business: selling shallots by mail order under the name Le Jardin du Gourmet. Before he moved to his present location, he worked out of Ramsey, New Jersey, and when I started ordering shallots from him, I assumed his premiere "Jersey" shallots were named after the Garden State.

I was wrong. The shallots came from the Isle of Jersey, the largest of the English Channel islands. The ease of growing and the delectable savor of Jersey shallots made them Raymond's No. 1 choice for his customers in this country. Other varieties just do not measure up to his high standards. "If there's no purple in the meat of the shallot when you cut it," he says, "then it isn't a real shallot. It's probably one of those 'potato onions' disguised as a shallot."

The "Frog's Leg" shallot, so called because it is

shaped like the thigh of a frog, is French, and much bigger than the Jersey, with bulbs about the size of a small egg. Restaurants favor this variety because it's so big, making it easier to use in the kitchen, and you will also see it in food stores. But Ray doesn't think it has the delectable flavor of the Jersey.

Shallots can be grown almost exactly like garlic. Plant them in the fall, as with garlic, and the extra growing time will result in bigger yields the following year: about six bulbs for every one planted, ranging from the size of a dime to the size of a quarter. Plant them early in the spring and you'll still get a crop, only the bulbs will be smaller and fewer.

Plant shallots 2 inches deep at 4-inch intervals, perhaps along one border, or in rows 6 inches apart. Fertilize the planting area and mix a handful of limestone into the soil if necessary to sweeten it up to about pH 7.5.

Shallots grow quickly in the cool weather of early spring or late fall. The hollow stems reach a height of about 8 inches. Some people clip the stems and use them as greens, rather like chives, but I prefer not to: rainwater can get into the stems and cause rotting. By late summer, with growth finished, the leaves get floppy and die down, a signal to dig up the bulbs that have formed in loose clusters. Remember to save enough from your harvest to replant another row of shallots for next season. Before bringing shallot inside, clean soil off bulbs (but *not* by washing them in water), and store in an onion basket or pantry out of reach of sunlight. Do not store in a refrigerator because they will absorb moisture and turn soft. Stored properly, shallots keep three to four months.

SORREL

RUMEX ACETOSA OR SCUTATUS

A very hardy perennial growing in loose-leaf clusters to 12 inches in the first year, with a lemony tart flavor.

Sorrel is a summery tonic to the palate. Its unique lemony tart flavor and bright yellow-green color infuse freshness in salads or the classic cold soup that bears its name.

Although this herb is a perennial, I recommend treating sorrel as a biennial when you grow it in the garden. That's because it bolts early in the second growing season, after which its leaves may become tough and bitter.

Sorrel is easily started from seed in the garden, as soon as the garden soil has warmed. The small oval seeds have a shiny, burgundy color. For maximum production, sow the seed as for any salad crop. Mark a row 3 to 4 feet long and ¼ inch deep. Sow the seed, cover with sand, and keep moistened until germination, in about eight days. When the seedlings are 2 inches high, thin, leaving about 3 to 4 inches of space between the strongest plants.

Begin harvesting leaves when they are 4 to 6 inches high, about six weeks from sprouting. When a substantial harvest is required, cut the leaves down to ground level, as the plant will grow back vigorously. Harvesting can continue several weeks past the first frost in your area. In late fall, sorrel leaves assume a reddish tint but flavor does not change.

Early in the next spring, the sorrel will resume growing and may be harvested when leaves reach 4 inches high. If allowed to remain in the garden into the warm weather of June, seed stalks will form and shoot up to 3 to 4 feet high. Instead, dig up the entire row and sow a fresh crop. This will ensure a steady supply of tender leaves with the desirable fresh sorrel flavor. Also, this will prevent the herb from wantonly self-sowing throughout your garden.

Sorrel seeds are marketed under several names. The variety called Nobel is the sorrel of choice among French chefs, who contend its somewhat broader leaves are more succulent than other varieties.

This herb may be grown indoors in a pot or window box. Sow the seeds in September or early October for a crop that will be ready for the holidays.

TARRAGON

ARTEMISIA DRACUNCULUS SATIVA

A hardy spreading perennial growing in a bush to 24 inches, with shiny green, narrow leaves possessing a bittersweet licorice flavor.

"Taste before you buy" should be the caveat for people shopping for their first tarragon plants. Unlike most herbs, French tarragon is impossible to start from seed (it doesn't produce seed) and may only be propagated from cuttings or root division. As a result, most gardeners prefer the convenience of buying a young plant from a nursery or garden center.

However, Russian tarragon (*Artemisia Dracunculus*) can be started from seed, and some commercial growers unwittingly put it into the market labeled as "tarragon." You'll be disappointed if you fail to taste-test the plant before buying. To the eye, Russian tarragon resembles French tarragon, but the coarse, weedy flavor of its leaves makes it unsuitable for the kitchen garden. For making classic French sauces like béarnaise and hollandaise or for spiking omelets, marinades, and stuffings with that enticing tarragon flavor, only French tarragon will do.

Tarragon suffers in wet conditions so be sure to locate your young plant in a particularly well-drained section of the garden. The plant can be put out in the early spring several weeks before the last frost date. Cut fresh sprigs as needed beginning about six to eight weeks after the transplant. This herb takes longer to become established than many other perennials, but once it reaches 6 to 8 inches high, you can harvest from it selectively. After the first year, the plant will be a more generous producer for you. You can cut it to within 2 inches of the ground as needed every month throughout the growing season.

As a member of the Artemisia plant family, tarragon requires a period of dormancy during the winter months. It does poorly in Southern gardens where there are no prolonged periods of freezing temperatures.

Mulching will keep the tarragon in hibernation and prevent it from reviving prematurely during a midwinter warm spell. After you've cut the plant to the ground toward the end of fall, wait for the soil to freeze solid to a depth of 1 inch—it will take three consecutive nights in the 20s for this to happen. Then mulch the tarragon with a 6-inch layer of salt hay. If this superb natural insulator is unavailable in your area, substitute a thick layer of leaves held in place by small branches or narrow boards.

There are two good methods for bringing tarragon indoors over the winter. One is to dig up the entire plant in the fall and make a root division. Put half of the plant back into the ground, then plant the other half in a 4-inch clay pot. Bury this pot in the ground for at least three good freezes. This will give the plant time to recoup its energies and prevent premature growth indoors, which would weaken it. When you're ready to mulch the garden tarragon, dig the potted tarragon out and bring it inside.

Alternatively, make a root division, wash off the roots of your new plant thoroughly, then place in a sealed plastic bag in the vegetable bin of your refrigerator. Leave it in cold storage for two months, then take it out and plant in a pot; within four weeks you can begin to harvest tarragon again.

When harvesting, handle tarragon leaves very carefully, as they bruise easily and lose their aroma. Dry in bunches hung up in a dark, dry area or on screens or trays. Or freeze sprigs in plastic ziplock bags.

Remove mulch from the garden in late winter or very early spring to prevent fungus from developing as the weather warms.

THYME

THYMUS VULGARIS

A perennial herb growing in a semibush form to 12 inches, with delicate stems and tiny green aromatic leaves.

Common thyme is an herb of uncommon value to the gardener and the cook. Its slightly pungent flavor tames strong meats and fishes and enhances soups and ragouts. As an attractive, compact grower, it can be used to embellish gardens of every shape, size, and design, in containers or in the ground, indoors and out.

Also known as English thyme, common thyme is only one of over three hundred varieties of this species, the third largest family of herbs, after sage (over five hundred) and mint (over four hundred). I recommend it because it is a relatively hardy perennial. French thyme (*Thymus vulgaris* var.) has grey-green, narrow, more pointed leaves, and a sweet flavor that is often preferred in French cuisine. However, it is much less hardy than common thyme and may not survive harsh Northern winters even when mulched. German thyme (*Thymus vulgaris* var.) is a more compact bush than English or French thyme— it's sometimes called dwarf thyme—and withstands cold well, but it does not offer the same leaf production as the English variety.

Thyme is best started from seed in pots indoors, about eight weeks prior to the expected date of the last frost for your area in the spring, then transferred to the garden. Thyme seed is so small, like tiny grains of sand, and germinates so slowly, that direct sowing into the garden soil is somewhat unpredictable. Young plants should be located where soil drains the best in your garden, as thyme, like tarragon, dislikes wet feet.

In the first year, cut sprigs beginning six weeks from the date of transplant, when the plants are 4 to 5 inches high, but leave at least 2 inches on the stems. In succeeding years you can begin the harvest earlier in the season, and more often. But avoid cutting into woody stems. Make your final harvest after the first fall frost. When the ground has frozen, following three consecutive days of freezing temperatures, mulch the plant with salt hay or some other suitable material. Thyme has a tendency to winterkill but mulching should prevent that. Remove mulch in the late winter to prevent any danger of rot when the growing season resumes.

Thyme begins to get too woody and untidy for my taste in its third or fourth growing season, and I usually replace the plant with vigorous young seedlings when that happens.

To harvest for storing, cut 6 inches of leafy tops and flower clusters before blossoms actually appear. It's easy to dry thyme on screens or trays because it doesn't hold that much moisture to begin with. When it becomes brittle, strip the leaves or run through a coarse sieve, then store in an opaque container.

Thyme takes other forms that will also be of interest to gardeners even if some of these varieties are not suitable as kitchen herbs.

There are the "walking-on" thymes (*Thymus Serpyllum* and *Thymus praecox*), so called because they tolerate being trod upon, delightfully releasing their aromas under foot. As low-growing, creeping varieties, they make excellent fillers on terraces and flagstone or brick pathways. Most cooks do not consider them sufficiently aromatic for kitchen uses.

Another group of creeping thymes feature fuzzy, wool-like leaves. The best-known varieties are wooly thyme (*Thymus pseudolanuginosus*), Hall's wooly thyme (*Thymus pseudolanuginosus* 'Hall's wooly'), and wooly stemmed thymes (*Thymus pseudolanuginosus* var.). The novel leaf surface makes the wooly thymes interesting to grow, but they have no culinary use. Also, their leaves tend to collect moisture and they are prone to rotting in wet areas or during prolonged rainy periods. The wooly thymes are best in rock gardens or other high and dry spots in your landscape.

Some thymes have decorative value because of their variegated leaves. Golden lemon thyme (*Thymus citriodorus* 'Aureus') has foliage edged with sharply

defined splashes of yellow, while silver-edged thyme (*Thymus vulgaris 'Argenteus'*) offers leaves with contrasting white and green. Their pronounced thyme fragrance also makes them suitable for use in recipes or as garnishes.

Adventurous cooks might enjoy experimenting with the large group of diversely flavored thymes. The names speak for themselves: caraway thyme (*Thymus Herba-barona*), nutmeg thyme (*Thymus Herba-barona* var.), lemon thyme (*Thymus × citriodorus*), Doone Valley lemon thyme (*Thymus pulegioides 'Doone Valley'*), oregano thyme (*Thymus vulgaris* var.), and many others. The lemon-flavored thymes go especially well with chicken and fish and make fine teas. Caraway thyme is the traditional seasoning for the English baron of beef, hence its botanical name, *Herba-barona*.

Oregano thyme can also be used interchangeably with true oregano in many Italian dishes, as one customer told me in no uncertain terms one day. An elderly Italian gentleman with a deep, heavily accented voice came in looking for oregano. I took him over to our oregano varieties and he sampled a leaf from each one, shaking his head each time and saying "No, no, 'atsa no oregano!" Then I took him out to a test plot of Oregano Maru in one of the gardens and he shook his head without even sampling it this time, as if to suggest I had a lot to learn about oregano. Finally I gave up and let him wander around our property on his own. About ten minutes later I heard him give a whoop over by the thyme garden. There he was, bending over a patch of oregano thyme. " 'Atsa oregano!" he said, as he straightened up and shoved a handful of it under my nose.

I shrugged and sent him home with six complimentary pots of oregano thyme, unlabeled.

SWEET VIOLET

VIOLA ODORATA

*A hardy perennial growing to 4 inches,
with serrated heart-shaped leaves
and sweet-scented purple blooms.*

© ROBERT MAIER, EARTH SCENES

This dainty and aromatic flower was prized by the Greeks and Romans for its spring beauty and fragrance. It was antiquity's flower of fertility, used in perfumes and love potions.

Today the sweet violet is as popular as ever. It's the first herb to flower in the early spring, and invariably we sell out of it within two or three weeks. I've never been successful at germinating sweet violet seed, in spite of the claims of some advertisers, so we propagate the plant by dividing the many runners it puts forth. Violets can be set in the garden in early spring, but select a semishady location so that the plants won't wither in the summer heat.

Violets that bloom in purple, white, or yellow are sometimes offered to the public as sweet violets, but they may not possess the characteristic sweet fragrance of the true sweet violet, which is always purple. Before buying, conduct a sniff-and-taste test, as I advised on the subject of tarragon.

Sweet violet is an excellent rock garden plant and companion to other spring-flowering perennials such as candytuft and yellow alyssum. It will produce plenty of flowers to harvest for salads and desserts long before the other edible flowers in your garden have even begun to bud.

HERB	COMMON VARIETIES	TASTE	BEST WITH	HOW TO USE	HERB COMBINATIONS
Tarragon	French is the only kind you want.	Piquant, mild licorice flavor.	Seafood, poultry, veal, fruit, herb butters, marinades, salad dressings, and vinegars. Use in blend known as *fines herbes*.	Use sprigs or strip leaves from stem. Use whole or chopped.	Excellent combined with basil, bay, chervil, fennel, garlic, parsley, and shallots. Classic *fines herbes* blend contains tarragon, parsley, chervil, and chives. Tarragon also blends well with cress, dill, mint, savory, sorrel, and thyme.
Thyme	English, French, German, Lemon Thyme	Spicy, slightly sweet flavor.	Chicken, veal, vegetables, marinades, soups, stews, Creole dishes.	Use sprigs or strip leaves from stem. Use whole.	Good herb for combining with basil, bay, chives, garlic, marjoram, oregano, parsley, rosemary, sage, savory, and tarragon.

SWEET VIOLET

VIOLA ODORATA

*A hardy perennial growing to 4 inches,
with serrated heart-shaped leaves
and sweet-scented purple blooms.*

© ROBERT MAIER, EARTH SCENES

This dainty and aromatic flower was prized by the Greeks and Romans for its spring beauty and fragrance. It was antiquity's flower of fertility, used in perfumes and love potions.

Today the sweet violet is as popular as ever. It's the first herb to flower in the early spring, and invariably we sell out of it within two or three weeks. I've never been successful at germinating sweet violet seed, in spite of the claims of some advertisers, so we propagate the plant by dividing the many runners it puts forth. Violets can be set in the garden in early spring, but select a semishady location so that the plants won't wither in the summer heat.

Violets that bloom in purple, white, or yellow are sometimes offered to the public as sweet violets, but they may not possess the characteristic sweet fragrance of the true sweet violet, which is always purple. Before buying, conduct a sniff-and-taste test, as I advised on the subject of tarragon.

Sweet violet is an excellent rock garden plant and companion to other spring-flowering perennials such as candytuft and yellow alyssum. It will produce plenty of flowers to harvest for salads and desserts long before the other edible flowers in your garden have even begun to bud.

SALAD HERB GARDEN

Of all the specialized gardens, this is my favorite. It is simple, easy to maintain and harvest from, and as much a source for our daily meals as the local grocery store. Adjust its size to your own space requirements and its contents to your own palate. I always include several rows of arugula in the garden simply because our family uses so much of it, and I sow succession crops of it to guarantee tender young leaves for our salads.

The plan for this garden measures only 50 square feet, but it produces more bounty for the table than many gardens much larger in size. If you can locate the garden against a wall or barrier with a southern exposure, add a small plastic cold frame to cover it for the winter and you will be able to harvest zest for your salads almost year-round.

CHIVES SORREL SALAD BURNET WINTER SAVORY DWARF BASIL RED BASIL ARUGULA FLAT PARSLEY ARUGULA LETTUCES ARUGULA CURLED PARSLEY CHICORIA BORAGE NASTURTIUM MUSTARD SUMMER SAVORY CHERVIL

ITALIAN HERB GARDEN

My grandmother never had an herb garden as such, for she grew all the herbs she needed amid the plants in her substantial vegetable garden. This garden, then, is a concentrated version of the kitchen herbs that were so important to her cooking.

The garden's practical design enables cultivating and harvesting with minimal time and effort. If you don't have a yard, the containers of rosemary, bay, thyme, sage, parsley, and oregano can be arranged on a deck or patio. Bring the containers inside in the late fall if you have an enclosed location that receives plenty of sun. Large boxes or barrels are suitable for the annuals that demand more growing room and occasional fertilizing.

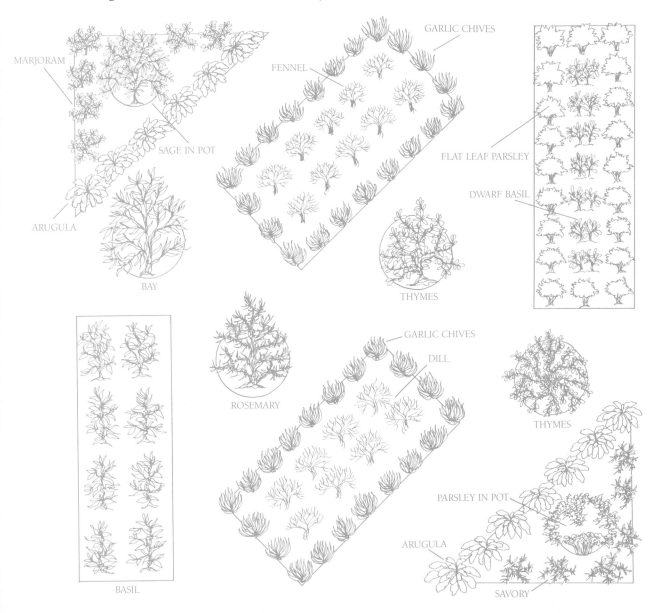

FISH-HERB GARDEN

Formerly, during trout season, an avid fisherman friend of mine would pack his freezer with the trout he caught. But he would draw on his supply for meals only once or twice a month, simply because he knew only one recipe for cooking trout. Then one year his wife put in her first herb garden. Now he has become an expert at creating various herbal combinations to season his fish. His freezer never becomes overstocked with trout, and he never tires of catching and cooking it.

There are fifteen herbs featured in this garden, enough variety to prepare your own favorite fish with innumerable flavor combinations. In half the garden, I have confined the annual herbs in rows, and the rest of the space I have assigned to perennials. This is a functional layout that can be applied to many specialized herb gardens.

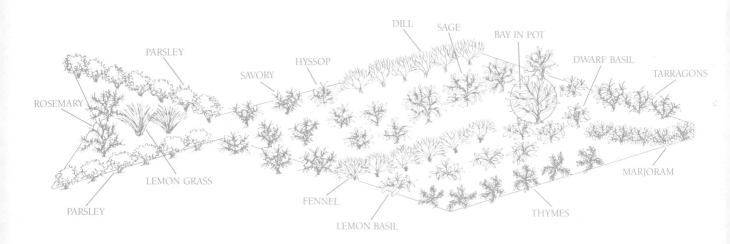

ROSEMARY   PARSLEY   SAVORY   HYSSOP   DILL   SAGE   BAY IN POT   DWARF BASIL   TARRAGONS

PARSLEY   LEMON GRASS   FENNEL   LEMON BASIL   THYMES   MARJORAM

DESSERT HERB GARDEN

This rock garden plan features the herbs commonly used in fruit or dessert dishes. The several different kinds of mint are in containers set amid rocks or atop a flat stone, to minimize the intrusion of these feckless growers into the rest of the garden.

Rock gardens are especially hospitable to herbs because they are usually very well drained and offer plenty of air and light circulation. Flat stones are handy for stepping from place to place within the garden.

I've limited this garden to herbs that I enjoy as embellishments to dessert courses. All of them have a sweet or fruity taste or flavor and with a little imagination can be used to brighten any number of dishes. For example, the leaves of the scented geraniums, if placed under the wax paper in the bottom of a tray containing sponge cake, will impart the flavor of the particular geranium to the cake.

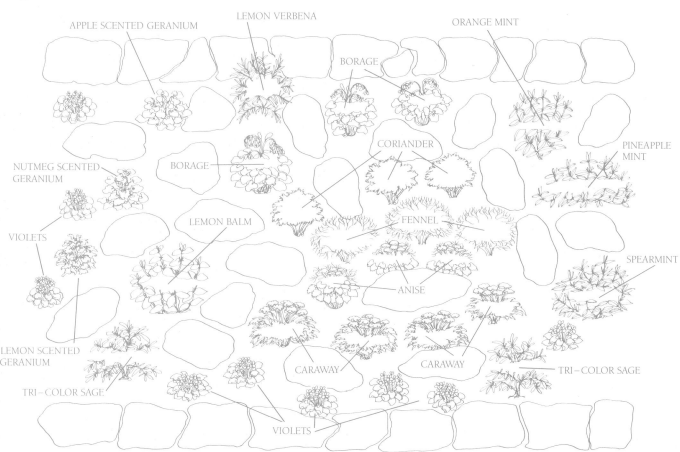

EDIBLE FLOWER GARDEN

Properly planned and cared for, this garden should give you attractive and colorful blooms to harvest for your favorite recipes from early spring to late fall. This is the order in which the herbs should flower if all goes well and the blossom colors.

violets (perennial)—white, purple

violas or pansies (perennial)—white, yellow, purple, blue

chives (perennial)—lavender

calendula (annual)—orange, yellow

lemon thyme (perennial)—pale lavender

lavender (perennial)—lavender

nasturtium (annual)—yellow, orange, red

borage (annual)—blue

anise hyssop (perennial)—dark blue

hyssop (perennial)—white, pink, blue

bee balm (perennial)—reds, pink, white, lavender

winter savory (perennial)—white

pineapple sage (annual)—red

If you decide to include several colors of hyssop, chances are you will end up with one faded color after several years of cross-pollination, unless you succeed in harvesting flowers before that occurs. Generally, it's a good idea to cut flowers early in the blossoming stage, rather than late, to maximize production by the plants. "The more you pick, the more they come," as my father used to say. Also, be sure to fertilize the garden at three to four-week intervals in the growing season. Flowering herbs simply require more organic feed to perform well.

Most of the perennials in this garden will flower more profusely in the second and subsequent years. All annuals should be removed at the time of the first frost in the fall, to keep the garden clean for the following spring. The calendula will bloom rapidly in the heat of summer, then falter except in areas where nights are cool. A fall crop of this striking orange-yellow bloom can be attained by sowing new seed in August.

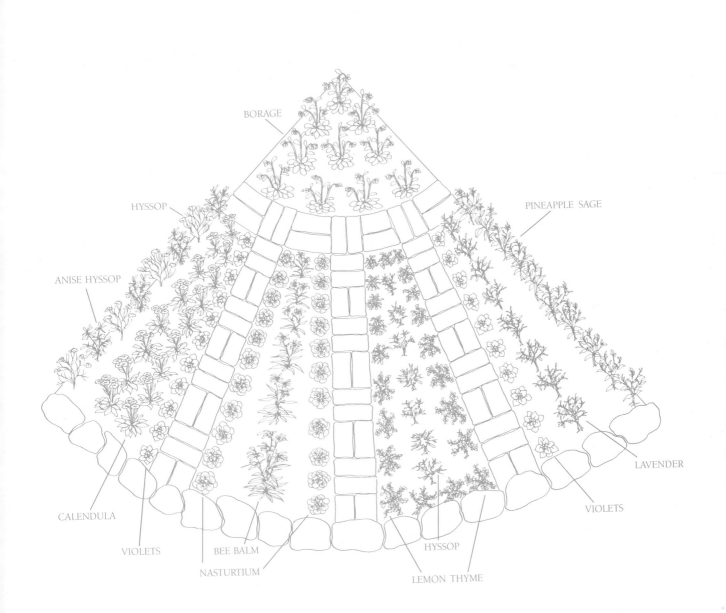

BORAGE

HYSSOP

PINEAPPLE SAGE

ANISE HYSSOP

CALENDULA

VIOLETS

BEE BALM

NASTURTIUM

HYSSOP

LEMON THYME

VIOLETS

LAVENDER

HERBS IN THE GARDEN

SALT-SUBSTITUTE GARDEN

For people on restricted diets or for cooks interested in reducing their reliance on salt to flavor food, this garden is the answer. Savory (both the summer and winter varieties) is the mainstay for herbal salt substitution, and when blended with other herbs, it will help you to produce appetizing dishes consistently. The blends of herbs are listed in order of recommended volumes, but the proportions should be adjusted according to your personal tastes and preferences. Both fresh and dried herbs are suitable for making the blends, always bearing in mind that larger quantities of fresh herbs are usually required to achieve the same degree of tang or savor.

SALAD BLEND

basil
parsley
lovage
marjoram
dill
tarragon
savory

SOUP BLEND

basil
lovage
parsley
marjoram
thyme
savory
bay

BEEF AND VEAL BLEND

basil
lovage
parsley
thyme
marjoram
savory
sage

FISH BLEND

basil
lemon balm
dill
fennel (leaves)
savory
rosemary
rue

POULTRY BLEND

sage
thyme
savory
parsley
lovage
marjoram
basil

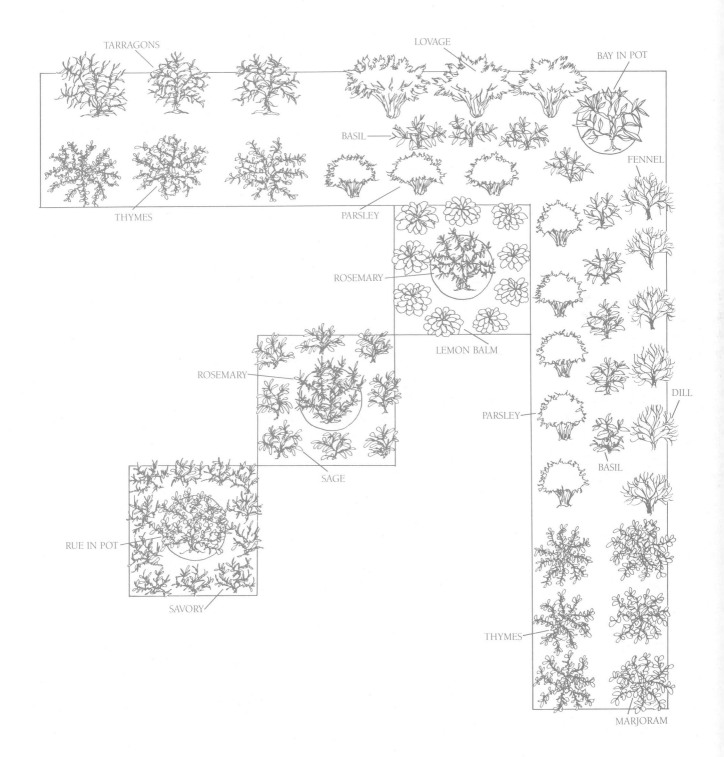

TARRAGONS

LOVAGE

BAY IN POT

BASIL

FENNEL

THYMES

PARSLEY

ROSEMARY

LEMON BALM

ROSEMARY

PARSLEY

DILL

BASIL

SAGE

RUE IN POT

SAVORY

THYMES

MARJORAM

HERBS IN THE GARDEN

KITCHEN HERBS

HERB	COMMON VARIETIES	TASTE	BEST WITH	HOW TO USE	HERB COMBINATIONS
Arugula (Roquette)		Pungent, peppery bite.	Best for salads, butters, sautéed with other greens, egg dishes.	Use leaves whole or shred.	Good with basil, borage, cress, dill, lovage, mint, and sage.
Basil	Sweet Bush, Sweet Fine, Small Leaf (minimum), Lettuce Leaf, Dark Opal	Sweet, with warm, clovelike flavor.	Tomatoes, cheese (particularly goat and mozzarella), poultry, eggs, vegetables, authentic pesto sauce.	Use whole or shred leaves by hand.	Combines well with bay, garlic, marjoram, oregano, savory, and thyme in cooked dishes. Goes well with chives, dill, garlic, mint, nasturtium, parsley, and watercress when used fresh.
Borage		Faint taste of cucumber	Best in salads, fruit drinks, teas, and vinegars.	Use blossoms and leaves whole. Leaves can be cooked as a vegetable.	Good with arugula, cress, dill, chervil, and parsley.
Burnet		Flavor resembles cucumber.	Green salads, cream and cottage cheese, vinegars.	Use leaves whole.	Fine with chervil, parsley, rosemary, and tarragon.

HERB	COMMON VARIETIES	TASTE	BEST WITH	HOW TO USE	HERB COMBINATIONS
Caraway		Slight cumin flavor.	Breads, cakes, cookies, soups, stews, vegetables such as beets, cabbage, and potatoes.	Use chopped leaves or seeds. Hollow stems can be cooked as a vegetable and candied like angelica.	Use with bay, garlic, parsley, and thyme.
Chervil		Slight anise flavor.	Salads, egg dishes and omelets, soups, sauces. One of the essential herbs for the French *fines herbes* along with chives, parsley, and tarragon.	Chop leaves or use whole. Best used fresh or cooked briefly.	Can also be used with borage, cress, dill, lemon balm, and sorrel.
Chives	Garlic Chives	Delicate, onion-like flavor.	Herb butters, potatoes, vegetables, eggs, fish, soups, salads, sauces.	Snip or use whole fresh stems. Chives need little cooking. Use flowers too.	Goes well with basil, chervil, coriander (cilantro), cress, dill, lemon balm, marjoram, nasturtium, oregano, parsley, sorrel, tarragon, and thyme.
Coriander (Cilantro)	"Slo-bolting"	Distinctive, minty flavor and aroma.	Affinity for avocados and hot chili peppers. Use with chicken; seafood; in Chinese, Thai, Mexican, and Indian dishes; seviche; tomato and other sauces.	Use whole, snipped, or chopped fresh leaves and tender stems. Don't dry it and don't cook it. Add just before serving.	Can be combined with chives, garlic, marjoram, oregano, and parsley.

HERB	COMMON VARIETIES	TASTE	BEST WITH	HOW TO USE	HERB COMBINATIONS
Cress	Watercress, Upland Cress	Peppery flavor.	Salads, soups, sandwich fillings; stir-fried as a vegetable.	Use leaves and tender young stems. Best flavor when used raw.	Cress harmonizes with bay, borage, chervil, chives, dill, garlic, marjoram, parsley, savory, shallots, sorrel, and tarragon.
Dill	Dill Bouquet	Refreshing, slightly sweet flavor with a hint of caraway.	Seafood, potatoes, cucumbers, chicken, salads, carrots, tomatoes, eggs, salad greens, biscuits, and breads.	Snip or chop leaves. Most flavorful raw but stands up well to cooking.	Goes with basil, bay, borage, chervil, chives, garlic, mint, nasturtium, parsley, sorrel, tarragon, and watercress.
Fennel		Slight anise flavor. Similar to dill in most respects.	Excellent for fish, sauces, soups, stuffings, and salads.	Chop leaves or use seeds.	Fennel goes well with basil, cress, coriander (cilantro), chives, garlic, oregano, parsley, sage, shallots, and tarragon.
Garlic	Elephant Garlic	Sweet, pungent, stronger than onion flavor.	Use with meats, fish, roast lamb, salads, salad dressings, pasta sauces, vegetables, cheese dishes, garlic bread.	Cook whole unpeeled buds, whole or chopped peeled cloves. Tame pungency by blanching and long cooking.	Robust flavor can add subtlety or intensity to food. Goes well with most herbs; use sparingly with chervil, chives, lemon balm, and mint.
Leek		Mild onion flavor.	Use alone as a vegetable or in soups, sauces, and stuffings for chicken, fish, and meats. Use julienne strips as a garnish.	Trim and cook whole; chop or julienne white bulb.	Can be combined with bay, dill, parsley, tarragon, and thyme.

KITCHEN HERBS

HERB	COMMON VARIETIES	TASTE	BEST WITH	HOW TO USE	HERB COMBINATIONS
Lemon Balm		Sweet, citrusy flavor.	Excellent in salads, fresh fruit compotes, custards, fish, chicken, butter sauces, rice, tea, and summer beverages.	Use leaves whole or chop.	Overpowered by stronger herbs. Can be used with chervil, chives, dill, fennel, mint, parsley, shallots, and very carefully with garlic.
Lemon Verbena		Strong aromatic lemon flavor.	Use in place of lemon zest in desserts, soups, salads, fruit dishes, summer coolers.	Strip leaves from stems. Use whole or chopped.	Can be combined with basil, chives, mint, parsley, and tarragon.
Lovage		Flavor similar to celery, but harsher.	Add to stuffings, soups, stews, egg dishes; chop leaves over fish and meat.	Use leaves and tender stems sparingly in place of celery.	Goes well with garlic, marjoram, oregano, parsley, and thyme.
Marjoram (Sweet)		Sweet, mild flavor.	Use on almost any meat or vegetable, poultry and game, fish, beans, pizza, stuffings, fish sauces, cheese and egg dishes.	Strip leaves from stems. Use whole or chopped.	One of the most compatible herbs—goes well with basil, bay leaf, chives, coriander (cilantro), garlic, oregano, mint, parsley, rosemary, sage, savory, and thyme.

HERB	COMMON VARIETIES	TASTE	BEST WITH	HOW TO USE	HERB COMBINATIONS
Mint	Spearmint, Peppermint, Orange Mint	Cool and refreshing flavor depending on variety. Fruited flavors have distinct flavor of name with mint overtones with exception of pineapple mint.	Peas, lamb, veal, green or fruit salad; fish, poultry, Middle Eastern dishes, cucumbers; steep for tea or iced beverages.	Use sprigs, whole, snipped, or chopped leaves.	Use carefully with other herbs; can be combined with basil, lemon balm, nasturtium, parsley, tarragon, and watercress.
Nasturtium		Flowers taste honey sweet; leaves have a peppery bite.	Salads, soups, sandwiches, and as a garnish.	Use flowers and leaves whole or chopped.	Good with basil, chives, cress, dill, mint, and parsley.
Oregano	Greek Oregano, True Oregano	Robust, pungent flavor similar to marjoram but stronger.	Tomatoes, lamb, pork, beef, chicken, salad dressings, bean soup, seafood, all types of vegetables, Italian, Greek, and Mexican dishes.	Strip leaves from the stems. Use whole or chopped.	Flavor blends well with basil, bay, chives, coriander (cilantro), garlic, marjoram, mint, parsley, savory, and thyme.
Parsley	Curly, Flat-Leaf	Faint celery-like flavor. Italian flat–leaf variety has stronger flavor; curly variety better for garnishing.	Virtually all food. Enhances the flavors and appearance of most foods.	Snip or chop leaves.	One of the herbs of *bouquet garni,* with bay and thyme. Combines well with all other herbs.

HERB	COMMON VARIETIES	TASTE	BEST WITH	HOW TO USE	HERB COMBINATIONS
Rosemary	Prostrate, Foresteri	Piquant, pine-like flavor.	Lamb, poultry, pork, grilled meats, vegetables, marinades, breads.	Use sprigs or strip leaves from stems. Use whole or chopped.	Goes well with bay, garlic, marjoram, oregano, parsley, sage, savory, and thyme.
Sage	Grey, Dwarf, Golden, Tricolor, Purple	Aromatic, woodsy flavor.	Predominant seasonings in sausage and bread stuffings, game, fatty meats, vegetables, veal.	Use whole or chopped.	Works well with other robust herbs such as bay, garlic, marjoram, oregano, parsley, rosemary, savory, and thyme.
Savory	Summer, Winter	Peppery taste with summer savory having a more delicate flavor than the winter variety.	Known as the "bean" herb. Also use with tomatoes, fish, poultry, stews, pork and veal, salads.	Use sprigs or chop leaves.	Both varieties combine well with basil, bay, garlic, marjoram, oregano, parsley, rosemary, sage, tarragon, and thyme.
Shallots	'Frog Leg,' 'Jersey'	Mild onion flavor.	Excellent cooked whole as a vegetable; fish and seafood, pasta, poultry and game, mustards, soups, sauces (especially *beurre blanc* and *Béarnaise*).	Peel and use whole or chopped.	Combines well with basil, bay, garlic, marjoram, oregano, rosemary, sage, tarragon, and thyme.
Sorrel		Spinachlike greens with a sour, lemony tang.	Excellent in soups, green salads, sauces, as garnish.	Use leaves whole or shredded. Add during last minutes of cooking.	Can be used with basil, chives, dill, garlic, parsley, and tarragon.

HERBS IN THE GARDEN

HERB	COMMON VARIETIES	TASTE	BEST WITH	HOW TO USE	HERB COMBINATIONS
Tarragon	French is the only kind you want.	Piquant, mild licorice flavor.	Seafood, poultry, veal, fruit, herb butters, marinades, salad dressings, and vinegars. Use in blend known as *fines herbes*.	Use sprigs or strip leaves from stem. Use whole or chopped.	Excellent combined with basil, bay, chervil, fennel, garlic, parsley, and shallots. Classic *fines herbes* blend contains tarragon, parsley, chervil, and chives. Tarragon also blends well with cress, dill, mint, savory, sorrel, and thyme.
Thyme	English, French, German, Lemon Thyme	Spicy, slightly sweet flavor.	Chicken, veal, vegetables, marinades, soups, stews, Creole dishes.	Use sprigs or strip leaves from stem. Use whole.	Good herb for combining with basil, bay, chives, garlic, marjoram, oregano, parsley, rosemary, sage, savory, and tarragon.

HERBS IN
THE KITCHEN

Cooking with Arugula (Roquette)

Italians and other Europeans devour arugula by the bowlful. The flavor is very robust; if you're not familiar with arugula, take it easy at first. Its flavor has been described as a combination of peanuts and horseradish with a pungent, peppery bite. Nobody ever describes arugula as delicate.

A few years ago, arugula was virtually unknown in the United States; now it's appearing in restaurants, recipes, and salads from coast to coast.

Use arugula fresh for salads; cook it with other greens. Blend shredded arugula with melted butter for seafood, potatoes, and pasta. For a colorful salad that highlights arugula's distinctive flavor, combine arugula, radicchio, and marinated goat cheese. Add a little Dijon mustard to the vinaigrette dressing.

Arugula quickly sautéed with broccoli rabe in olive oil, garlic, and lemon can be served as part of an antipasto or as a warm salad. Make a salad of arugula and cherry tomatoes. Sprinkle with coarsely grated mozzarella and offer a dressing made with a sharp mustard such as green peppercorn or green herb. Arugula lovers like it alone, dressed with a simple garlic vinaigrette.

Add arugula to a vegetable frittata; use arugula as part of a bed of summer greens to hold grilled quail and red peppers. Use arugula as a base for a salade niçoise, composed of the vegetables and other herbs that you have in the garden. Serve warm red-skinned potato salad over arugula. Toss linguine with arugula, pieces of sun-dried tomato, and a generous sprinkling of grated Parmesan cheese.

Arugula will not dry or freeze successfully.

Veal Loaf with Arugula (Roquette) Sauce

Everyone loves a good meat loaf. Here it becomes company fare with a pungent sauce made with fresh arugula. Serve it as part of a special Sunday lunch along with a cold pasta salad, cheeses, ripe olives in oil and herbs, crisp French bread, and sweet butter. Offer a bowl of champagne grapes and green plums for dessert.

1	onion, minced
1	bunch scallions, minced
2	celery ribs, minced
1	carrot, shredded
1	small sweet green pepper, minced
1	small sweet red pepper, minced
1	garlic clove, minced
1	tablespoon chopped fresh thyme
1	teaspoon salt
½	teaspoon freshly ground black pepper

Freshly grated nutmeg

¼	teaspoon cayenne pepper
1½	pounds veal, coarsely ground
1	egg, lightly beaten
½	cup soft bread crumbs
3	very large tomatoes, sliced

Arugula (Roquette) Sauce (recipe follows)
Arugula (Roquette) leaves, for garnish

Preheat oven to 375°.

In a large mixing bowl, combine onion, scallions, celery, carrot, green and red peppers, garlic, thyme, salt, black pepper, a pinch of nutmeg, and cayenne pepper. Add veal, egg, and bread crumbs; mix well. Form into a loaf and place in a lightly greased baking dish. Bake for 45 to 50 minutes.

Remove loaf from baking dish and cool to room temperature. Cut into thin slices. Spoon some of the sauce onto a large serving platter. Alternate loaf and tomato slices on sauce. Garnish with arugula leaves. Pass remaining sauce separately.

Arugula (roquette) sauce:

4	cups firmly packed well-washed arugula (roquette) leaves
2	eggs, at room temperature
1	egg yolk, at room temperature
⅓	cup white wine vinegar
1	tablespoon Dijon mustard
2	cups olive oil

Salt, to taste

Blanch arugula in boiling water for 30 seconds. Drain and plunge into a large bowl of ice water. Drain well; squeeze dry. Coarsely chop.

In a food processor or blender, combine eggs, yolk, vinegar, mustard, and salt, to taste. Add arugula and process for 1 minute. With machine running, slowly add olive oil through feed tube in a thin stream until mixture is the consistency of thin mayonnaise. Chill for up to two hours (the sauce becomes bitter if made any further ahead).

SERVES 6

Chicken Paillard with Vinegar Sauce and Arugula (Roquette)

Grilled chicken paillard has become a popular offering of restaurants, prepared with a myriad of seasonings and sauces. This version, served on a bed of arugula, makes a wonderful warm luncheon salad or entree for a quick supper, teamed with risotto and a bowl of fresh fruit.

3   whole chicken breasts, split, boned, and skinned
½   cup olive oil
1   garlic clove, minced
1   tablespoon minced fresh thyme
1   tablespoon minced fresh parsley
1   bay leaf
2   whole cloves
4   cups rich chicken stock (preferably homemade)
2   Granny Smith apples, cored and sliced
2   tablespoons cider vinegar
Salt and freshly ground black pepper, to taste
About 6 cups arugula (roquette)

Place chicken breasts between 2 pieces of wax paper and pound with a mallet until very thin. Combine ¼ cup olive oil, garlic, thyme, parsley, bay leaf, and whole cloves in a shallow dish large enough to hold the chicken breasts in one layer. Add chicken to oil-herb mixture, turning once to coat well. Cover and marinate, refrigerated, for 3 hours.

Meanwhile prepare sauce: In a large saucepan, bring chicken stock to a boil. Add apples and vinegar; simmer for 30 minutes, until the apples are very tender. Remove apples from sauce and puree apples until smooth in a food processor or blender. Return apple puree to saucepan and continue to cook the sauce over low heat until thick. Season with salt and pepper, to taste. Keep warm.

At serving time, remove chicken from marinade and grill over medium coals or under a preheated broiler about 1 minute per side. Cut the chicken breasts into thick slices.

Stem, wash, and dry the arugula. Toss with remaining ¼ cup olive oil and season with salt and pepper, to taste. Divide arugula among 6 serving plates. Arrange chicken slices on arugula and spoon sauce over chicken breasts.

SERVES 6

Arugula (Roquette) Salad with Warm Walnut Oil and Raspberry Vinegar

In the summer, compose a salad of arugula and other greens available in the garden or market, fresh herbs for seasoning, and edible flowers for color and subtle flavor accents (page 91). Experiment with the amounts of greens and herbs to achieve the right balance for your personal taste. Offer a crock of warm walnut oil and a carafe of raspberry vinegar; mix the dressing right on the salad.

Arugula (Roquette)
Choice of basil, borage blossoms, cress, chicory, dandelion greens, dill, lavender, lovage, mint, mâche, mustard, sage leaves, nasturtiums, pansies, and other edible flowers.
Warm walnut oil
Raspberry vinegar

Cooking with Basil

When you're cooking with fresh basil and you're not sure you've added enough, add more! There's no need to be timid with this popular herb. In the kitchen, fresh basil is king: it can be used by the handful with little risk as it improves the flavor of almost any food, vegetable or protein. Many cooks claim basil as their favorite kitchen herb.

Basil is the essential ingredient of many Italian, French, Greek, and Southeast Asian dishes. Its sweet, warm, clovelike flavor with a licorice undertone is an absolute must in Italian cooking—spaghetti, lasagne, pizza, and the garlicky pesto from Genoa all use generous amounts. Italians seldom eat tomatoes, cooked or raw, without basil. Slices of luscious ripe tomatoes and mozzarella cheese, sprinkled with green olive oil and a generous handful of chopped fresh basil, is a simple but lusty classic.

When summer vegetables are at their best, so is fresh basil. Stuff sweet red or yellow peppers with cooked rice combined with chopped fresh basil, minced scallions, minced Italian plum tomatoes, and crumbled feta cheese. Bake at 350° until tender, about 40 minutes. Stuff baby raw vegetables with ratatouille made with lots of fresh basil for a light and healthful hors d'oeuvre.

French cooks make pistou, a basil paste with garlic and olive oil that is beaten into vegetable soup. It also shows up in their sauces, salads, butters, and as a frequent garnish. Thai cooks find fresh basil excellent for stir-frying with beef, seafood, and poultry. A Thai stir-fry combines strips of boneless chicken breast, garlic, grated lime zest, straw mushrooms, shredded bamboo shoots, chopped fresh red chili peppers, lots of fresh basil, and oyster sauce (found in gourmet shops and many supermarkets). It is served over chopped cabbage or lettuce leaves and garnished with basil.

Basil is almost as aromatic in the herb garden as it is in a simmering pot, sending forth its exotic, spicy fragrance as people brush by. Be careful: bees also love its pretty flowers. The flowers, ranging in color according to the variety from creamy white to white tinged with pink or lavender to deep rose-pink, also have a mild basil flavor and are lovely when scattered over salads, sauces, or scrambled eggs.

For best aroma and flavor, shred basil gently with your fingers instead of chopping it with a knife. Add this herb during the last minutes of cooking or

use fresh; the flavor will fade if it's held in heat too long. Handle the fresh leaves with care: the slightest bruise will blacken them.

Toss shredded basil onto zucchini and yellow summer squash that have been briefly sautéed in olive oil and garlic; sprinkle with freshly grated Parmesan cheese. Basil adds an aromatic twist to sandwiches and hamburgers when used in place of lettuce.

Just before serving, garnish hot spinach soup with basil; stir the shredded leaves into melted butter to pour over steamed carrots or boiled potatoes. Stuff red and yellow cherry tomatoes with a mixture of goat cheese, minced red peppers, and minced onion. Sauté in butter until warm and stir in a generous amount of fresh basil. These are simply lovely with lamb or beef.

Italians stir-fry eggplant, tomatoes, garlic, onion, and fresh basil, topping the dish with shredded mozzarella cheese as soon as it's removed from the pan. Next time you make red-skinned potato salad, add lots of fresh basil.

Next to sweet basil, the most common variety used in cooking is lettuce leaf basil (also called large-leaf). Use it as you would sweet basil. Its leaf texture makes it especially nice for salads or the centuries-old custom of wrapping foods for cooking, such as shrimp, chicken pieces, or fish. Dark opal basil is also loved for its deep purple color and fragrant deep rose-pink flower spikes. Use it for butters, heavy cream sauces, in salads and stir-fries. It colors vinegars magenta. Scatter its rosy flowers onto salads and sauces.

The season for fresh basil can be extended by making basil puree in a food processor or blender, using 8 cups washed and dried basil leaves and 4 tablespoons olive oil. Transfer the puree to a jar and float a thin layer of olive oil on top. Cover and refrigerate (or freeze, using plastic containers) for later use. Each time you use the puree stir in the olive oil on top, replacing it with another thin layer after each use. Basil preserved in oil will keep for up to one year in the refrigerator and longer in the freezer.

Basil puree is marvelous on grilled chicken or fish, stirred into gazpacho, or spooned into pears that have been poached in white wine, lemon peel, and a little sugar. During the winter when basil growing in your kitchen window is being used lovingly leaf by leaf, pull the basil puree out of the refrigerator or freezer. Spread it on slices of peasant bread and top with minced sun-dried tomatoes and ripe olives. Pop under the broiler until hot and bubbly; it'll stir up memories of summer warmth.

Fresh basil dries well, but loses some of its flavor, which can be recaptured by soaking the dried basil in a little white wine or vermouth. Chop the reconstituted basil and use as fresh.

Basil freezes easily. Tear the leaves into small pieces, place in ice trays, and cover with water. Freeze and store the frozen cubes in plastic bags. Defrost the cubes in a strainer and use as fresh. Basil can also be frozen by laying the whole leaves on a baking sheet. Freeze and then pack the frozen leaves into plastic bags. Use straight from the freezer.

A favorite Italian method of preserving basil is to layer the fresh leaves in coarse salt in a container with a tight-fitting lid. This method will turn the leaves dark but will not affect the flavor. Be sure to rinse off the salt before using. Salt-preserved basil will keep for 4 to 6 months, stored in a dark, cool place.

Fresh Tomato Soup with Basil Dumplings

Plum tomatoes and dumplings made with fresh basil are a wonderful combination in piping hot soup. It's great served in front of a blazing fire at the end of a brisk fall day devoted to raking leaves. A splash of gin is the secret ingredient. Keep the rest of the meal simple: cheese, crisp apples, and pears.

¼	cup olive oil
2	large onions, sliced
2	shallots, minced
2	garlic cloves, minced
2	carrots, peeled and finely diced
2	celery ribs, diced
1	sweet red pepper, seeded and diced
2	tablespoons fresh lemon juice
1	teaspoon sugar
3	cups well-seasoned chicken stock (preferably homemade)
3	pounds very ripe fresh Italian plum tomatoes, peeled, seeded, and diced
1	tablespoon gin
1	cup all-purpose flour
1	teaspoon baking powder
Salt and pepper, to taste	
3	eggs
2	tablespoons vegetable oil
¾	cup torn fresh basil leaves

Heat olive oil in a large, heavy soup pot. Add onion, shallots, and garlic. Sauté over medium heat, stirring occasionally, for 5 minutes. Add carrots, celery, and red pepper, lemon juice, sugar, and chicken broth. Simmer for 15 minutes. Strain out vegetables; return broth to the pot. Puree vegetables in a food processor or blender and return to soup pot. Add tomatoes and gin; simmer for 10 minutes, or until soup begins to thicken. Watch carefully and don't allow it to burn.

Meanwhile, combine flour, baking powder, and ½ teaspoon salt in a large bowl. Add eggs and oil; beat until dough is sticky. Stir in ½ cup basil. Drop dough by ½ teaspoons into a large pot of boiling salted water. Simmer dumplings, uncovered, until they rise to the surface and then 3 to 4 minutes longer, turning periodically, until they are cooked through. (Test one by cutting in half to be sure center is no longer raw.)

Drain dumplings in a colander, rinse under cold water, and drain again. Set aside until ready to add to the soup. Add dumplings to the hot soup and serve at once. Garnish with remaining basil.

SERVES 4

Steamed Fish with Ginger and Fresh Basil

If you have access to very fresh fish, this is a spectacular dish and will delight anyone who is fond of fish and Chinese black beans. Serve with steamed rice, carrot puree, a cucumber salad with fresh mint, and blackberry ice.

1½–2-pound whole fish such as red snapper or sea bass
2   ounces Chinese fermented black beans
2   small fresh red chili peppers, seeded and finely chopped
1   tablespoon minced fresh ginger
1   garlic clove, minced
3   scallions, minced
2   tablespoons dry white wine
1   tablespoon peanut oil
1   tablespoon soy sauce
3   sprigs fresh coriander (cilantro)
1   cup fresh basil leaves, finely shredded

Wash the fish and pat dry. Place fish on rack for steaming.

Rinse the black beans; drain thoroughly. Coarsely chop beans and combine with chilies, ginger, garlic, and scallions. Spread the bean mixture over the fish. Sprinkle with wine; drizzle with oil and soy sauce. Place fish in steamer; lay coriander sprigs on top of fish. Steam, covered, for 15 to 20 minutes, or until fish flakes easily. Transfer fish to heated serving platter. Sprinkle with fresh basil and serve.

SERVES 4

Gratin of Fresh Raspberries with Fresh Basil

An exhilarating summer dessert (right), this has just a suggestion of fresh basil flavor. Since it must be served immediately, it cannot be prepared in advance but it does go together quickly. Serve with fluted glasses of champagne; raspberries seem to have an affinity for champagne.

3   cups fresh raspberries, rinsed and drained
10 fresh basil leaves, torn
4   egg yolks, at room temperature
2   tablespoons water
2   tablespoons Framboise liqueur
¾   cup crème fraîche or heavy cream, whipped to soft peaks
1   tablespoon sugar

In a food processor or blender, puree 1 cup raspberries and the basil. Spoon into 6 ½-cup soufflé dishes or ramekins. Divide remaining whole raspberries among the dishes. In the top of a double boiler, whisk egg yolks until foamy. Whisk in water and cook, whisking constantly, until pale yellow. Whisk in Framboise and continue cooking, whisking constantly, until mixture is very fluffy and mounds slightly.

Remove from heat and whisk until cool. Fold in whipped cream or crème fraîche and sugar. Spoon mixture over raspberries and place under the broiler until lightly browned around the edges, about 2 to 3 minutes. Watch carefully and do not let the topping get too brown. Serve at once.

SERVES 6

Wonton Pumpkin Ravioli with Basil Sauce

A velvety pumpkin-mousse ravioli with a marvelous basil sauce is a fabulous way to officially welcome autumn back into the kitchen when the herb garden is still brimming with fresh basil and early pumpkins arrive at the roadside stands. Fresh wonton skins are increasingly available at supermarkets and make fine ravioli. Serve with a green salad with toasted goat cheese, followed by a big fall fruit dessert.

4	shallots, minced
2	tablespoons unsalted butter
1	cup fresh pumpkin puree
3	eggs, at room temperature
¼	cup dry bread crumbs
1	cup freshly grated Parmesan cheese
2	tablespoons minced fresh basil leaves

Salt and freshly ground black pepper, to taste
1¼ pounds wonton skins
Basil and Coriander Pesto Sauce (recipe follows)

In a small saucepan, sauté shallots in butter over low heat until limp and golden. Add pumpkin puree and simmer about 4 minutes, stirring constantly to prevent scorching. Remove from heat and whisk in egg, bread crumbs, Parmesan cheese, and minced basil. Season with salt and pepper, to taste.

Scoop 1 rounded teaspoon of filling onto the center of a wonton skin. (Cover remaining skins with a dampened paper towel while you're working to prevent them from drying out.) Brush the edges of the skin with a little water and cover with a second skin. Press around the filling so the two skins seal tightly. Trim edges with a pastry wheel. Place filled ravioli on a lightly floured cloth. Repeat until all of the filling is used.

Bring a large pot of salted water to a boil; add ravioli. After they rise to the surface, cook until tender, about 1 minute for al dente. Remove with a slotted spoon and drain. Toss ravioli with Basil and Coriander Pesto Sauce and serve immediately.

Basil and coriander (cilantro) pesto sauce:

¼	cup shelled pistachio nuts
¼	cup pine nuts
3	garlic cloves
2	small jalapeño chili peppers
1	1-inch piece fresh ginger, peeled
1	cup firmly packed fresh basil leaves
¼	cup fresh coriander (cilantro) leaves
3	tablespoons fresh lime juice

About 1 cup olive oil
Salt and freshly ground black pepper, to taste

Blanch pistachio nuts in boiling water for 2 minutes. Drain and rub the nuts briskly between towels to remove the skins. Place pistachios, pine nuts, garlic, chili peppers, ginger, basil, and coriander in the work bowl of a food processor or blender. Process to a fine paste. Add lime juice and process for 10 seconds. With machine running, add enough olive oil in a thin stream to make a mayonnaise consistency. Add salt and pepper, to taste.

SERVES 4

Eggplant Pizza

The humble rustic pizza has become sophisticated, with exotic toppings of duck sausage, smoked salmon, golden caviar, goat cheese, crabmeat, and lobster. The possibilities are almost endless—experiment with different toppings and herbs. Add wine or beer, a simple salad, and you have one of America's favorite meals.

Dough:

1	envelope active dry yeast
1	cup lukewarm water
3	cups unbleached flour
1	teaspoon salt
1	tablespoon olive oil
1	tablespoon thyme (or other herb) honey

In a large mixing bowl, dissolve yeast in ¼ cup lukewarm water. Let stand for 10 minutes.

Add flour, salt, olive oil, honey, and remaining ¾ cup lukewarm water. Mix well until dough forms a ball. Sprinkle on more flour if dough is too sticky.

Knead on a floured surface for 10 minutes, until smooth and elastic. Place dough in an oiled bowl, cover with a cloth, and set in a warm place until it doubles in bulk, about 1 hour.

Punch down dough and let rest for 10 minutes. Divide dough into 4 equal pieces and roll each piece into a flat circle about 10 inches in diameter. (At this point, you can use the pizza dough immediately or freeze for up to 2 months, well wrapped, for future use. Thaw completely before using.)

Pizza:

2	tablespoons olive oil
1	teaspoon dried red pepper flakes
1	cup shredded Italian Fontina cheese
1	cup shredded mozzarella cheese
2	baby Japanese eggplants, sliced lengthwise in ¼-inch slices
2	plum tomatoes, sliced into rounds
½	cup goat cheese, cubed
½	cup fresh basil leaves, torn
2	tablespoons capers

Cornmeal
Fresh basil sprigs, for garnish

Preheat oven to 500°.

Brush each of the pizza rounds with olive oil and sprinkle with red chili flakes. Divide Fontina and mozzarella cheese evenly over the dough circles. Top with eggplant, tomato slices, goat cheese, fresh basil, and capers.

Place pizzas on a baking sheet that has been dusted with cornmeal. Bake until pizza is brown around the edges and the cheese is bubbling, about 10 to 12 minutes. Remove from oven and garnish with fresh basil sprigs.

MAKES 4 8-INCH PIZZAS

Stuffed Zucchini Blossoms with Ratatouille and Basil

Zucchini blossoms are prepared in many different ways in Italy: whole, fried in batter, stuffed, and fried. The version given here (right) is lighter and makes a stunning vegetable to serve with Roasted Sea Bass with Lemon Thyme Crust (page 213). For the appetizer, pair fresh figs with thinly sliced prosciutto. Finish the meal with biscotti (almond cookies flavored with raisins, chocolate, or glacéed fruit) for dipping in grappa liqueur scented with a whole pear.

3   tablespoons olive oil
1   onion, finely chopped
1   garlic clove, minced
1   zucchini, finely chopped
1   yellow crookneck squash, finely chopped
1   small sweet yellow pepper, seeded and finely chopped
1   small sweet green pepper, seeded and finely chopped
1   small eggplant, finely chopped
2   ripe tomatoes, peeled, seeded, and finely chopped
1   teaspoon minced fresh thyme leaves
1   teaspoon minced fresh rosemary leaves
1   teaspoon chopped fresh mint
1   tablespoon chopped fresh flat-leaf parsley
20 large fresh basil leaves, torn
Salt and freshly ground black pepper, to taste

8   small zucchini with blossoms attached

Preheat oven to 400°.

In a heavy skillet, heat 1 tablespoon olive oil over medium heat. Add onion, garlic, chopped zucchini, yellow squash, peppers, and eggplant. Cook until softened, about 5 minutes. Add tomatoes, thyme, rosemary, mint, and parsley. Cook for about 5 minutes over high heat until liquid is almost absorbed and mixture has thickened. Remove from heat and stir in basil leaves. Add salt and pepper, to taste. Set aside.

Open zucchini blossoms very gently and remove centers; try to avoid tearing. Fill a large bowl with cold water and several ice cubes. Bring a large saucepan of lightly salted water to a boil; carefully add zucchini and blanch for 15 seconds. Drain and immediately place in ice water. Drain zucchini and blot dry with paper towels. With a sharp knife, carefully cut zucchini lengthwise into ½-inch-thick slices. Do not cut through the blossoms.

Brush a large baking sheet with 1 tablespoon olive oil. Carefully open each zucchini blossom and fill three-quarters full with ratatouille mixture. (You'll have some ratatouille left over for another use.) Twist flower tips to enclose mixture and place on prepared baking sheet. Brush zucchini with remaining olive oil and sprinkle with salt and pepper, to taste. Cover with a sheet of aluminum foil and bake for 10 minutes, or until tender when pierced with a fork.

Carefully lift zucchini from baking sheet and place on heated serving plates, pressing lightly into a fanlike pattern.

SERVES 4

Oysters on the Half Shell with Two Basil Sauces

Oysters served on the half shell with two heady basil sauces would make a dazzling first course for a barbecue that includes a good steak, grilled leeks, and Vegetable Chili (page 172). Combine fresh berries with crème fraîche and threads of caramel for dessert.

5–6 dozen very fresh tiny oysters
Basil–Red Pepper Sauce (recipe follows)
Basil-Walnut Sauce (recipe follows)

With an oyster knife, shuck the oysters curved side down to save their juices. Loosen the oysters from their muscles with the knife. Spoon one of the sauces on one half of the oysters, the other sauce on the remaining oysters. Arrange 5 or 6 of both types on individual oyster plates over a bed of crushed ice. Serve at once.

Basil–red pepper sauce:

2 cups fresh basil leaves, finely shredded
1 sweet red pepper, peeled, seeded, and cut into fine julienne strips
3 tablespoons olive oil
3 tablespoons fresh lemon juice
1 garlic clove, finely minced
Salt and freshly ground black pepper, to taste

Combine all ingredients, mixing well.

Basil-walnut sauce:

2 cups fresh basil leaves, finely shredded
¼ cup grated Parmesan cheese
¾ cup chopped walnuts
1 garlic clove, finely minced
3 tablespoons olive oil

Combine all ingredients, mixing well.

SERVES 6

Cooking with Burnet

For a little zing in your salads and soups, try this small parsley-size herb with the cucumber flavor. Eat only the tender young leaves; the older leaves are strong and can be used for flavoring but should be removed before serving.

Toss a few leaves into vegetable juice or tomato juice; perk up a Bloody Mary with a sprig of burnet. Chop the leaves finely and scatter over salads, soups, or fish. The texture is similar to that of parsley.

For a quick sandwich, spread equal parts of Roquefort and cream cheese onto black bread; sprinkle generously with chopped fresh burnet. For herb toast, butter whole wheat bread lightly and sprinkle with chopped burnet. Broil until toasted.

Fill pita bread with sliced tomatoes, sliced avocado, sliced radishes, alfalfa sprouts, and chopped burnet for a healthful lunch. Mix finely chopped burnet, parsley, and chives into butter with a minced clove of garlic. Use to baste chicken while roasting or grilling.

Whirl fresh burnet, buttermilk, and plain yogurt in a blender for a refreshing midmorning drink. Offer a cooler made with chilled sparkling water and a sprig of fresh burnet.

Make lovely tea sandwiches with *pain de mie* or extrathin bread—white, whole wheat, or pumpernickel—lightly spread with unsalted butter. Top with any of the following: avocado slices and chopped burnet; mustard sprouts and burnet leaves; egg salad and chopped burnet; thin slices of Brie cheese and burnet leaves; thinly sliced plum tomato, mashed avocado, and burnet leaves; steak tartare, minced red onion, and burnet leaves with a generous grinding of black pepper; a mixture of finely chopped burnet leaves, fresh dill, and summer savory.

Make the best of herb vinegars by filling a wide-mouthed quart jar half full of loosely packed burnet leaves. Fill the jar with white wine vinegar; tightly cover and place on a sunny windowsill for several days. Use the vinegar to flavor salad dressings and marinades.

Couscous Salad with Burnet

Couscous is a staple in the North African countries of Algeria, Morocco, and Tunisia. The golden color of couscous along with the lightness of its grain makes an attractive background for chopped burnet leaves. Serve this colorful salad with cold medium-rare tenderloin beef and sliced tomatoes with sun-dried tomato vinaigrette.

2	cups chicken stock (preferably homemade)
3	tablespoons olive oil
1	teaspoon ground cumin

Dash ground cinnamon
Dash ground ginger

1	cup quick-cooking couscous
¼	cup dried currants
¼	cup chopped pitted dates
1	cup diced zucchini
½	cup diced carrots
½	cup diced red onion
2	tablespoons fresh lemon juice

Salt and freshly ground black pepper, to taste
¼	cup pine nuts

Chopped fresh burnet

In a heavy saucepan, bring chicken stock, 2 tablespoons olive oil, cumin, cinnamon, and ginger to a boil. Stir in couscous and continue to cook until most of the liquid is absorbed, about 2 minutes. Remove from heat and stir in currants and dates. Cover tightly and let stand for 15 minutes. Add zucchini, carrots, and onion.

In a small bowl, combine lemon juice and remaining 1 tablespoon oil. Pour over couscous; toss to coat thoroughly. Refrigerate overnight to blend flavors.

To serve, bring to room temperature. Toss with pine nuts; sprinkle generously with chopped burnet.

SERVES 4 TO 6

Sweet Potato Slices with Burnet and Crème Fraîche

These sweet potato slices offer a vibrant accent of color as a casual canapé with an interesting contrast of flavors. Beautifully simple and light.

5   large sweet potatoes or yams, about 3 pounds (select potatoes that are long and narrow)
1   teaspoon salt
1   teaspoon freshly ground white pepper
½   cup sour cream
1   cup crème fraîche (or 1 additional cup sour cream)
Finely chopped fresh burnet

Peel potatoes and slice ¼-inch thick. Cover with cold water and let soak for 15 minutes. Bring a large pot of fresh water to a boil; add potatoes, salt, and white pepper. Reduce heat and simmer until potatoes are tender, but still firm, about 5 minutes.

Drain and dry potatoes on paper towels. In a small bowl, combine sour cream and crème fraîche. Place one teaspoon cream mixture on each slice; garnish with chopped burnet. Chill for up to one hour before serving.

MAKES ABOUT 48 HORS D'OEUVRES

Cooking with Caraway

Caraway is not an herb whose absence from your kitchen herb garden would limit your cooking repertoire, but it certainly adds to certain recipes a fresh, clean, unique flavor similar to that of cumin. The plant is dainty with delicate, frondlike leaves, white umbrella-shaped flowers, and a slight aroma of carrots. The familiar small crescent-shaped seeds ripen to almost black with lighter-colored stripes about a month after the flowers appear. The roots are thick and tapering, resembling a small parsnip. All of the plant can be used in cooking.

The small, dark-brown, pungent seeds, well-known for the flavor they give to cakes, cookies, and breads—particularly rye bread—also brighten cabbage, onion and potato dishes, cheese, sauerkraut, Brussels sprouts, cauliflower, pickles, soups, and goulash. For an unusual snack, lightly dip fresh fruit such as apple, pear, or pineapple slices into crushed caraway seeds. Sprinkle the seeds onto pot roasts and stews. In Austria, you're likely to be served red cabbage with caraway seeds to accompany roast goose. The flavor of caraway seed is very strong; use it sparingly.

The young green leaves are similar to carrot leaves and have a delicate flavor. Try adding them, finely chopped, to salads or soups. The thick tapered roots can be boiled and eaten as a vegetable, dressed with a little melted butter or a cream sauce.

Caraway Pound Cake

This simple pound cake with a dream of a glaze is pretty enough for the afternoon tea table or an extravagant dessert for a late evening dessert party.

1½   cups (3 sticks) butter, at room temperature
1   pound (3¾ cups) confectioners' sugar
6   eggs
1   teaspoon vanilla
2¾   cup sifted cake flour
1   teaspoon grated orange zest
2   tablespoons caraway seeds
¼   teaspoon mace

Glaze:
1½   cups sifted confectioner's sugar
2–3 tablespoons fresh orange juice
2   tightly packed tablespoons grated orange zest

Preheat oven to 300°.

Heavily butter a 10-inch (12-cup) plain or decorative tube pan. Dust with flour. Set aside.

Using an electric mixer and a large bowl, beat butter until creamy. Sift confectioners' sugar; gradually add to butter, beating until mixture is light and fluffy. Beat in eggs, one at a time, beating well after each addition. Beat in vanilla. Gradually beat in cake flour. Stir in grated orange zest, caraway seeds, and mace.

Transfer batter to prepared pan and smooth top. Bake for 1½ hours until a wooden pick inserted in center comes out clean. Cool in pan for 5 minutes. Turn out onto a rack to cool completely.

In a small bowl, combine sugar and orange juice. Pour over the top of the cooled cake, letting the glaze run down unevenly on the sides. Sprinkle with orange zest. Cut the cake into thin slices.

SERVES 10 TO 12

Caraway Rye Breadsticks

These breadsticks smell wonderful as they're baking. Generously sprinkled with caraway seeds and coarse salt, they are delicious served warm from the oven with a crock of sweet butter and a glass of wine.

1   envelope active dry yeast
1   teaspoon sugar
1   cup hot water (about 110°)
¼   cup olive oil
1   teaspoon salt
¾   cup rye flour
About 2¼ cups all-purpose flour
1   egg, beaten with 1 tablespoon water
Caraway seeds
Coarse salt

In a large bowl, combine yeast, sugar, and ½ cup water. Stir to dissolve. Let stand for 10 minutes until foamy. Stir in remaining ½ cup water, olive oil, salt, rye flour, and all-purpose flour, ½ cup at a time, until dough is smooth and elastic. If dough is sticky, add additional flour, 1 tablespoon at a time.

Turn out onto a floured surface and knead for 5 minutes. Pat or roll the dough into a rectangle about 16 × 8 inches. Place on a well-oiled baking sheet. Brush top with additional oil. Cover with a cloth and set in a warm, draft-free place to rise until doubled in bulk, about 45 minutes.

Preheat oven to 400°.

Cut the dough crosswise into 4 strips. Cut each strip into 8 strips. Roll each strip between your hands to form a rope about 12 inches long. Place the ropes 1 inch apart on lightly oiled baking sheets. Brush with the beaten egg and sprinkle with caraway seeds and coarse salt. Bake breadsticks for 15 minutes or until golden. Cool on racks.

MAKES 32 BREADSTICKS

Sweet Potato Salad with Caraway

Caraway leaves join with sweet potatoes and haricots verts, the tiny French green beans, in this unusual potato salad. Grill a chicken with rosemary and lemon juice, mix a green salad, and take everything outdoors to your favorite picnic spot. A small basket of fresh figs makes a nice dessert.

1¼ pounds sweet potatoes or yams, peeled
1   pound *haricots verts* (or tender young green beans)
1   large onion, cut in half and thinly sliced
½   cup dry white wine
2   garlic cloves, minced
2   tablespoons olive oil
¼   cup crème fraîche
1   tablespoon Dijon mustard
3   tablespoons chopped fresh caraway leaves
Sprigs of fresh caraway

Drop the potatoes as you peel them into a large saucepan of cold, salted water. Bring to a boil and cook until tender but still firm.

Drain potatoes and slice into ¼-inch slices. Steam *haricots verts* over rapidly boiling water until just tender. Combine potatoes, *haricots verts*, and onion. Toss gently.

In a small saucepan, bring white wine to a boil. Reduce heat, add garlic, and simmer for 5 minutes. Remove from heat and whisk in oil, crème fraîche, Dijon mustard, and caraway leaves. Toss vegetables with dressing. Garnish with caraway sprigs.

SERVES 6

COOKING WITH CARAWAY

Cooking with Chervil

Chervil is the most delicately flavored ingredient in the mixture known as *fines herbes* (a combination of chervil, parsley, chives, and tarragon). It's indispensable in the French kitchen and rapidly gaining importance with cooks elsewhere.

The dainty, feathery leaves are most flavorful during cool weather and just prior to flowering. Like chives, chervil benefits from constant cutting, so don't hesitate to use plenty in your summer recipes. The flavor, remotely like that of anise or tarragon (but more subtle) dissipates quickly when cooked; add fresh chervil just before serving. Because of its delicate nature, chervil is considered a blending herb and can be used generously and in combination with most other herbs, helping to smooth out their flavors.

Fresh chervil has great impact on fish, egg dishes, poultry, sauces, soups, and vegetables. It brightens a summer salad with just a handful of its sprightly sprigs. Add chopped fresh chervil to chicken soup just before serving; the delicate aroma wafts up.

Stuff veal chops with a mixture of mascarpone or cream cheese, a little grated Parmesan cheese, equal amounts of fresh basil, fresh chervil, fresh chives, a few sage leaves, and salt and pepper. Bake in a 350° oven for 30 minutes. Deglaze the roasting pan with white wine. Add some chopped fresh chervil and pour the sauce over the chops. Your butcher can cut a deep pocket in each chop to hold the stuffing.

Sprinkle chopped chervil leaves over carrot or cucumber salad. Spread black bread with ripe avocado and sprinkle with chopped fresh chervil for a luscious light lunch. Chervil on buttered new potatoes makes a refreshing change from the usual parsley or mint. Add lots of fresh chervil to a vinaigrette marinade for mushrooms or carrots. Sprinkle it over slices of cantaloupe, honeydew, or cranshaw melon.

Add chervil to a smoked salmon or trout mousse; pipe onto leaves of Belgian endive, into cherry tomatoes or snowpeas. Watching calories? Sprinkle chopped fresh chervil into a steaming baked potato. You won't miss the butter.

Since dried chervil has virtually no taste, you're better off freezing it for future use. To freeze, snip or chop the leaves and pack tightly into ice trays. Top with water and freeze. When frozen, store in plastic bags. Defrost in a strainer and use as fresh.

Whole Lobster with Chervil Dressing

Lobster is expensive unless you live close to the source, but this beautiful and sophisticated dish is perfect for an important dinner. The lobsters are steamed on a bed of fresh herbs, then the finished dish is garnished with more fresh herbs and whatever edible flowers are available. The presentation is stunning; the flavor, sublime.

Serve a first course of angel hair pasta tossed with a delicate sauce of fresh herbs, unsalted butter, and a little cream. Leave out the cheese and pass the pepper mill, instead. For dessert, poached pears with a chocolate sauce and chopped pistachios would make a worthy ending. Pour an excellent champagne throughout.

1	cup fresh chervil leaves
1	cup fresh basil leaves
1	cup fresh tarragon leaves
1	cup fresh flat-leaf parsley
3	bay leaves
2	cups dry white wine
6	whole black peppercorns
2	lemons, sliced
4	1½-pound lobsters

Chervil Dressing (recipe follows)

12	cherry tomatoes
1	zucchini, cut into matchstick-size julienne strips
1	yellow summer squash, cut into matchstick-size julienne strips

Additional fresh herbs and edible flowers for garnish

Place herbs in the bottom of a large pot; add wine, peppercorns, and lemons. Top with the lobsters, cover and bring to a boil. Reduce heat and steam the lobsters for 8 to 10 minutes.

Remove lobsters from the pot. Crack the claws.

Pour some of the Chervil Dressing onto the serving plates. Arrange the lobster over the sauce. Arrange the vegetables, fresh herbs, and flowers around the lobster. Serve with picks and lobster crackers.

Chervil dressing:

1½	cups fresh chervil leaves
1	medium onion, chopped
3	shallots, chopped
¾	cup white wine vinegar
3	egg yolks
¾	cup olive oil

Salt and freshly ground black pepper, to taste

In a food processor or blender, combine chervil, onion, shallots, vinegar, egg yolks, and olive oil. Process until blended. Do not overprocess or the dressing will separate. Add salt and pepper to taste. Makes about 1½ cups.

SERVES 4

COOKING WITH CHERVIL

Grilled Eggplant Salad with Fresh Chervil

A beautiful summer salad—the eggplant emerges tasting slightly smoky, sweet, and intense. Although you could serve this hot, the flavor of the eggplant is best at room temperature. It's a perfect salad to serve with grilled chicken or fish.

2	large tomatoes, peeled, seeded, and chopped
4	shallots, minced
¼	cup chopped fresh chervil
¼	cup olive oil
3	tablespoons white wine vinegar

Salt and freshly ground black pepper
2	small white eggplants
2	small purple eggplants

Additional olive oil for brushing eggplants
Chopped fresh chervil

In a large bowl, combine tomatoes, shallots, and ¼ cup chopped fresh chervil. Add ¼ cup olive oil and vinegar. Season with salt and pepper, to taste. Chill for 30 minutes to combine flavors.

Meanwhile, cut eggplants into thin slices lengthwise. Sprinkle with salt and pepper; brush both sides with additional olive oil. Grill over low coals until browned on both sides, brushing with olive oil as needed to keep moistened. Remove from grill and keep warm.

To serve, divide tomato-chervil mixture among 4 chilled salad plates. Arrange eggplant slices over tomatoes and sprinkle with chopped chervil.

SERVES 4

Salmon Scallops with Fresh Chervil Sauce

A combination of dazzling flavors, this salmon dish echoes the colors of summer. Buy the best salmon you can find; ask your fish market to cut the salmon into scallops. Complement the salmon with cucumbers quickly sautéed in unsalted butter and chopped fresh tarragon. Start the meal with globe artichokes smothered with herbs and end with a tart, cool tangerine sorbet garnished with candied citrus peel.

Salmon:

4   salmon scallops
3   shallots, minced
Freshly ground white pepper, to taste
1   cup dry white wine

Place salmon scallops in a poaching pan or shallow large skillet with cover. Sprinkle on shallots and season with white pepper, to taste. Pour on wine. Bring to a boil, reduce heat, and cover. Poach for 5 to 8 minutes, or until salmon is opaque and flakes with a fork. Keep fish warm while making sauce.

Chervil sauce:

2   tablespoons unsalted butter
2   tablespoons fresh lemon juice
½   cup dry white wine
2   shallots, minced
1   garlic clove, minced
1   small tomato, peeled, seeded, and coarsely chopped
¼   cup crème fraîche
1   cup coarsely chopped fresh chervil

In a small saucepan, combine butter, lemon juice, wine, shallots, garlic, and tomato. Bring to a boil; reduce heat and simmer, uncovered, for 20 minutes. Strain sauce through a fine sieve. Whisk in crème fraîche and stir in chervil. Return to stove to heat through; do not boil. Pour sauce over and around salmon.

SERVES 4

Cooking with Chives

Bright green chives growing in a pretty pot in a sunny kitchen window, jetting out of the side pocket of a strawberry jar planted with herbs on the patio, or growing in great clumps, sporting their fluffy flowers, in the garden—no matter how or where chives are grown, the flavor of these graceful, slender, dark green stalks are often just what's needed in the good cook's garden to jazz up a finished dish. Although seldom used alone in a recipe, chives can be the perfect addition or garnish for just about any dish. Use them finely snipped (always use scissors as chopping with a knife crushes out the juices) or left in long strips.

Chives have a delicate, oniony flavor with a hint of pepperiness. Since chives thrive on constant cutting, scatter them generously over salads, soups, eggs, or cheese dishes. A simple chive butter that's excellent with grilled vegetables such as eggplant, tomatoes, summer squash, or freshly picked corn can also be spread onto muffins or biscuits hot from the oven. Chive mustard made with minced chives and any grainy mustard is wonderful served with grilled fish or chicken. Stir chives into hollandaise to pour over steamed asparagus or cauliflower. Adding chives to an omelet or scrambled eggs makes these simple dishes very special.

Fresh chives have found their way into all the cuisines of the Northern Hemisphere. In France, chives are used for simple sauces, basic vinaigrettes, and egg dishes. The Germans add chives to mayonnaise and the Russians use them with lamb and beet dishes (a single chive makes a lovely garnish for a bowl of borscht). The Japanese use chives for a garnish for their clear soups and add the popular white-blooming garlic chives to fish and vegetable stews. In China, garlic chives, also called Chinese chives, add strong flavor to egg dishes and stir-fried beef, and in Thailand, several spicy noodle dishes call for ample amounts of garlic chives.

Both the common round-blade and flat-leaf garlic chives produce sweet edible flowers, a tiny ball of lavender or white blossoms. Scatter the chive flowers over salads or dip them in a light batter and fry gently until golden brown for an interesting accompaniment to fish or poultry. Steep the lavender blossoms in white wine vinegar for a beautifully colored and flavored salad vinegar.

Always use chives fresh. Chives do not dry well and frozen chives lose their flavor after three or four months. If you are going to freeze chives for a shorter period of time, it's best to freeze the whole leaves in plastic bags and snip off what you need, straight from the freezer.

Garlic Chive Polenta Layered with Three Vegetables

Polenta has become very popular with diners everywhere. Here, it is teamed with fresh vegetables and pancetta to make a rustic main course that can be assembled well beforehand and baked when needed. If instant polenta is not available, yellow corn meal can be substituted. This needs only the accompaniment of a simple Boston lettuce salad, a satisfying dessert, and a bottle of excellent red wine.

Spinach layer:
6   tablespoons unsalted butter
1   garlic clove, minced
1   pound fresh spinach, well washed
Salt and pepper, to taste

Tomato layer:
3   medium tomatoes, peeled, seeded, and chopped
1   tablespoon chopped fresh thyme

Mushroom layer:
4   ounces pancetta, minced
4   ounces fresh mushrooms, sliced
1   tablespoon chopped fresh oregano
1   tablespoon dry white wine

Polenta:
4   cups chicken stock (preferably homemade)
1   box (13 ounces) instant polenta
½   cup minced fresh garlic chives
2   tablespoons minced flat-leaf parsley
⅔   cup grated Romano cheese
Salt, to taste

Preheat oven to 350°.

Melt 2 tablespoons butter in a heavy skillet with cover over medium heat. Add garlic and cook for 2 minutes. Add spinach and sauté over high heat until just wilted. Remove from heat; drain and season with salt and pepper, to taste. Set aside.

Wipe out skillet; heat 2 tablespoons butter over medium heat. Add tomatoes and thyme. Cook, stirring occasionally, until the moisture has evaporated and the mixture is thick. Season with salt and pepper, to taste. Set aside.

Wipe out skillet; sauté pancetta over low heat for about 15 minutes, until golden brown. Remove with a slotted spoon; set aside. Discard excess grease. Add mushrooms, oregano, and wine to skillet and cook over medium heat until mushrooms are barely tender and liquid has been absorbed, about 4 minutes. Season with salt and pepper, to taste. Set aside.

In a large saucepan, bring stock to a boil. Gradually whisk in polenta. Lower heat and cook, stirring constantly, until thickened, about 1 minute. Whisk in garlic chives, parsley, remaining 2 tablespoons butter, and Romano cheese. Taste for salt.

Spoon ¼ of the hot polenta into a well-buttered loaf pan (10½ × 5 × 2½ inches) that has been lined with parchment paper. Top polenta with spinach layer. Cover spinach with the second quarter of polenta. Top with tomato mixture. Cover tomatoes with the third quarter of polenta. Top with mushroom mixture and then remaining polenta. Cover pan with buttered parchment paper and bake for 30 minutes or until set.

Remove from oven and let stand for 5 minutes. Remove top parchment paper and invert onto serving platter. Remove remaining parchment paper. Let stand about 10 minutes and slice. Serve warm.

SERVES 6 TO 8

Radicchio Leaves Filled with Smoked Trout Mousse and Chives

With a delicate contrast of colors and flavors, baby radicchio leaves are filled with smoked trout mousse for a spectacular hors d'oeuvre (left). Use a star tip when piping on the mousse and garnish each with a tiny spray of fresh chives. The trout mousse can be prepared ahead and refrigerated until ready to use. Pipe the mousse onto the radicchio no more than an hour before serving.

6	ounces smoked trout
6	ounces cream cheese, at room temperature
¾	cup crème fraîche

Few drops of fresh lemon juice

1	tablespoon fresh or bottled grated horseradish

Salt and pepper, to taste

25–30	very small radicchio leaves (about 4 small heads)
1	bunch of fresh chives

Remove and discard the skin and bones of the smoked trout. Finely chop trout in a food processor. Add cream cheese and crème fraîche; process until smooth. Add lemon juice and horseradish; season with salt and pepper, to taste. Cover and refrigerate until ready to use.

When ready to assemble hors d'oeuvres, soften mousse with a wooden spoon and place in a pastry bag with a star tip. Pipe about 1 tablespoon of the mousse onto each radicchio leaf and garnish with 2 or 3 fresh chives.

MAKES 25 TO 30 HORS D'OEUVRES

Chilled Zucchini Soup

An extremely rich, smooth version of an iced soup that is filled with the flavors and colors of summer. If a coarser texture is desired, do not put the mixture through a sieve. Make this soup just as the first zucchini are being picked from the garden. Topped with a spray of chives, it makes a delightful beginning to any summer meal.

¼	cup olive oil
6–8	medium zucchini, trimmed, scrubbed, and diced
½	cup chopped fresh chives
1	teaspoon chopped fresh thyme
4	cups crème fraîche or heavy cream

Salt and freshly ground pepper, to taste

In a large, heavy saucepan, heat oil over medium heat. Add zucchini; reduce heat to low and cook, covered, for 10 to 15 minutes, or until zucchini are very tender but not browned. Cool slightly and stir in chives, thyme, and 2 cups crème fraîche.

Puree in batches in a food processor or blender until smooth. Stir in remaining crème fraîche and chill for several hours. Add salt and pepper, to taste. Serve cold.

SERVES 6 TO 8

Cooking with Fresh Coriander (Cilantro)

A clump of fresh coriander with its tiny white flowers tinged with lavender floating above lacy green fernlike foliage is a most pleasant sight in any kitchen herb garden. When the flowers ripen and dry, they turn into the better-known coriander seed, but it is the pungent, uniquely flavored leaves of fresh coriander that have taken over Southwestern cooking in the United States and have long been an essential herb in Indian, Middle Eastern, Latin American, Portuguese, and Asian kitchens.

One of the oldest known herbs, coriander is mentioned in the Old Testament and probably grew in the Hanging Gardens of Babylon. Ancient Greek, Roman, and Chinese cooks thought highly of it. Just when or where the leaves were first used to flavor food, no one knows. Coriander was one of the first herbs grown in the American colonies (for the seeds) but it wasn't until recently that the fresh leaf began to be used in the United States.

Fresh coriander leaves have a flavor that is entirely different from the flavor of the seeds and the two are not interchangeable in recipes, although they can both be used in the same recipe for an interesting synergistic effect. But try substituting coriander seeds for fresh coriander leaves in a seviche, a Cantonese roast chicken, a Mexican salsa, or an Indian chutney, and you'll notice the difference. Fresh coriander leaves have a strong, slightly woodsy taste often described as orange peel mixed with sage. Coriander seed is quite different in flavor—much more subtle, slightly sweet, with a hint of cumin and anise.

Select very fresh coriander leaves for cooking as its flavor deteriorates with age. The leaves should be glossy green with no yellow or mold. To keep it fresh once it's picked, store it in a container with 2 to 3 inches of the stems in water. Place a plastic bag over the top and secure it with a rubber band or kitchen string. Stored this way, coriander stays fresh for about a week.

Don't bother to dry fresh coriander as the flavor will not hold. Instead, the coriander leaves can be frozen individually in plastic bags or preserved in a light oil. Another method of preserving fresh coriander is to puree the fresh leaves with a little water and freeze the puree in ice trays. Once frozen, store in plastic bags. One cube will equal about 1 tablespoon of the fresh herb.

Fresh coriander is highly aromatic, but quickly loses its flavor when cooked. Sprinkle some chopped fresh coriander leaves onto a hot, brothy soup and the fragrance wafts up. Tuck a bunch of leaves inside a roast chicken or fish for a Chinese-style dish with the flavor of coriander permeating the food as it cooks. Since fresh coriander combines well with spicy foods such as garlic and hot chili peppers, sprinkle it over bowls of your best homemade chili or stir it into guacamole dip.

Stir coriander into cooked rice along with slivers of fresh coconut, thinly sliced pitted dates, or dried apricots and grated lemon zest. Coriander seems to have an affinity for avocados and oranges. Make a quick, interesting salad from sliced avocado, sliced

oranges, sliced papaya, sliced red onion, a handful of fresh coriander leaves, and a vinegar and oil dressing spiked with canned diced green chili peppers.

Thai cooks excite and tease the palate with fresh coriander, calling on it to help accentuate the differences of flavor, texture, and temperature in their cooking. They use it extensively—chopped stems as well as leaves—in sauces, soups, and salad. Moroccans make a spicy hot eggplant dip flavored with fresh coriander, and a lamb or chicken stew with dried fruits, sweet spices, lemon, honey, and lots of fresh coriander. Lebanese cooks rely on fresh coriander for lentil soup and their fabulous tabbouleh; the Mexicans consider fresh coriander an essential herb for everything from enchiladas to chicken mole and turkey sausages.

Orange Gazpacho

Ladle this cooling soup into chilled clear glass mugs for a summery, sippable first course while herb-wrapped steaks and garden vegetables are grilling. The dazzling combination of the fruit and vegetable flavors is heightened by the fresh coriander. A swizzle stick in the form of a fresh scallion makes a pretty garnish.

2   large ripe tomatoes, peeled, seeded, and finely chopped
1   medium cantaloupe, seeds and rind removed and finely chopped
1   cucumber, peeled and chopped
1   large onion, chopped
1   sweet yellow pepper, chopped
1   sweet red pepper, chopped
2   jalapeño peppers, minced
1   garlic clove, minced
¼   cup chopped fresh coriander (cilantro)
Grated zest of 1 orange
Grated zest of 1 lime
1½ cups fresh orange juice
3   tablespoons fresh lime juice
Salt and freshly ground black pepper, to taste
Sprigs of fresh coriander (cilantro), for garnish

In a food processor or by hand, finely mince together tomatoes, cantaloupe, cucumber, onion, yellow pepper, red pepper, jalapeño peppers, garlic, and ¼ cup fresh coriander. Put the minced vegetables and herbs in a large bowl, add orange and lime zests, and stir in orange and lime juices. Season to taste with salt and pepper. Chill for at least one hour. Ladle into chilled soup bowls and garnish with sprigs of fresh coriander.

SERVES 4

Spicy Thai Shrimp Soup with Fresh Coriander (Cilantro)

This version of the most popular soup in Thailand is lively in flavor yet lean in calories. An aromatic hot-tart soup that features shrimp, it relies on fresh coriander to help provide the surprising flavor contrasts. Precede the soup with some Chinese dim sum (steamed dumplings, potstickers, or steamed pork buns). Follow the soup course with fresh fruit and pour a selection of Chinese and Japanese beers.

3   quarts chicken stock (preferably homemade)
2   6-inch stalks fresh lemon grass, sliced
1–2 red chili peppers, seeded and thinly sliced
Zest of 1 lime
½   pound fresh straw mushrooms
1   pound large shrimp (12–15 per pound), shelled and deveined
⅔   cup lime juice
4   scallions, sliced
½   cup chopped fresh coriander (cilantro)

In a large soup pot, combine broth, lemon grass, chili peppers, and lime zest. Bring to a boil; cover and simmer for 15 minutes. Lift out lime zest and discard. Add mushrooms and shrimp; simmer for 4 minutes. Stir in lime juice.

Transfer shrimp to serving bowl. Pour in broth. Sprinkle with scallions and coriander.

SERVES 4

California Seviche with Fresh Coriander (Cilantro)

This stunning version of a South American favorite is a cool, streamlined first course that deserves your most dramatic presentation. Follow with steak or chicken grilled with fresh rosemary, asparagus with a squeeze of orange, and baked whole unpeeled onions for a spectacular dinner full of interesting California twists. Thin slivers of a classic lemon tart make an elegant finale.

½ pound bay scallops
½ pound sea bass, cut into ½-inch cubes
1 cup fresh lime juice
¼ cup chopped fresh coriander (cilantro)
4 scallions, minced
1 teaspoon freshly ground black pepper
3 tablespoons red wine vinegar
6 tablespoons vegetable oil
1 garlic clove, minced
Salt and freshly ground black pepper, to taste
1 large, ripe avocado
24 cherry tomatoes, halved
Lemon juice
1 medium red onion, minced
½ cup diced jicama

In a large shallow glass bowl, combine scallops and sea bass with lime juice, coriander, scallions, and pepper. Tightly cover and refrigerate for 6 to 8 hours, or overnight. Stir occasionally.

In a small bowl, whisk together vinegar, olive oil, and garlic. Add salt and pepper, to taste. Cover and chill.

To serve, peel and slice avocado; sprinkle with lemon juice to prevent darkening. With a slotted spoon, remove scallops and sea bass from the marinade. Combine with tomatoes, avocado, red onion, and jicama. (A jicama is a brown root vegetable available in Mexican markets and, more and more, the produce section of supermarkets. Peel and you'll find a white, sweetish, juicy, crunchy flesh.) Toss very gently with the vinaigrette. Spoon into individual serving bowls and garnish with fresh coriander leaves.

SERVES 6 to 8

Grilled Tuna with Pecan Coriander (Cilantro) Butter

Grilled fresh tuna is succulent, moist, and surprisingly unfishy in flavor with many of the same qualities as a buttery filet mignon. The zesty coriander butter is Southwestern in inspiration and would be equally good with grilled swordfish. Serve with tomatoes stuffed with tabbouleh; grill small leeks and large yellow peppers alongside the tuna. For dessert, heap chunks of iced watermelon into a pretty bowl.

6   tuna steaks, about 1½ inches thick
1   tablespoon olive oil
Salt and freshly ground black pepper, to taste
2   tablespoons fresh lime juice
1   cup pecans, lightly toasted and coarsely chopped
½   cup fresh coriander (cilantro) leaves
½   cup fresh parsley leaves
1   small onion
1   large garlic clove
1   small fresh jalapeño pepper chili, stemmed
¼   cup (½ stick) well-chilled unsalted butter, cut into 4 pieces

Brush tuna with olive oil and 1 tablespoon lime juice. Season with salt and pepper, to taste. Cover with plastic wrap and refrigerate for 2 to 3 hours.

Toast pecans by spreading them evenly on an ungreased baking sheet. Place in a 400° oven for 3 to 4 minutes, or until lightly toasted. In a food processor or blender, combine pecans, coriander, parsley, onion, garlic, and jalapeño. With on/off turns, mince fine.

With machine running, drop in butter pieces and process until smooth, stopping as needed to scrape down the sides of the work bowl or blender. Add remaining lime juice and blend until smooth. Remove coriander butter from processor or blender and cream in pecans.

Grill tuna steaks over hot coals or under a preheated broiler for 4 minutes per side or until medium rare. Do not overcook. Top the hot steaks with a tablespoon of the prepared butter.

SERVES 6

Moroccan Lamb Stew

Deliciously seasoned with fresh coriander, lemon, honey, and sweet spices, this stew conjures up images of spice markets and cities of intrigue. A fine example of the use of fresh green coriander in Morocco, this exotic blend of fruit and spices also uses the coriander seed. It's even more delicious made a day or two in advance of serving. The stew is rich so needs only a green salad (garnished with sliced oranges, slivers of red onions, and chopped fresh mint) and French bread for mopping up the sauce. Pass a tray of dried fruit for dessert.

3   tablespoons olive oil
1   large onion, thinly sliced
1   tablespoon chopped fresh ginger
1   teaspoon ground coriander
3½   pounds boneless lamb, cut into 1-inch cubes
1   cup moist dried apricots
12   large sprigs fresh coriander (cilantro)
2   bay leaves
1   sprig fresh thyme
3   sticks whole cinnamon
2   tablespoons honey
2   tablespoons lemon juice
Salt and freshly ground black pepper, to taste

In a heavy Dutch oven, heat olive oil. Add onion, ginger, and ground coriander. Sauté for 2 minutes. Add lamb and stir to coat with the onion mixture. Cover and cook over low heat for about 1 hour, adding a little water if necessary to prevent sticking. Stir in apricots. Tie 6 sprigs of fresh coriander, bay leaves, thyme, and cinnamon together with kitchen string. Place on top of meat; cover and simmer until apricots are tender, about 10 minutes.

Remove from heat and discard coriander-cinnamon bouquet. With a slotted spoon, remove lamb and apricots to a heavy serving platter. Keep warm. Stir honey into pan juices; boil to reduce and thicken the sauce. Stir in lemon juice and season with salt and pepper, to taste. Pour the heated sauce over the lamb. Coarsely chop remaining fresh coriander and sprinkle over lamb.

SERVES 6

Snow Crab Claws with Salsa Fresca

The crab claws (left) are full of sweet meat and the spicy dipping sauce is one of the hottest you've ever tasted. Fresh coriander helps to add the nip. This sauce is best when made at least 4 hours in advance. It's also delicious with tortilla chips and as a jazzy topping for grilled fish or meats. You'll find the snow crab claws in the freezer section of most supermarkets.

24   frozen snow crab claws

Defrost frozen crab claws overnight in the refrigerator or for 2 to 3 hours at room temperature. Serve the crab claws, thoroughly chilled, on a bed of chopped ice, accompanied by a bowl of the sauce for dipping.

SERVES 6

Salsa fresca:
1   sweet red pepper, finely chopped
1   sweet yellow pepper, finely chopped
4   ripe tomatoes, seeded and finely chopped
1   small red onion, finely chopped
1   garlic clove, finely minced
1   serrano chili pepper, finely minced
1   jalapeño chili pepper, finely minced
Juice of 1 lime
3   tablespoons olive oil
½   cup finely chopped fresh coriander (cilantro)
¼   cup finely chopped flat-leaf parsley
Salt and freshly ground black pepper, to taste

Combine all ingredients and chill, covered, in the refrigerator for at least 4 hours before serving.

MAKES ABOUT 2 CUPS

Cooking with Cress

Cress evokes childhood memories of picking the fresh green growth from the banks of a nearby creek, nibbling on the cold peppery leaves. Whether grown wild on the banks of a stream or in the herb garden, you'll want plenty of cress for use in salads and a superb cress soup. Of the several varieties of cress, watercress is the best known to the cook and most widely used. Garden cress is similar in flavor to watercress but slightly sharper and its leaves are smaller and a paler green.

Although not an aromatic herb, cress adds a peppery flavor (often described as a combination of the flavors of parsley, spinach, and mustard greens) to everything from green or vegetable salads to pasta, fish, chicken, potatoes, soups, and grains. Add minced cress leaves to hollandaise, béarnaise, and beurre blanc. Add finely minced cress leaves to crepe batter, compound butters, and crème fraîche (for topping grilled fish or chicken paillards). Include some minced cress in soufflés or fish mousse.

Chinese cooks use watercress for its pungent flavor in broth soups at the end of a rich meal and in stir-fry recipes with meat or chicken.

Cress is the traditional English sandwich stuffer or topping on finger sandwiches for the tea table. Mix fresh cress with radish, alfalfa, and bean sprouts for a crunchy filling for sandwiches or crepes—or toss with a mustard vinaigrette for a salad rich in texture and flavor.

For an elegant first course, arrange rolled slices of lightly smoked salmon on a bed of watercress. Add slices of hard-cooked egg and offer a dill vinaigrette. Sprinkle on capers; add a few nasturtium blossoms for a beautiful presentation.

If you grow arugula (roquette) in your garden, combine equal amounts of finely chopped watercress and arugula with grated onion, a dash of Tabasco, a squeeze of lemon, and just enough sour cream to bind. Offer the spread in a pretty bowl, surrounded with toast points.

Add some sprightly sprigs of cress to gazpacho. Tuck the tender stems into pita bread filled with rare roast beef. Top with a dollop of sour cream and the best caviar that you can afford for a peasant sandwich worthy of a special occasion.

For a refreshing and healthful drink, throw some watercress in a blender with cold tomato juice, some fresh basil leaves, and a dash of Tabasco. Chopped cress is excellent mixed with mayonnaise as a salad dressing. Add the leaves to potato salad, chicken salad, or seafood salad, just before serving.

Cress is best eaten raw or cooked briefly. It will not dry or freeze. To keep cress fresh once picked, store it in the refrigerator with the stems in water and the leaves covered by a plastic bag. Plan to use the cress within a day or two.

Lady Apple and Blue Cheese Salad with Pomegranate Dressing

Rich with autumn colors, this spectacular salad has a combination of flavors that makes it perfect for a roast chicken or duck dinner. The tart, stylish dressing is especially good with fresh watercress.

12 lady apples*
Fresh lemon juice
4   cups watercress leaves and tender stems
¼   pound blue cheese, crumbled
⅓   cup olive oil
3   tablespoons raspberry vinegar
1   shallot, minced
¼   cup pomegranate seeds from 1 pomegranate**
Salt and freshly ground black pepper, to taste

Cut apples in half lengthwise; stem and core. Rub cut surfaces with lemon juice. Wash and thoroughly dry watercress. Tear watercress into bite-size pieces and divide equally among 4 chilled salad plates or shallow bowls.

Arrange 6 apple halves on each plate; sprinkle with blue cheese. Whisk together oil, vinegar, and shallot. Stir in pomegranate seeds. Sprinkle salads with salt and pepper, to taste. Spoon on dressing.

SERVES 4

*Lady apples are very small white apples with a red blush that are available from mid-October through December. If not available, substitute wedges of red or yellow Delicious apples or seckel pears.

**To remove the seeds, cut the pomegranate in quarters and remove the flesh from the shell with a spoon. Remove and discard the connecting pulp.

Stir-fried Watercress with Walnuts

This vegetable is light and versatile; it can go with any number of entrees such as fish, poultry, or beef. Cooked in this manner, watercress tastes as fresh as watercress eaten raw.

6   cups watercress leaves and tender stems
2   cloves garlic, finely minced
½   cup broken walnut pieces
2   tablespoons olive oil or walnut oil
1   tablespoon balsamic vinegar
Salt and freshly ground black pepper, to taste

Wash and thoroughly dry watercress. Sauté walnuts in oil over medium-high heat until they are lightly browned. Add garlic; sauté for 1 minute. Add watercress and stir-fry until watercress is wilted, about 15 seconds. Add vinegar and toss for another 5 seconds. Season with salt and pepper, to taste. Serve at once.

SERVES 6

Cooking with Dill

Dill is wonderful for pickles, but good cooks reach for its lacy foliage and slightly bitter seeds for a far wider range of foods. Although native to the Mediterranean, dill is not used in the food of that region except in Greece and Turkey. It is popular in eastern Europe—Russia and Poland, particularly—and in France, England, Germany, and the Scandinavian countries, where it grows wild. The Swedish make a marvelous "dilly bread" and use copious amounts of fresh dill to pickle salmon (gravlax) in a brine of salad oil, sugar, salt, whole white peppercorns, red onion, and Cognac. In Finland, they make a memorable buttermilk soup with fresh dill, and in Denmark, most open-faced sandwiches are garnished with a sprig of dill. Here, fresh dill on new potatoes, fresh green beans, fresh asparagus, or cold soups is a sure sign that spring is here.

Thick veal chops can be cooked many ways; they are a standout when stuffed with goat cheese mixed with fresh dill, lemon zest, and freshly ground black pepper. Dust with seasoned bread crumbs and sauté in oil, about 5 minutes per side, until crispy brown. Have your butcher cut a deep pocket in each chop to hold the stuffing.

Dill is particularly tasty with eggs and poached fish, especially salmon. Don't forget to add dill when making a salmon soufflé. Add fresh dill to a pasta dough for angel hair or fettuccine: toss the cooked pasta with a dressing made with shredded smoked salmon, olive oil, lemon juice, finely minced shallots, and chunks of ripe tomatoes. Sprinkle more fresh dill over the finished dish.

Grilled chicken is a favorite for a quick meal. Before grilling, marinate the chicken for 30 minutes in plain yogurt and lots of fresh dill. This will become a favorite. The same marinade can be used for a leg of lamb with equal results. Let the lamb marinate for up to 2 hours.

Use fresh dill when making potato salad, coleslaw, fresh beets, crepes, biscuits, muffins, carrot or beet sorbet, and hollandaise sauce. An interesting condiment for lamb or fish combines fresh dill with shredded daikon (Japanese radish), and minced onion, bound with a small amount of sour cream or plain yogurt.

Add chopped fresh dill to cream cheese for filling hollowed-out blanched baby squashes for crudités. Spread the same dill cheese on apple slices that have been dipped in lemon juice to prevent darkening; sprinkle with chopped walnuts. For another easy hors d'oeuvre, cream fresh dill and softened unsalted butter for spreading on split tiny corn muffins; fill with thin slices of smoked turkey or ham.

The best way to preserve the sharp flavor of fresh dill (described by many as a mixture of anise, parsley, and celery) is to freeze the leaves immediately after harvesting. The fresh sprigs can be frozen in plastic bags and used straight from the freezer. Chopped fresh dill can be frozen in ice trays, covered with water. Store the frozen cubes in plastic bags and defrost in a strainer, using as fresh.

Dill's pleasant aroma, a combination of mint, citrus, and fennel, is fairly delicate and almost lost in cooking or drying. The fresh leaves also lose some of their flavor during cooking. Add fresh dill toward the

end, sprinkle it on after the dish is finished, or supplement the flavor of the leaves with dill seeds. Somehow, the fresh dill flavor manages to survive in soufflés.

The unripe seeds of dill have been used for hundreds of years to flavor vinegar. Gather the seedheads and steep (include a part of the stem) in one pint of vinegar per seedhead. Let stand for one to two weeks; strain and use for salads. The dried seedheads are used for making pickles. The small yellow-green flowers, borne in large umbrellalike clusters, are lovely in bouquets and as a garnish for a fish platter holding a cold poached salmon with the obligatory green mayonnaise and cucumbers.

Steak Salad with Dill Dressing

A whole meal salad that can be varied, according to the freshest vegetables in the market, this hearty cold beef salad travels well and deserves to star at your next picnic or tailgate supper. Pack the dressing in a separate container to spoon over the assembled ingredients just before serving.

Offer mugs of a sippable soup before, and serve the salad with crusty rolls and glasses of Pinot Noir Blanc. Since the setting is casual, try big, casual oatmeal cookies—dotted with white chocolate—and a basket of plump green figs and seedless red grapes for a self-service dessert. Don't forget to include a thermos of hot coffee.

2   pounds boneless sirloin steak, 1 inch thick
1   pound *haricots verts* (or very young green beans), trimmed
1   pound yellow squash, sliced
16 small new potatoes, scrubbed and quartered
1   pint cherry tomatoes, cut in half
2   bunches watercress, well washed and bottom stems removed

Dill dressing:
1½ cups dry vermouth
1   red onion, finely minced
2   garlic cloves, minced
3   tablespoons olive oil
¼   cup heavy cream
¼   cup crème fraîche
2   tablespoons Dijon mustard
¼   cup chopped fresh dill

Broil or barbecue the steak for 5 minutes on each side, until medium rare. Cut into thin slices, about ½-inch thick. Pack into a container and chill.

Steam *haricots verts* and squash over boiling water until just tender. Drain and refresh under cold water. Drain well and set aside.

Place potatoes in a saucepan with lightly salted cold water. Bring to a boil; reduce heat to simmer and cook until fork tender, about 10 minutes. Drain well and toss with squash and *haricots verts*. Pack into a container and chill.

Pack cherry tomatoes and watercress in separate containers and chill.

Make dressing by bringing vermouth to a rapid boil in a small saucepan. Add onion and garlic; reduce to ⅓ cup. Transfer to a bowl and whisk in remaining ingredients. Pour into a container and chill.

At the picnic site, arrange watercress in a large shallow serving bowl. Arrange vegetables over watercress and top with steak slices. Scatter the tomatoes over the salad. Whisk Dill Dressing and spoon some over the salad. Offer the remaining dressing to spoon over individual servings.

SERVES 8 TO 10

Dilled Grits Soufflé

Mix lots of fresh dill, grits, and a combination of cheeses into a hearty soufflé for a wonderful brunch surprise. Serve with baked country ham and fresh fruit. If you're serving Bloody Marys, add a sprig of fresh dill. The soufflé won't wait, so be sure to have everything else ready to serve.

1	cup milk
1	cup water
½	cup quick-cooking grits
5	tablespoons unsalted butter
½	teaspoon freshly ground black pepper
5	egg yolks, slightly beaten
4	ounces sharp Cheddar cheese, grated
2	ounces Swiss cheese, grated
8	egg whites
¼	cup minced fresh dill

Preheat oven to 400°. Butter a 3-quart soufflé dish and set aside.

In a heavy saucepan, combine milk and water. Bring to a boil; stir in grits and cook, stirring, for 5 minutes or until thick and smooth. Remove from heat. Add butter and pepper. Stir until butter melts. Stir a small amount of the hot mixture into the egg yolks; add the egg yolks to the saucepan, stirring until well blended. Stir in cheeses, reserving 1 tablespoon of each cheese for a topping.

Beat egg whites until stiff. Add one-third of the egg whites to the grits to lighten the mixture. Fold in remaining egg whites and dill.

Pour soufflé mixture into prepared pan. Sprinkle with reserved cheeses. Bake for 35 to 40 minutes or until puffed and set. Serve at once.

SERVES 10 TO 12

Cold Carrot and Tomato Soup with Fresh Dill

Make this summery soup (right) the day before to serve as part of a no-work weekend lunch. Serve with cheese—a soft blue and a good white Vermont Cheddar are nice with the soup—black bread, and green and black olives. A speedy little lunch.

3	pounds fresh, ripe tomatoes
3	tablespoons unsalted butter
2	onions, coarsely chopped
2	shallots, coarsely chopped
6	carrots, coarsely shredded
2	russet potatoes, peeled and coarsely chopped
4	cups rich chicken stock (preferably homemade)
3	tablespoons minced fresh dill

Salt and freshly ground black pepper, to taste
Sour cream
Fresh dill sprigs, for garnish

Blanch tomatoes in boiling water for 1 minute to loosen skins. Peel and coarsely chop. In a large saucepan, melt butter over medium heat. Add onions, shallots, and carrots. Sauté for 5 minutes. Add potatoes and chicken stock; simmer, covered, for 10 minutes. Add tomatoes and continue to cook, stirring occasionally to prevent sticking, for 15 minutes.

Puree in batches in a food processor or blender. Return to saucepan and add dill, salt, and pepper. Simmer for 5 minutes. Chill for several hours. Serve cold with a dollop of sour cream and a sprig of fresh dill.

SERVES 6

Endive with Smoked Salmon and Fresh Dill Mustard Sauce

This simple-to-make smoked salmon hors d'oeuvre looks as beautiful as it tastes. Individual leaves of Belgian endive make excellent bases for light cocktail fare. Here they're filled with thinly sliced smoked salmon (lox can be substituted) and a dollop of a sweetly pungent mustard sauce with lots of fresh dill. Another time, fill the endive with a small amount of julienned beets and top with the same mustard sauce. Serve with ice-cold vodka, aquavit, or dry white wine.

4–5 heads of endive
2½ pounds smoked salmon, thinly sliced
Dill Mustard Sauce (recipe follows)
Fresh dill, for garnish

Separate the endive leaves by cutting a small slice off the bottom of each endive and carefully loosening the leaves. Arrange a small slice of salmon on each endive leaf. Garnish with a dollop of the Dill Mustard Sauce and a small sprig of fresh dill.

MAKES ABOUT 50 HORS D'OEUVRES

Dill mustard sauce:
5   tablespoons Dijon mustard
2   teaspoons dry mustard
4   tablespoons sugar
3   tablespoons white wine vinegar
½   cup light vegetable oil
½   cup sour cream
½   cup chopped fresh dill

In a food processor or blender, combine mustards, sugar, and vinegar. Process until smooth. With motor running, add oil in a very slow stream until mixture is thick. Stir in sour cream and dill.

MAKES ABOUT 2 CUPS

Cooking with Fennel

For Italian and French cooks, fennel is an essential kitchen herb. Its delicate anise flavor is valued for fish, sausages, salads, breads, and pasta. For years, the bulb and tender young stems of Florence fennel (also called finocchio), have been a familiar vegetable in American kitchens but increasingly, the herb fennel is becoming popular—its leaves and seeds are also used with poultry, pork, soups, and cooked vegetables such as cabbage, peas, beans, potatoes, and cauliflower. All parts of this graceful Mediterranean plant can be used in cooking.

The feathery green leaves are wonderful with fish. Stuff whole fish with the leaves and stalks before roasting or grilling. Add the leaves to a poaching liquid or to a basting sauce. For a quick fish butter, combine ¼ cup (½ stick) unsalted butter, 2 teaspoons lemon juice, salt and freshly ground black pepper to taste, 2 tablespoons finely chopped fennel leaves, and a dash of Pernod.

Stir the chopped leaves into hot tomato soup to heighten its flavor; add them to meat loaves and polenta. Sprinkle them over salads or into marinades. Chopped fresh fennel does wonders for white bean salad.

Add the crushed fennel seeds to crumb toppings for casseroles, press them into pork chops before grilling, or stir them into bread dough, steamed cabbage, or a spicy sausage sauce for pasta. Use fennel seed in combination with the chopped fresh leaves as an aromatic stuffing poked into slits cut in a pork roast.

Treat the hollow stalks as you would celery in cooking. Eat them raw or simmer the stalks in water or chicken stock as a vegetable to be served with butter. They can also be sautéed in garlic and olive oil. Add them to soups or stews (at the last as they cook quickly). Children love the licoricelike flavor of fennel; let them use a fresh fennel stalk as a straw for sipping orange juice. In the South of France, the dried fennel stalks are the bed on which grilled sea bass is flamed. Try adding a few sprigs of fresh rosemary to the fennel for a fantastic flavor and aroma.

The root can be thinly sliced and simmered in chicken stock until tender for a simple fennel soup, adding salt and freshly ground black pepper, to taste. The clusters of lovely yellow flowers in late summer and early fall are beautiful as a garnish.

Make fennel vinegar and then use the vinegar for *beurre blanc* fennel sauce. The leaves can be dried but they will lose some of their pungency. Fresh fennel leaves can be frozen for up to two months, packed in small bunches in plastic bags. Use them as you would fresh.

Flamed Tuna with Fennel and Tangerine Sauce

This is a variation of the famous French method of flaming fish with fennel using fresh tuna, which is deliciously meaty when cooked in this manner. Start with Cold Carrot and Tomato Soup with Fresh Dill (page 130); serve wild rice and a julienne of zucchini and carrots with the fish. End the meal with fresh strawberries and snifters of Cognac.

4   thick tuna steaks (about 6 ounces each)
Salt and freshly ground black pepper, to taste
¼   cup olive oil
2   tablespoons chopped fresh fennel leaves
2   tablespoons chopped flat-leaf parsley
Dried fennel stalks
Cognac for flaming, warmed
Fresh fennel sprigs, tarragon sprigs, and edible
        flowers, for garnish
Grated zest of 2 tangerines
Tangerine Sauce (recipe follows)

Sprinkle tuna with salt and pepper, to taste. In a small bowl, combine olive oil, fennel, and parsley. Grill tuna over hot coals about 3 to 4 minutes per side, until brown on the outside but slightly pink inside, basting with fennel oil.

Arrange fish over dried fennel stalks on a flame-proof platter. Pour over warm Cognac and flame. Spoon sauce onto individual serving plates. Arrange tuna over sauce and garnish with herbs and edible flowers. Sprinkle with tangerine zest. Serve with remaining Tangerine Sauce.

Tangerine sauce:
½   cup fresh tangerine juice
2   teaspoons chopped fresh tarragon
¼   cup unsalted butter, cut into 4 pieces

Bring tangerine juice and tarragon to a boil in a small saucepan. Whisk in ¼ cup butter, piece by piece, until sauce thickens.

SERVES 4

Monkfish with Pinot Noir Sauce

This is a very pretty dish to place in front of a diner, but it's surprisingly easy to prepare and the combination of flavors is terrific. Monkfish, called lotte *in France, has a flavor and texture similar to lobster, but it's much less expensive and is becoming more readily available. Fluffy lemon rice and a sauté of zucchini and spinach would be a welcome counterpoint to the richness of the Pinot Noir sauce.*

3   tablespoons olive oil
2   shallots, minced
½   cup Pinot Noir
1   tablespoon chopped fresh fennel leaves
1   tablespoon chopped fresh tarragon
½   cup bottled clam juice
2   tablespoons (¼ stick) unsalted butter
1   tablespoon fresh lemon juice
Salt and freshly ground black pepper, to taste
¾   pound monkfish fillets, trimmed of
    membranes
3   tablespoons olive oil
2   sprigs fresh fennel
2   sprigs fresh tarragon

Preheat oven to 400°.

In a medium saucepan, heat 1 tablespoon oil over high heat. Add shallots; sauté until soft, about 2 minutes. Add wine, fennel, and tarragon. Cook until liquid is reduced by half. Add clam juice and cook until reduced to 3 tablespoons. Remove from heat and whisk in butter. Strain the sauce through a fine sieve. Add lemon juice and season with salt and pepper, to taste. Set aside and keep warm.

In a large, heavy ovenproof skillet, heat the remaining 2 tablespoons olive oil over high heat. Add the monkfish fillets and sauté 1 minute per side until lightly browned.

Arrange 1 sprig of fennel and 1 sprig of tarragon on each fillet. Bake for 6 to 8 minutes, or until fish is opaque throughout. Spoon 2 tablespoons sauce on each of 2 warmed serving plates. Place a roasted fillet on top.

SERVES 2

Country Crayfish Soup

Fresh crayfish are available in fish markets during the summer months and in the freezer section of many supermarkets all year. Crusty bread, a green salad, and fresh fruit are all you need to complete this meal. Serve an earthy white wine.

1   tablespoon unsalted butter
1   tablespoon olive oil
4   garlic cloves, minced
1   large onion, chopped
3   tablespoons minced fresh fennel leaves
3   large fresh tomatoes, peeled, seeded, and
    chopped
1   cup light beer
Juice of 1 fresh lemon
1   sprig fresh tarragon
Salt and freshly ground black pepper, to taste
20–36 crayfish, washed and cleaned
Chopped fresh flat-leaf parsley, for garnish

In a large heavy saucepan, heat butter and oil over medium heat. Add garlic and onion; sauté until barely limp. Add fennel, tomatoes, beer, lemon juice, and tarragon. Simmer slowly for 30 minutes. Add salt and pepper, to taste. Add crayfish and cook for 10 minutes. Serve in shallow soup bowls and garnish with chopped flat-leaf parsley.

SERVES 4

Cooking with Garlic

The sight of garlic bulbs drying in a sunny place for two or three days speaks to a garlic fanatic of marvelous dishes to come. Love it or hate it, garlic is the most widely used herb in the world and its influence circles the globe.

Often called the rose of Provence, garlic is usually associated with the Mediterranean, but it's used lavishly in Mexican, South American, Caribbean, Indian, Middle Eastern, and Chinese cooking—nearly every cuisine except Japanese—to add warmth and excitement to every dish it touches. Garlic has infiltrated nouvelle and other trendy cuisines, where it is used freely as an ingredient or roasted whole and served as a vegetable. Try to envision a world without the Caesar salad; the *bagna cauda* of Piedmont; a simple roast chicken stuffed with garlic cloves and fresh green herbs; a bowl of steaming Mexican garlic soup to cool you down on a hot summer day; a jar of homemade pesto sauce to spoon over pasta or poached fish; the incredibly garlicky golden mayonnaise of Provence, aioli; or plump cloves of roasted garlic to squeeze onto rounds of crusty bread spread with chèvre or Brie—all depend on the ample use of fresh garlic for their flavor and character.

Roasting helps tame the potent odor and harsh flavor of raw garlic, giving it a mild, subtly sweet flavor similar to that of chestnuts. When selecting fresh garlic for roasting, look for good-size bulbs with large, firm cloves. Place the unpeeled heads in a shallow baking pan, drizzle with a little olive oil, and bake for about 1 hour at 325°, or until centers are soft and buttery. (If you're serving duck or quail, drizzle the garlic with honey instead of the olive oil

and sprinkle with curry powder.) To eat, pluck off the cloves and squeeze their contents out of the skins onto crackers, slices of meat, or servings of cooked vegetables such as cauliflower, broccoli, green beans, or new potatoes.

Blanching also tames garlic, taking away the hot sting and most of the lingering aftertaste. Don't bother to peel the cloves before blanching; just break the garlic head apart into cloves and drop into rapidly boiling water. Boil until tender and drain in a colander. When cool enough to touch, slip off the skins. A bonus—your hands won't reek of garlic.

There is no substitute for fresh garlic. Nothing can compare with its fresh, sweet taste. Garlic salt, flakes, powder, or commercially packed chopped garlic in oil simply lack the flavor of fresh garlic. When garlic is mashed or pureed, it is strongest, releasing the maximum of its volatile oils. Sprinkling a little salt on the chopping board will help keep the minced garlic from sticking to the knife, and rubbing your hands with salt after handling garlic will take away the odor. Take great care when sautéeing garlic; it burns very quickly and turns acrid.

Push slivers of garlic into a pork or beef roast; the garlic saturates the meat with a wonderful intense flavor. If you only want a faint whisper of garlic, rub a heated serving platter for fish or chicken (even vegetables) with a clove of garlic. Use whole, peeled garlic cloves and remove them from the dish after a minute or two. After just that long, the garlic will have imparted a hint of flavor. Garlic lovers add minced fresh garlic just minutes before finishing a dish so that it retains its potent flavor. Try a mixture of minced garlic and parsley strewn over grilled chicken or steamed fresh vegetables. The French always remove any tiny green shoots inside the garlic clove, which they claim interfere with digestion.

Store garlic in a string bag filled loosely with whole garlic heads in a cool, dry place. Since garlic has a high oil content, it will keep well for up to a month in an airy place away from the sun. Garlic should not be refrigerated as the cold temperature and moisture cause it to lose potency and soften. Garlic will not freeze; it turns mushy.

One garlic clove yields about 1 teaspoon minced garlic.

Tangerine Aioli

Fruited versions of aioli are not unheard of. Catalonian cooks offer some marvelous renditions using pureed pears or apples. Here, the fruity overtones come from fresh lemon juice and frozen tangerine juice concentrate with a mild spike of ground nutmeg. Offer this sweet-tart garlicky dip as a casual appetizer, surrounded with apple wedges, pear wedges (mix both with some fresh lemon juice to preserve color), fresh strawberries, broccoli, and carrots.

3   tablespoons fresh lemon juice
2   tablespoons frozen tangerine juice
     concentrate, thawed
2   egg yolks
2   garlic cloves, minced
½   teaspoon ground nutmeg, preferably freshly
     grated
1   cup salad oil

In a food processor or blender, combine lemon juice, tangerine juice concentrate, egg yolks, garlic, and nutmeg. Process until smooth. With the motor running, slowly pour oil through the feed tube. Process until mixture is the consistency of mayonnaise. Transfer aioli to a serving bowl; cover and chill for several hours to ripen flavor. Bring to room temperature before serving.

MAKES ABOUT 1½ CUPS

138

Garlic Roasted Fillet of Beef with Two Sauces

This expensive cut of beef is more tender but less flavorful than other cuts of beef. Garlic slivers amply supply the flavor, and the two sauces provide a dramatic presentation. Start with California Seviche with Fresh Coriander (page 121); then with the beef, serve a colorful tumble of baby vegetables such as fiddlehead greens (the tips of young ferns), baby corn, carrots, pattypan squash, and turnips. Fresh raspberries drizzled with herb honey would make a perfect finale.

1   fillet of beef tenderloin (2–2½ pounds), trimmed
2   garlic cloves, thinly sliced
Olive oil for brushing
Salt and freshly ground black pepper, to taste

Cognac-mustard sauce:
1   tablespoon unsalted butter
1   garlic clove, blanched in boiling water for 2 minutes
1   tablespoon Cognac
1   tablespoon Dijon mustard
1   cup crème fraîche

Fresh tomato butter sauce:
3   tablespoons olive oil
2   pounds ripe tomatoes, peeled, seeded, and finely diced
1½   teaspoons chopped fresh thyme
1   garlic clove, blanched in boiling water for 2 minutes
¼   cup dry red wine
¼   cup red wine vinegar
¼   cup crème fraîche
3   tablespoons butter, cut into small pieces

Preheat oven to 450°.

Cut ¾-inch-deep slits in meat. Insert garlic slices into slits. Place fillet on a rack in a heavy roasting pan. Brush with olive oil and season with salt and pepper, to taste. Roast to desired doneness, about 30 minutes for medium rare. Let roast stand for about 20 minutes before slicing against the grain and at a slight angle.

Meanwhile prepare sauces: To make Cognac-Mustard Sauce, melt butter in a small saucepan. Peel and mince garlic. Add to butter and sauté over medium heat until garlic is soft but not browned. Stir in Cognac and mustard. Whisk in crème fraîche and keep warm.

To make the Tomato Butter Sauce, heat the olive oil in a medium skillet. Add tomatoes and cook until tomatoes are thick and most of the liquid is absorbed. Stir in thyme, then salt, and pepper to taste. Set aside.

Peel and mince garlic. Combine with wine and wine vinegar in a nonaluminum pan. Cook over high heat until almost all of the liquid is absorbed. Whisk in crème fraîche and reduce by half. Add the butter, one piece at a time, whisking constantly until mixture is thick and foamy. Stir in reserved tomatoes and keep warm.

To serve, spoon Fresh Tomato Butter Sauce onto one side of heated serving plates. Arrange slices of roasted fillet in the center of the plate and spoon Cognac-Mustard Sauce along the other side of the fillet slices. Serve at once.

SERVES 4

Mediterranean Garden Soup with Rouille

When your vegetable garden or the nearby roadside stand is brimming with red, ripe tomatoes, yellow and green zucchini, deep purple eggplant, and fat leeks, a pot of soup redolent with fresh herbs makes a perfect supper. Greenings or the young tender tops of the growing garlic are added for a mild garlic flavor. For panache, top the soup with Rouille, a scrumptious, rosy pink version of aioli made from garlic and pimentos with a hot pepper kick. By itself, Rouille is great on crackers, steamed fish, broiled chicken, or clams on the half shell. The soup needs only the addition of some crusty peasant-style bread.

3   quarts well-seasoned chicken stock (preferably homemade)
1   cup dry white wine
¼   cup small dried white beans, soaked in water for 2 hours
3   small red-skinned potatoes, cut into 1-inch dice
1   large onion, cut into 1-inch dice
2   leeks, trimmed, cut into 2-inch julienne strips and rinsed thoroughly
2   carrots, cut into 2-inch julienne strips
3   celery stalks, cut into 2-inch julienne strips
1   zucchini, cut into 1-inch dice
1   yellow crookneck squash, cut into 1-inch dice
1   small eggplant, cut into 1-inch dice
2   large, ripe tomatoes, peeled, seeded, and chopped
½   cup garlic greenings, chopped
1   teaspoon minced fresh rosemary
1   teaspoon minced fresh thyme
1   tablespoon minced fresh basil
2   teaspoons minced fresh flat-leaf parsley
Salt and freshly ground black pepper, to taste

In a large soup pot, bring stock and wine to a boil. Reduce heat; drain beans and add to pot. Simmer for 15 minutes. Add potatoes, onion, leeks, carrots, and celery. Cook for 15 minutes. Add zucchini, yellow squash, eggplant, tomatoes, and herbs. Cook until all vegetables are tender. Season with salt and pepper, to taste. Ladle into heated soup bowls and dollop with Rouille.

Rouille:
3   egg yolks
5   garlic cloves, finely minced
1   thick slice of French bread, broken up
3   tablespoons fresh lemon juice
3   canned red pimentos
¼   teaspoon dried hot red pepper flakes
Salt and freshly ground black pepper, to taste
1   cup olive oil

Combine egg yolks, garlic, bread, lemon juice, pimentos, and red pepper flakes in a food processor or blender. Process until mixture is smooth. Scrape down the sides of the processor with a rubber spatula.

While processor is running, add olive oil very slowly through the feed tube, drop by drop, until fully incorporated and the mixture has the consistency of thick mayonnaise. Add salt and pepper, to taste. Cover and store in refrigerator for up to 1 week. Makes about 1 cup.

SERVES 6 TO 8

Red Pepper Pasta with Garlic Pistachio Sauce

Add a vegetable puree to pasta dough and it gives the noodles color and a delicate flavor. This pasta takes on a new dimension when you add fresh red chili peppers and top it with a garlic sauce with the unexpected addition of chopped pistachios. The ultimate degree of hotness is up to you; go slowly at first unless you already know that the sky's the limit when it comes to hotness in food. Serve as a side dish with broiled fish or alone as a light supper or lunch.

3   medium sweet red peppers
1–2 fresh red chili peppers
2–2½ cups all-purpose flour
Pinch salt
1   egg
¼   cup olive oil
4   garlic cloves, peeled
½   cup chopped pistachios
1   tablespoon tiny capers
Salt and freshly ground black pepper, to taste

Roast peppers over an open flame or under a broiler until blackened. When thoroughly charred, place peppers in a brown paper bag to steam (this will enable you to peel them more easily). As soon as peppers are cool enough to handle, peel off the black skins with a small paring knife. Seed and remove ribs. Remove seeds from hot peppers. Puree sweet peppers and hot peppers in a food processor until smooth and set aside.

Mix flour and salt briefly in processor. Add egg and pureed peppers to flour mixture. Process until dough is stiff and smooth and forms a ball. If dough feels sticky, add about 1 more tablespoon flour and process to blend. Cover dough with plastic wrap and let rest for about 30 minutes.

Using a pasta machine (manual or electric), make fettuccine. Dry slightly on pasta rack for an hour or less. If prepared longer than 1 hour ahead, place pasta on a tray and cover with plastic wrap.

Bring 2½ quarts lightly salted water to a boil in a 5- to 6-quart pan. Quickly drop in noodles, a few at a time, and stir to prevent sticking. Cook, uncovered, until tender to bite, about 2 to 3 minutes. Do not overcook. Drain in a colander, shaking out excess water. Set aside and keep warm.

Heat olive oil in a small skillet; add garlic and chopped pistachios. Sauté over low heat until nuts are lightly toasted. Remove from heat and stir in capers. Toss the pasta with the garlic-pistachio mixture. Season with salt and pepper, to taste. Serve at once.

SERVES 4

Barbecued Game Hens, Thai Style

Barbecued chicken is extremely popular in Thailand, with street vendors everywhere grilling highly seasoned chickens over hot coals. For a casual patio buffet, split Cornish game hens are particularly well suited for this method of cooking. Each half makes one serving. Poussins (little chickens that have been specially fed), squab, or quail can be substituted for the game hens. Garlic is present for pungency in the coating before grilling and in the accompanying sauce. Serve with baked sweet potatoes, a salad of cold vegetables, and perhaps a mango or papaya mousse for dessert.

4	Cornish game hens
¼	cup minced fresh coriander (cilantro)
1	tablespoon freshly ground black pepper
12	garlic cloves, minced

Ask your butcher to cut the hens in half lengthwise. In a small bowl, combine minced fresh coriander, pepper, and minced garlic. Rub this mixture evenly over the hens. Grill hens over a bed of hot coals, about 6 inches from the source of heat. Turn hens every 5 minutes for even browning, allowing 25 to 30 minutes total cooking time. Arrange hens on a heated platter and serve with Thai Sauce.

Thai sauce:

2	red hot chili peppers, seeded and finely chopped
3	tablespoons dark brown sugar
1	tablespoon honey
2	12-inch stalks fresh lemon grass
1	tablespoon coarsely chopped fresh ginger
6	garlic cloves, minced
4	shallots, minced
¼	cup soy sauce
¼	cup minced fresh coriander (cilantro)

In a food processor or blender, combine all ingredients and process until smooth. Serve cold.

SERVES 8

Bruschetta

A slice of toasted crusty bread doused with extra-virgin olive oil, rubbed with fresh garlic, and sometimes strewn with ripe tomatoes and fresh herbs is southern Italy's version of garlic toast. A glorious late-afternoon snack, Bruschetta needs only glasses of cool white wine, a quiet spot, and the accompaniment of good friends. It is a marvelous example of simple Italian country food.

12	pieces crusty Italian bread, sliced 1 inch thick
⅓–½	cup extra-virgin olive oil
2	large, ripe tomatoes, peeled, seeded, and diced
2	tablespoons chopped fresh oregano
24–36	fresh basil leaves, torn into small pieces
12	garlic cloves, peeled and cut in half lengthwise
	Salt and freshly ground black pepper, to taste

Toast bread slices over a grill or in a very hot (425°) oven until lightly browned on both sides. Remove from heat and brush lavishly with olive oil. Arrange the toasted bread on a large platter.

In a small serving bowl, combine tomatoes, oregano, and basil leaves. Place garlic cloves in a separate serving bowl. Serve Bruschetta warm with your guests rubbing their slice of bread with a cut garlic clove, topping the bread with some of the tomato-herb mixture, and sprinkling to taste with salt and pepper.

SERVES 4

Cooking with Leeks

Leeks are the cornerstone of French cooking and an essential herb in nouvelle cuisine, where they most often are used in julienne strips. To French and other European cooks, leeks are too beautiful to be merely chopped up and added to a recipe—they cook them gently and serve them whole as a side dish, napped with a sauce or vinaigrette.

In this manner, leeks are treated much like asparagus. A simple lemon butter made with fresh chervil is marvelous over steamed leeks, topped with bread crumbs and popped under the broiler for a few seconds. Or, poach leeks in lightly salted water and serve with a tarragon butter, sprinkled with grated Parmesan cheese. Another sauce that complements poached leeks is quickly made by combining sour cream, prepared horseradish, salt, and freshly ground black pepper, to taste. Pour the sauce over the hot cooked leeks, cover, and chill for about 1 hour. Serve cold.

Leeks are terrific in soups and are an essential ingredient in vichyssoise. They also make a wonderful Dutch soup, cooked in a simple milk broth that is served with shreds of Edam or Gouda cheese to sprinkle onto the soup at the table. Stuff sautéed leeks under the skin of a boneless chicken breast or into the cavity of a whole fish; bake and serve with a lemon sauce.

Start a meal with a terrine made with this aristocrat of the onion family. The mild onion flavor is superb. Poach leeks in fresh tarragon and chicken stock, press flat in a terrine with a heavy weight and chill for at least 8 hours or up to 2 days. Pour off any liquid that accumulates; slice and top with a vinaigrette made with Dijon mustard.

The best parts of the leek are the white bulbous end and the lower stalk. On a young leek from your herb garden, more of the green part is tender and edible than that of most market leeks.

Dirt has a way of lurking between layers of the leaves; leeks should be well washed before using. Split the leeks in half lengthwise to within ½ inch of bulb end, or split large stalks completely through. Strip away the outer 2 or 3 layers of leaves and hold each leek under running water, gently separating the layers to wash thoroughly.

When preparing leeks whole, trim them the French way: cut off root ends and trim the tops to a point by making diagonal cuts from each side to the center. Split and clean as described above.

Five-Grain Pilaf with Leeks

This is a crunchy pilaf with the unexpected addition of leeks and toasted pecans. The wheat berries, rye berries, and millet are readily available at natural food stores. Serve this delicious pilaf as an accompaniment for grilled, sautéed, or roasted meat or poultry.

6   tablespoons (¾ stick) unsalted butter
2   cups thinly sliced leeks (white part only)
½   cup pearl barley
½   cup wild rice
¼   cup wheat berries
¼   cup rye berries
¼   cup millet
2   bay leaves
1   tablespoon chopped fresh thyme
3   cups beef stock (preferably homemade)
½   cup dry red wine
1   cup toasted pecans, chopped
Salt and freshly ground pepper, to taste

Preheat oven to 350°.

Melt butter in a heavy ovenproof casserole over medium heat. Add leeks and cook until soft, stirring occasionally, about 6 minutes. Add barley, wild rice, wheat berries, rye berries, and millet. Stir and cook for 3 minutes. Add bay leaves and thyme. Mix in stock and wine. Bring to a boil. Cover tightly and bake until liquid is absorbed, about 35 to 40 minutes. Stir in pecans and add salt and pepper, to taste.

NOTE: Toast pecans on an ungreased baking sheet in a 250° oven for approximately 10 minutes, stirring frequently. Cool.

SERVES 8

Beet Soup with Leeks

This is a light version of borscht, a cooling way to begin a family meal or light summer luncheon (below). It's a snap to throw together and can be served cold with a dollop of sour cream or hot as a dressy first course.

1   pound beets, peeled and grated
¼   cup red wine vinegar
2   medium carrots, peeled and sliced
2   leeks, trimmed, washed, and sliced
4   cups rich chicken stock (preferably homemade)
1   pound green cabbage, thinly sliced
Salt and freshly ground black pepper, to taste
Sour cream
Sprigs of fresh dill, for garnish

Soak ½ cup of the grated beets in vinegar; set aside. In a large soup pot, simmer carrots and leeks in chicken stock for 10 minutes. Add remaining beets and cook until tender, about 15 minutes. Add the cabbage and cook for 3 minutes.

Add the vinegar and reserved beets. Season the soup with salt and pepper, to taste. Serve the soup hot, warm, or chilled, with a dollop of sour cream and a sprig of fresh dill.

SERVES 4 TO 6

Cooking with Lemon Balm

Lemon balm conjures up images of bees humming around dark green crinkly mint-shaped leaves and darting in and out of clusters of small white flowers. It also signals the possibility of a shady refuge from the hot summer sun and a tall, soothing cooler full of the sweet, lemony scent of fresh lemon balm.

Fresh lemon balm imparts a subtle lemon flavor and fresh lemon fragrance, making it especially nice for fruit dishes, custards, and tea. Early fresh leaves can be chopped and added to salads; just cut down somewhat on the vinegar or lemon juice.

Cut the leaves into slivers and sprinkle over fish or add to poached fruit where a lemony flavor is desired. Lemon balm can be used in stuffings, sauces, or any dish in which you would use lemon thyme. It enhances the flavor of vegetables, light grains, roast chicken, steamed vegetables, and fruit salads. Lay fish or chicken over a bed of lemon balm leaves before baking; you won't need any other seasonings. Stir the minced leaves into cooked rice or into clarified butter for dipping artichoke leaves.

Stir chopped fresh lemon balm into plain yogurt and sprinkle with any kind of fresh berries. The minced leaves can be added to a cooked soft custard to pour over fresh fruit. Add the leaves to iced tea or place sprigs of fresh lemon balm in a tall chilled wine glass with white wine; add a splash of sparkling water for a summer spritzer.

For a late-night soothing tea, steep lemon balm leaves in a cup of boiling water. Stir in honey and lemon juice, to taste.

Dried lemon balm is mainly used for tea. For other uses, it's better to freeze the leaves for later use, packed into plastic bags. They'll keep well for up to 2 months.

Glazed Raspberry Tarts with Lemon Balm

These rich little tarts are perfect to follow a special summer meal with cups of espresso and a lemon twist. Also excellent for afternoon tea.

½   cup all-purpose flour
1   tablespoon sugar
3   tablespoons very cold butter
1   egg yolk
½   teaspoon cider vinegar
3   ounces cream cheese, softened
1   tablespoon confectioners' sugar
2   tablespoons minced lemon balm
Fresh raspberries
¼   cup red currant jelly
Lemon balm leaves, for garnish

Preheat oven to 300°.

Stir together flour and sugar. With a pastry blender, cut in butter until mixture resembles coarse meal. With a fork, stir in egg yolk and vinegar. Work dough with your hands until it forms a smooth, noncrumbly ball. (To make dough in a food processor: in a work bowl fitted with steel blade, combine flour, sugar, and butter with on/off motion until mixture resembles coarse meal. Add egg yolk and vinegar. Continue processing until dough forms a ball.)

Press a rounded tablespoon of dough into each of 6 tart pans that are 2 to 2½ inches in diameter, forming an even layer on bottom and sides of pans. Prick the pastry with a fork, line with aluminum foil, and fill with dried beans or pie weights. Bake for 20 minutes, or until golden brown. Let cool in pan; invert to remove and set aside. Discard beans.

In a small bowl, cream together cream cheese, confectioners' sugar, and lemon balm. Spread 1 tablespoon cheese–lemon balm mixture on the bottom of each cooled tart shell. Arrange berries in tart shells.

In a small saucepan, melt jelly; brush over berries. Refrigerate tarts until ready to serve.

MAKES 6 SMALL TARTS

Chicken and Papaya Salad with Honey Lemon Balm Dressing

Everyone loves chicken salad, but this version is far from the usual rendition with its coat of heavy mayonnaise. Comfortable with almost anything, chicken goes light in this summery salad of papaya and avocado that is bursting with flavor and color. Bright beets are a surprise addition and toasted walnuts add a nice crunch. The tangy dressing is made with fresh lemon balm and honey.

2   tablespoons unsalted butter
2   whole chicken breasts, skin and bones intact
Salt and freshly ground black pepper, to taste
3   tablespoons fresh lemon juice
¼   cup olive oil
¼   cup dry white wine
2   tablespoons finely chopped lemon balm
2   tablespoons finely chopped onion
1   small bunch beets (4 or 5)
2   ripe papayas
2   ripe avocados
2   heads Belgian endive
1   small head red leaf lettuce
1   small head Boston lettuce
12   sprigs fresh watercress, tough stems removed
½   cup toasted walnuts, coarsely chopped

Preheat oven to 350°.

Butter a baking dish with unsalted butter. Place chicken in baking dish, skin side up. Sprinkle with salt and pepper, to taste, and 1 tablespoon lemon juice. Cover tightly with aluminum foil.

Bake for 25 to 30 minutes. Cool chicken and shred. Place in a glass bowl. Combine olive oil, wine, lemon balm, and onion. Pour over chicken and marinate, refrigerated, for 2 hours, stirring once or twice.

Place beets in cold water; bring to a boil, reduce heat, and cook over medium heat until tender, about 15 to 20 minutes. Peel beets and cut into fine julienne strips. Chill.

Cut papayas in half and discard seeds. Peel and slice lengthwise into ½-inch wedges. Cut avocados in half, remove the pits, and slice lengthwise into ½-inch wedges. Sprinkle avocado slices with remaining 2 tablespoons lemon juice to prevent darkening.

On each serving plate, prepare a bed of endive, red leaf lettuce, Boston lettuce, and watercress. With a slotted spoon remove the chicken from the marinade, discarding marinade. Arrange chicken, papaya, and avocado on lettuce. Arrange a clump of beets in one corner; sprinkle with walnuts and drizzle on the dressing.

Honey lemon balm dressing:
2   shallots, chopped
2   tablespoons honey
3   tablespoons chopped lemon balm
2   tablespoons dry white wine
2   tablespoons fresh lemon juice
1   tablespoon Dijon mustard
⅔   cup olive oil

Combine all ingredients in a food processor or blender; process until well blended.

SERVES 4

Rhubarb Lemon Balm Tea Bread

*Rhubarb bread is marvelous for tea. Serve with lots
of sweet butter; it's also good spread with cream cheese.*

1½   cups firmly packed brown sugar
⅔   cup vegetable oil
1   cup buttermilk
1   egg
1   teaspoon vanilla extract
1   teaspoon baking soda
1   teaspoon salt
2½   cups all-purpose flour
1½   cups chopped uncooked fresh rhubarb
½   cup sugar
⅓   cup finely chopped fresh lemon balm
1   teaspoon grated lemon zest
1   tablespoon unsalted butter, at room
       temperature

Preheat oven to 350°. Grease a 9 × 5-inch loaf pan.
Line bottom and sides with wax paper.

In a large bowl, combine brown sugar and oil;
beat well. In a small bowl, beat together buttermilk,
egg, and vanilla. Add to brown sugar mixture. Blend
thoroughly. Combine baking soda, salt, and flour.
Gradually stir into brown sugar mixture. Fold in
rhubarb. Transfer batter to prepared bread pan.

In a small bowl, combine sugar, lemon balm,
lemon zest, and butter. Sprinkle mixture over batter.
Bake for 50 to 60 minutes, or until a tester inserted
in the center of the loaf comes out clean. Let cool in
pan for 10 minutes. Turn out onto racks. Remove
wax paper when loaf is cool.

MAKES 1 LARGE LOAF

Crepes Filled with Lemon Balm and Kiwi

These wonderful little crepes are perfect as a dessert or can be served at a summer weekend brunch with icy wake-up drinks, spicy sausages, and eggs scrambled with Brie and fresh tarragon. Crepe batter needs to sit in the refrigerator at least an hour to rest before using; it can be made the evening before.

3   cups cold milk
6   eggs
½   teaspoon salt
3   cups all-purpose flour
1   tablespoon sugar
3   tablespoons unsalted butter, melted
5   tablespoons chopped fresh lemon balm
Melted unsalted butter for frying crepes
8   ripe kiwis, peeled and finely chopped
Superfine sugar
Confectioners' sugar

In a blender, combine milk, eggs, salt, flour, sugar, 3 tablespoons melted butter, and 3 tablespoons lemon balm at high speed for 2 minutes. Chill for 1 hour. Heat a 6- or 7-inch crepe pan over moderately high heat and brush pan with melted butter.

Pour about ¼ cup batter into pan, quickly tilting pan to coat the bottom. Pour back any excess batter into the bowl. Return pan to the heat and cook the crepe for about 1 minute or until it loosens from the pan and is light brown. Turn the crepe and cook for another 30 seconds. Remove crepe from pan and place on a plate.

Continue cooking crepes, brushing the pan lightly with butter each time, if necessary. Set crepes aside to cool.

Combine kiwi fruit and remaining 2 tablespoons lemon balm. Place a cooled crepe on a flat work surface. Place 1 teaspoon kiwi filling near the bottom edge of the crepe. Fold in the sides and roll as you would for egg rolls. Place the filled crepes on a buttered baking sheet. Repeat process until all crepes are filled.

When ready to serve, preheat oven to 400°. Sprinkle the crepes with superfine sugar and place in oven until warmed through. Remove from oven and dust with confectioners' sugar. Arrange on a serving platter.

MAKES ABOUT 25 CREPES

Microwave Lemon Balm Spanish Orange Marmalade

4   Spanish Seville oranges, unpeeled
3   tablespoons minced lemon balm
6   tablespoons granulated sugar

Cut oranges into quarters and finely chop in food processor. Transfer to a 1-quart glass bowl or measuring cup. Stir in lemon balm and sugar. Cook on medium power for 6 minutes or until slightly thickened, stirring every 2 minutes. Transfer to a glass jar with cover; refrigerate until redy to use. (Marmalade will continue to thicken as it cools.)

MAKES ABOUT 1 CUP

Cooking with Lemon Verbena

Lemon verbena, one of the most strongly aromatic herbs, fills the kitchen with a soft lemon fragrance. In cooking, use it in place of lemon zest. Its narrow, lemon-scented leaves are delightful in teas, fruit drinks, desserts, and jellies. The delicate spikes of white-to-pale-lilac blossoms share the lemon fragrance of the leaves and make a lovely garnish.

Add chopped leaves to a fish sauce or sprinkle them over a tomato salad for a pleasant citrusy tang. It's not really necessary to have a recipe for fruit salad; almost any combination of seasonal fruits can be combined to begin or end a meal. Include chopped fresh lemon verbena, according to taste.

Toss together orange and grapefruit sections; sprinkle with lots of chopped lemon verbena. Combine seedless green grapes, fresh blueberries, and casaba melon balls. Sprinkle with light rum and chopped lemon verbena. Mix cantaloupe balls, avocado slices, and wedges of tomatoes. Add salt, freshly ground black pepper, a splash of tequila, and a generous sprinkling of minced lemon verbena. Pile peeled and sliced kiwi in a stemmed glass with fresh raspberries. Fill the glass with white wine and add chopped lemon verbena. Or, try a combination of champagne grapes, champagne, and minced lemon verbena.

Fold sprigs of lemon verbena into damp guest towels. Roll up and place in a basket that can go into the microwave oven. Microwave on high for 30 seconds. Pass these refreshing lemon-scented towels to your guests between courses or while they're eating finger food.

Kiwi Fizz

On a hot summer day, surrender to the pleasures of the season with this refreshing fruit fizz (below). Find a quiet place to sit in the garden or on the porch and enjoy a lazy moment. Add a sprig of lemon verbena for a scented garnish.

2   ripe kiwi fruit
1   teaspoon honey
4   fresh lemon verbena leaves
¾   cup sparkling mineral water
Sprig of lemon verbena, for garnish

Peel and coarsely chop kiwi fruit. Puree with honey and lemon verbena leaves in a food processor or blender, adding a little mineral water as needed to obtain a smooth puree. Strain through a sieve, pressing pulp with a spoon to remove seeds.

Place kiwi puree in a tall chilled glass with crushed ice. Pour in mineral water and stir to combine. Garnish with sprig of lemon verbena.

NOTE: ½ cup cubed ripe honeydew melon can be substituted for the kiwi.

SERVES 1

Apricot Clafouti

Make this clafouti when apricots are at the peak of their season. A flat custardlike baked pudding, it's a snap to prepare and can bake while you're having the appetizer and main course. About as simple as dessert can be!

1   cup light cream
2   eggs
6   tablespoons granulated sugar
3   tablespoons chopped fresh lemon verbena
½   cup all-purpose flour
1   pound fresh apricots, pitted and sliced
Confectioners' sugar

Preheat oven to 350°.

Combine cream, eggs, sugar, and lemon verbena with a wire whisk until smooth. Gradually whisk in flour. Stir in apricots and pour mixture into a lightly buttered 3-cup shallow baking dish. Bake for 30 to 35 minutes or until the clafouti is golden and puffed. Let stand for 5 minutes. Dust with confectioners' sugar and serve warm.

SERVES 4

Blueberry Lemon Verbena Muffins

These moist, old-fashioned blueberry muffins with the lemony flavor of fresh lemon verbena are beautiful for a lazy summer brunch. But don't restrict them to the morning; offer these muffins in the late afternoon, as a surprise treat. No one will be able to resist. Lemon verbena also scents the sugar (made the day before) used as a topping.

6	lemon verbena leaves
1	cup superfine sugar
3	tablespoons minced fresh lemon verbena
1½	cups fresh blueberries
1	cup chopped walnuts
2	cups all-purpose flour
1	tablespoon baking powder
¾	cup granulated sugar
½	cup milk
⅓	cup safflower oil
1	egg

Bury lemon verbena leaves in superfine sugar in a tightly closed container. Let stand overnight before using.

Preheat oven to 400°. Generously grease a muffin tin with 12 cups, about 2½ inches in diameter.

In a medium bowl, combine lemon verbena, blueberries, and walnuts. In a large bowl, mix together flour, baking powder, and sugar. In a medium bowl, whisk together milk, safflower oil, and egg. Pour into flour mixture and stir until just blended.

Add the blueberry–lemon verbena mixture and gently fold together. (Batter should not be smooth.) Divide the batter into the cups of the prepared muffin tin. Sprinkle each muffin with a little of the lemon-scented sugar. (Use any remaining lemon sugar for tea.)

Bake for 25 minutes, or until golden. Remove from oven and let cool in muffin tin for 2 to 3 minutes. Remove muffins and cool on a rack.

MAKES 12 MUFFINS

Cooking with Lovage

Lovage is an old-fashioned herb with a distinctive flavor—like pungent celery with a hint of lemon and anise. If you've never eaten lovage, use it cautiously at first. Cut the leaves or tender stalks for soups and use a few chopped sprigs in salads. A little lovage goes a long way.

All parts of this magnificent Mediterranean herb are used in cooking. Use the leaves as you would any other aromatic herb in salads, stuffings, vegetable soups, and omelets. Cut and blanch the young hollow stalks as a vegetable, chop them into soups and sauces, or candy them as you would angelica for garnishing cakes. Use tougher mature stalks in chicken or beef stock.

Fill the cavity of a nonoily fish such as red snapper or trout with lovage stems and leaves. Baste with olive oil infused with chopped lovage leaves while grilling or baking. Flame with a splash of Pernod.

When cooked, fresh lovage is not as pungent in flavor. Lovage seeds dry well; sprinkle them over meat or into bread dough. Lovage seeds also make a flavorful herb butter. Grate the lovage roots to make tea or chop them and preserve in honey for basting ham and pork.

A preservation method that works well with lovage is the salt method; sprinkle ½ teaspoon salt per 1 cup of loosely packed chopped lovage. Alternate ½-inch-thick layers of chopped lovage with salt sprinklings until the container is full. Refrigerate. Use this lovage salt instead of table salt for cooking.

Lovage Frittata

Lovage and frittatas—huge thick omelets baked in the oven—are both native to the Mediterranean. Perfect for brunch, lunch, or supper, frittatas are wonderfully flexible and can be quickly made with whatever vegetables and herbs you have on hand. For a light Sunday lunch, serve this frittata with hot, crusty herb bread and an arugula (roquette) and garden lettuce salad. Offer iced cherries or champagne grapes and your best homemade cookies for dessert.

3   tablespoons olive oil
2   medium baking potatoes, peeled and thinly sliced
1   medium onion, peeled and thinly sliced
½   cup loosely packed lovage leaves
2   sweet red peppers, minced
8   eggs, lightly beaten
Salt and freshly ground black pepper, to taste
2   sprigs of fresh thyme

Preheat oven to 400°.

Pour the olive oil into an 8-inch baking dish.

Arrange potato and onion slices in the baking dish; bake for 20 minutes, or until potatoes are just tender. Sprinkle lovage and red peppers over the other vegetables. Pour eggs over vegetables and sprinkle with salt and pepper, to taste. Arrange thyme on top.

Bake until eggs are set, the sides are puffed and the top is golden brown, about 20 minutes. The frittata should be firm but not dry. Serve hot or at room temperature.

SERVES 4

Strasbourg Hens with Lovage Stuffing

Fresh lovage adds the perfect flavor accent to the stuffing for these game hens served with a beer sauce (right). Finish this country meal with two fresh vegetable purees, beet and carrot. For dessert, make a rhubarb crisp served with spoonfuls of crème fraîche.

1   small onion, minced
1   carrot, finely diced
⅓   cup finely chopped fresh lovage (use the tender young shoots and leaves)
2   tablespoons salted butter
1   bay leaf
1   sprig of fresh thyme
½   cup wild rice
2½   cups chicken stock (preferably homemade)
Salt and freshly ground black pepper, to taste
2   ¾-pound Cornish hens
2   slices bacon
1½   cups light beer, at room temperature
½   teaspoon sugar
1   carrot, peeled and cut in fine julienne strips
1   leek (white part only), washed and cut in fine julienne strips
Salt and freshly ground black pepper, to taste

To make stuffing, sauté onion, carrot, and lovage in butter for 10 minutes. Add bay leaf, thyme, and wild rice. Add 1 cup chicken stock. Bring to a boil; cover and reduce heat to low. Cook for about 30 minutes, stirring occasionally with a fork to prevent sticking. Add salt and pepper, to taste. When rice is tender, remove thyme sprig, drain off any excess liquid, and set stuffing aside to cool slightly.

Preheat oven to 350°.

While stuffing is cooling, debone hens by turning the hen breast side down on a cutting board. With a sharp knife, cut down both sides of the

backbone. Remove meat from the rib cage, cutting as close to the bone as possible. Cut away the whole carcass from the meat. Remove the thigh bones from each leg and turn the hen skin side up. (If you're on good terms with your butcher, ask him to debone the hens for you.)

Carefully loosen the skin from the meat. Insert ½ cup of prepared stuffing under the skin of each hen. Turn hen over and fasten skin closed with a small skewer. Tuck wing tips under breast and tie the drumsticks together with kitchen string. Place hens breast side up in a shallow baking dish.

Cut bacon slices in half and cover each hen with two strips. Roast for about 45 minutes, until golden brown. Remove hens from pan, remove skewers, and keep warm. Drain off the excess grease from the

roasting pan; add ½ cup beer to deglaze. Strain into a saucepan; add remaining 1½ cups chicken stock and set aside.

In a large heavy skillet, combine remaining 1 cup beer and sugar. Bring to a boil over medium-high heat. Add the carrot and leek. Cook about 3 minutes or until just tender. Lift out the cooked vegetables and keep warm. Add the vegetable juices to the reserved pan juices and reduce over high heat to thicken. Add salt and pepper, to taste.

Remove bacon from the roasted hens. Place on individual heated serving plates and garnish with julienne vegetables. Nap hens and vegetables with the reduced sauce.

SERVES 2

COOKING WITH LOVAGE

Cooking with Marjoram (Sweet)

Cooks who grow sweet marjoram in their kitchen herb garden can't believe how large a sweet marjoram plant gets by the end of summer. Fortunately, one can hardly have too much marjoram. This extremely versatile aromatic herb works well with all kinds of meats, fish, soups, and egg and cheese dishes. As a result, it is one of the most frequently used kitchen herbs.

Along with oregano and basil, sweet marjoram is one of the three essential herbs in Italian cooking. Risotto with zucchini blossoms is a traditional Italian dish and chopped sweet marjoram adds a spicy, fragrant flavor. For 2 cups raw Italian Arborio rice, add 3 tablespoons roughly chopped fresh sweet marjoram to the chicken broth. After the rice has cooked for 10 minutes, add several chopped zucchini blossoms (stems and pistils removed), salt and freshly ground black pepper, to taste. Cook the rice for another 10 to 15 minutes (Arborio rice takes a little longer to cook than long-grain rice); remove from heat and stir in unsalted butter and freshly grated Parmesan cheese.

Ladle piping hot polenta over a small mound of cold mascarpone cheese and top with a generous sprinkling of chopped fresh marjoram. Another Italian dish transformed to the sublime.

In England, marjoram is traditional with goose and chestnuts. It has an affinity with beans; use it in white bean salad or sprinkled over steamed green beans. Add it to bean, split pea, or lentil soup.

Toss cooked spaghetti with chopped sweet marjoram, finely minced garlic, olive oil, and a sprinkling of dried red pepper flakes. Marjoram's alluring flavor is also excellent with vegetables such as potatoes, carrots, turnips, cabbage, zucchini, and corn. Stir a generous amount into batter for corn bread and corn muffins.

Sprinkle the chopped leaves into vegetable juice or tomato juice, sprinkle it over eggplant, and add a generous amount to tomato-based pasta sauces. Use it with lamb, pork, veal, and ground meats. Add marjoram to stuffings for chicken and duck. Marjoram goes well with pheasant and rabbit.

For a variation on Roquefort grapes, combine cream cheese and a small amount of heavy cream until smooth. Coat seedless grapes with the cheese mixture and roll them in finely chopped fresh sweet marjoram. Place on wax paper and chill until ready to serve.

Sweet marjoram's mild flavor becomes stronger when dried. Sweet marjoram freezes well; pack small bunches in plastic bags, freeze, and use straight from the freezer. If you are planning to keep it more than a few months, it's better to dry your harvest.

Sweet Marjoram Blueberry Tartlets

Marjoram is a delicate herb that combines successfully with fruit. These tartlets are perfect for the tea table or as an accompaniment to roast goose or duck.

Sweet marjoram pastry:

2   cups all-purpose flour
½   teaspoon salt
Dash freshly ground black pepper
1   tablespoon minced fresh sweet marjoram
½   cup (1 stick) salted butter
5   tablespoons ice water

Blueberry filling:

3   tablespoons fresh lemon juice
1   tablespoon sugar
1   tablespoon Grand Marnier
1   cup fresh blueberries, washed, drained, and
     picked over
Grated lemon zest
8   tiny sprigs of fresh marjoram

Preheat oven to 350°.

To make pastry, combine flour, salt, pepper, and marjoram. Cut in butter until mixture resembles coarse meal. Stir in ice water, 1 tablespoon at a time, until dough can be formed into a ball. (If using a food processor, place flour, salt, pepper, marjoram, and butter in a work bowl fitted with a steel blade. Combine by turning machine on/off until mixture resembles coarse meal. Add water and continue processing until dough forms a ball.) Wrap in plastic wrap and chill for 1 hour.

On a lightly floured board, roll out dough to ¼-inch thick. If you're using 2–2½-inch tartlet pans, place 8 of them on top of the pastry. Using a sharp knife, cut the pastry slightly larger than each pan.

Press the pastry into the pans and, using your thumb, cut off the excess.

Or, for a single large tart, cut the pastry slightly larger than the pan and make a pretty edge with the tines of a fork. Prick the pastry with a fork, line with aluminum foil, and fill with dried beans or pie weights.

Bake for 10 to 15 minutes until golden. Transfer to a rack, remove the foil and beans. Let tartlet shells cool.

Meanwhile, in a small saucepan, combine lemon juice, sugar, and Grand Marnier. Bring to a boil and stir until sugar dissolves. Add blueberries and cook over medium heat for 5 minutes. Set aside to cool. Fill each tartlet shell with blueberry mixture or pour it all into the single large tart shell. Refrigerate.

When ready to serve, reheat in a 350° oven for 5 minutes. Sprinkle tartlets with grated lemon zest and garnish with small sprigs of marjoram.

SERVES 8

Grilled Corn Cakes with Sweet Marjoram–Red Pepper Marmalade

Serve these delicious little corn cakes at your next barbecue with grilled fish or chicken. They're full of fresh corn flavor and are easier to make than fritters—they keep well in a low oven until you're ready to serve. Any leftover red pepper marmalade can be used another time on hot biscuits or muffins.

1½ cups fresh corn kernels
½ cup milk
⅓ cup cornmeal
⅓ cup all-purpose flour
¼ cup (½ stick) unsalted butter
2 eggs
2 egg yolks
½ teaspoon salt
½ teaspoon freshly ground black pepper
2 tablespoons minced fresh sweet marjoram
Unsalted butter, melted, for brushing skillet
Sour cream
Sweet Marjoram–Red Pepper Marmalade (recipe follows)

In a large bowl, whisk together corn, milk, cornmeal, and flour. In a small bowl, whisk together butter, eggs, and egg yolks. Stir egg mixture into corn mixture. Stir in salt, pepper, and marjoram.

Heat a small skillet over high heat. Brush with unsalted butter. Drop batter into skillet to make small pancakes, about 3 inches in diameter. Cook for 2 minutes on each side until golden. Keep warm and repeat with remaining batter.

To serve, arrange 2 corn cakes on each plate. Garnish each with a dollop of sour cream and marmalade.

Sweet marjoram–red pepper marmalade:
3 sweet red peppers, seeded and ribs removed
1 large tomato, peeled and seeded
1 small onion, peeled
2 garlic cloves, peeled
2 tablespoons chopped fresh sweet marjoram
2 tablespoons red wine vinegar
1 teaspoon salt
Salt and freshly ground black pepper, to taste

Preheat oven to 450°.

In a baking dish with cover, place peppers, tomato, onion, and garlic. Sprinkle with marjoram. Cover and bake for 30 to 45 minutes, or until vegetables are very soft. Puree in a food processor or blender. Press through a coarse sieve. Stir in vinegar. Season with salt and pepper, to taste. Serve at room temperature.

Rack of Lamb with Sweet Marjoram and Lemon

This lamb roast makes a spectacular presentation for a special dinner party. It cooks quickly and smells wonderful as it's roasting. Surround the racks with pan-roasted vegetables (quartered roasting potatoes, quartered baby artichokes, baby carrots, whole peeled shallots, whole heads of unpeeled garlic, and fresh sprigs of sweet marjoram and rosemary). Drizzle the vegetables with olive oil; season with salt and freshly ground black pepper. Start the vegetables about 20 minutes before the lamb in a 400° oven and they'll be done by the time you're ready to serve the lamb.

2	3½–4-pound racks of lamb with 8 to 9 chops each

Salt and freshly ground black pepper, to taste

3	garlic cloves, finely minced
2	tablespoons fresh lemon juice
3	tablespoons chopped fresh marjoram
2	tablespoons olive oil

Unsalted butter, softened to room temperature

Have the butcher "french" the bone ends of racks. Season each rack lightly with salt and pepper, to taste.

Preheat oven to 500°.

In a small bowl, combine garlic, lemon juice, marjoram, and olive oil. Coat the meaty side of each rack with the garlic-marjoram mixture. Cover exposed bone tips with small pieces of foil.

Lightly butter a shallow baking pan (large enough to hold both racks of lamb). Place lamb in the baking pan, coated side up. Roast for 20 to 25 minutes, until golden brown on the outside but pink and rare inside. Remove from oven and place the bone sides together, intertwining the ends of the rib bones. Discard foil. Let the meat rest for 10 minutes. Arrange on warmed serving platter, surrounded by vegetables, for at-the-table carving.

SERVES 6

Cooking with Mint

Mint is synonymous with mint juleps (the symbol of Southern hospitality), tall icy glasses of tea served on the porch, mint chocolate ice cream, and the mint apple jelly that often accompanies a leg of lamb. It also adds sparkle to summer salads, most vegetables, and sauces for meat, poultry, and fish. The varieties most used for cooking are spearmint and applemint, although other varieties such as peppermint, pineapple, and the citrus mints—orange and grapefruit—are finding a place in contemporary cuisines and are popular for summer drinks, teas, and jellies.

Widely used around the Mediterranean and in Middle Eastern countries, mint is essential for tabbouleh and falafel. Indian cooks combine minced cucumber and onion, plain yogurt, cardamom seeds, and finely chopped mint for a condiment that cools the palate and is especially good with spicy foods. In Iran, a few dried currants would be added.

Greeks use mint in stuffed grape leaves and Italians sprinkle it chopped over sautéed zucchini. In Portugal, cooked fava beans are pureed with fresh mint and in Spain, grilled chicken marinated in Spanish sherry is served with a generous sprinkling of the chopped fresh herb. Virtually ignored by traditional French cooks, mint is used extensively in nouvelle cuisine.

Thai cooks use fresh mint for stir-fries, salads, and as a garnish. An interesting chicken salad with Thai flavors can be made by combining finely chopped cooked chicken, fresh lemon grass, red chili peppers, scallions, fresh coriander (cilantro), and chopped fresh mint. Sprinkle with lime juice and Thai fish sauce (available at gourmet shops and some supermarkets—if not available substitute soy sauce).

For a summer appetizer, combine fresh mint leaves, to taste, with equal parts of sour cream and mayonnaise to make a cool sauce for dipping blanched sugar snap peas. Marinate fresh pineapple in port and chopped fresh mint. Sprinkle chopped fresh mint over fresh corn salad.

Stir finely chopped mint into a sugar cookie recipe or your favorite recipe for rich vanilla ice cream. If you want the ice cream green, add a tablespoon of green crème de menthe. Add chopped mint to a sabayon made with lime juice; serve with fresh fruit of the season.

A mixture of chopped fresh mint and mascarpone cheese makes a wonderful dip for crisp apples and pears. Add mint to cantaloupe or strawberry soup; serve mint sorbet in lemon shells for a refreshing summer dessert.

Stuff a chicken with 5 sprigs of fresh mint before roasting or marinate chicken pieces in buttermilk and chopped fresh mint before grilling. Fresh mint also enlivens the flavor of cooked carrots, cabbage, cauliflower, peas, new potatoes, turnips, and beans. Sprinkle mint over tomatoes before broiling; scatter the fresh leaves over a quick sauté of cherry tomatoes, garlic, and olive oil. Sprinkle chopped mint into melted butter for cooked artichokes or sprinkle it over marinated artichoke hearts.

Serving Cajun or Caribbean food? For an interesting side dish, try fried bananas, rolling them first in chopped fresh apple or pineapple mint.

Mint loses its flavor when cooked for long periods of time; add the finely chopped leaves just before serving. Fresh mint leaves are more flavorful than dried. It's better to freeze the leaves for future use. Chop the mint and pack into ice trays. Cover with water and freeze. Store the frozen cubes in plastic bags and defrost in a strainer, using the mint as fresh.

Mint Chocolate Mousse Cakes with Raspberry Puree

Mint is a natural dessert herb. Combined with rich dark chocolate mousse cake floating in a puddle of raspberry puree and sprinkled with fresh raspberries, it's a heady experience for anyone who adores chocolate. Offer these little cakes with coffee or espresso.

4   tablespoons chopped fresh peppermint
½   cup boiling water
6   tablespoons unsalted butter, at room temperature, plus butter for greasing the molds
1½ ounces unsweetened chocolate
3   ounces semisweet chocolate
⅔   cup granulated sugar
3   large eggs, separated
9   tablespoons all-purpose flour
3   cups fresh raspberries
2   tablespoons superfine sugar

Make a "mint tea" by placing the peppermint in the boiling water and letting it steep for 30 minutes. Strain, discarding mint leaves. Set aside.

Preheat oven to 325°. Butter six ½-cup ramekins or molds. Line the bottom of each mold with a circle of wax paper and butter the paper.

Place 6 tablespoons of "mint tea" in the top of a double boiler over simmering water. Add the chocolates and melt, stirring until blended. Set aside.

Cream the butter and sugar together until light and fluffy. Beat in egg yolks and stir in reserved mint chocolate mixture. Stir in the flour. Beat egg whites until they hold a soft peak. Stir a little of the egg white into the chocolate mixture to lighten the batter. Fold in remaining egg whites.

Divide the batter between the six prepared molds. Place the molds in a baking dish. Fill the pan with boiling water until it reaches about halfway up the sides of the molds. Bake for 40 minutes. Remove baking dish from oven and allow molds to cool in the water.

Reserve 1 cup raspberries. Puree remaining 2 cups in a food processor or blender. Force through a fine sieve to remove seeds. Stir in superfine sugar.

When ready to serve, unmold the cakes by running a knife around the inside of each mold and inverting onto individual plates. Peel off wax paper. Surround each cake with raspberry puree and scatter the reserved raspberries around the cakes.

MAKES 6 LITTLE CAKES

Dried Fruit and Mint Chocolate Tartlets

Chocolate and mint are irresistible. Two-bite-size, these dessert cups are mint chocolate on the outside and a mixture of mint, dried fruit, and nuts on the inside. A delight for any chocolate fanatic, these mint chocolate dessert tarts make a pretty addition to a tea table and go well with coffee for dessert. They're tiny; allow 1 or 2 for a serving. You'll find the tiny paper baking cups for muffins in gourmet shops and some supermarkets.

9	ounces semisweet chocolate
32	small, fresh peppermint leaves
16	dried apricots, finely chopped
16	dried, pitted dates, finely chopped
16	dried figs, finely chopped
1	cup walnuts, finely chopped
3	tablespoons crème de menthe
32	paper muffin cup liners (2½-inch size)

Place chocolate and 16 of the mint leaves in the top of a double boiler over barely simmering (not boiling) water. Stir until chocolate melts. Remove from heat; discard mint leaves.

Stack 2 paper muffin cups together. With a ½-inch-wide brush, paint the inside bottom and about ½ inch up the inside of each muffin cup. Repeat process until 16 muffin cups have been painted with the mint chocolate. Set cups in muffin pans and refrigerate until chocolate is hard, about 1 hour. Use right away or wrap airtight and chill for up to 3 weeks.

For the filling, finely chop remaining mint leaves and combine with dried fruits and walnuts. Pour on crème de menthe and mix. Fill each chocolate cup with mint-fruit mixture. Refrigerate until ready to serve. Peel away paper before serving.

MAKES ABOUT 16

Three Mint, Three Melon Balls

Melon balls, tossed with fresh lime juice and a variety of fresh garden mints, are a snap to throw together in the spare minutes of a busy weekend (right). Suitable for brunch, lunch, or dinner, this dessert deserves your most elegant glass bowl for a spectacular presentation.

1   ripe, firm honeydew melon, halved and seeds removed
1   ripe, firm cranshaw melon, halved and seeds removed
1   ripe, firm cantaloupe, halved and seeds removed
3   tablespoons fresh lime juice
3   tablespoons chopped fresh grapefruit mint
3   tablespoons chopped fresh apple mint
3   tablespoons chopped fresh orange mint

With a melon-ball scoop, cut as many balls as possible from each melon half. Place in a large bowl. Add lime juice and chill. Sprinkle with the mints just before serving; stir gently.

SERVES 6

Currant Mint Chutney

Serve this zesty chutney with lamb—a refreshing change from the mint-flavored apple jelly that's usually served. It also works with grilled chicken and roast pork.

½   cup cider vinegar
½   cup firmly packed light brown sugar
½   teaspoon dry mustard
Dash salt
3   sun-dried tomatoes (packed in oil), minced
1   Granny Smith apple, peeled and chopped
1   large onion, minced
1   garlic clove, minced
6   tablespoons currants
⅓   cup firmly packed chopped fresh mint leaves

In a saucepan, combine vinegar, brown sugar, mustard, and salt. Bring the mixture to a boil over moderate heat. Remove from heat and let cool, stirring occasionally. Add sun-dried tomatoes, apple, onion, garlic, currants, and mint. Stir to combine thoroughly. Pack into a container with cover. Refrigerate. Bring to room temperature before serving.

Lemony Mint Custard

A very adult custard, this easy-to-make dessert tastes sublime and makes an elegant end to a dinner party. Present the custard in your prettiest stemmed glasses and follow with a selection of brandies and strong hot coffee.

12   egg yolks
1½   cups dry white wine
½   cup chopped mint
¾   cup lemon juice
⅔   cup sugar
Sprigs of fresh mint, for garnish

Beat yolks, wine, mint, lemon juice, and sugar in the top of a double boiler over gently simmering water until thick and light in color, about 15 minutes. Pour through a sieve, discarding mint leaves. Pour into stemmed glasses and chill. Garnish with sprigs of fresh mint.

SERVES 4

Pineapple Mint Julep

1   small pineapple (about 3 pounds), peeled and cored
½   cup firmly packed Kentucky mint leaves
½   cup sugar
4   cups crushed ice
1½   cups Kentucky bourbon
2   tablespoons fresh lime juice

Cut pineapple into chunks. Puree in a food processor or blender with mint leaves and sugar, scraping down the sides of the work bowl as needed. Add crushed ice and process until smooth, using on/off turns.

Pour pineapple-mint mixture into a large pitcher. Add bourbon and lime juice. Garnish with a large sprig of fresh mint. Pour into chilled glasses.

SERVES 6

Mint Sparkler

Juice of 3 fresh lemons
½   cup chopped fresh grapefruit mint
1   cup sugar
2   cups white sparkling wine
Lemon slices, for garnish
Mint sprigs, for garnish

In a large pitcher, combine lemon juice, mint, and sugar. Let stand for 30 minutes. Strain, discarding mint. Add sparkling wine and pour into chilled glasses over crushed ice. Garnish with a lemon slice and a sprig of fresh mint.

MAKES 2 DRINKS

Peppermint Flip

Crushed ice
½   cup chilled champagne
2   tablespoons brandy
1   egg yolk
1   tablespoon Peppermint Sugar Syrup (recipe follows)
Mint sprig, for garnish

Half fill a cocktail shaker with crushed ice. Pour in champagne, brandy, egg yolk, and Peppermint Sugar Syrup. Shake the mixture vigorously and strain into a chilled fluted champagne glass. Garnish with mint sprig and serve at once.

Peppermint sugar syrup:
1   cup water
1⅔   cup sugar
¼   cup chopped fresh peppermint

In a saucepan, combine water, sugar, and peppermint. Bring mixture to a boil, stirring and washing down any sugar crystals clinging to the sides of the pan with a brush dipped in cold water, until sugar is dissolved. Cook the syrup over moderate heat, undisturbed, for 5 minutes. Let cool and strain. Discard mint leaves. Keeps in the refrigerator for up to a month in a sealed jar. Use it to flavor iced tea or spoon over fresh fruit.

MAKES 1 DRINK

Mango-Mint Wine Cooler

1   large mango, peeled and flesh cut off the pit
2   cups fresh orange juice
2   tablespoons fresh lime juice
3   tablespoons Peppermint Sugar Syrup (see recipe above
2   cups white wine
Mint sprigs, for garnish
Orange twists (just twist a curl of orange zest over each glass)

In a blender, puree the mango with orange juice, lime juice, and mint syrup. Strain through a fine sieve into a large pitcher, pressing hard on the solids. Pour in white wine. Chill thoroughly. Serve in tall chilled wine glasses. Garnish each drink with an orange twist and sprig of fresh mint.

MAKES 4 DRINKS

Cooking with Oregano

Hot, spicy pizza heady with oregano; spanakopita with delicate layers of phyllo, spinach, feta cheese and lots of fresh oregano; fresh goat cheese marinating in olive oil and fresh oregano; fresh tomato salsa relying on fresh oregano for its snap—all are delicious examples of how good cooks throughout the Mediterranean and South America have long recognized oregano for its culinary versatility. Essential to the pizza and pasta dishes of Italy, equally at home with the pilaf and lamb of Middle Eastern countries, oregano is a basic herb in Mexican and South American kitchens. The Aztecs combined it with chili peppers to create a forerunner of chili powder.

Whenever you make tacos, spaghetti sauce, minestrone, barbecue sauce, navy bean soup, or stuffed grape leaves, oregano is the herb to use. Sprinkle chopped fresh oregano into stir-fried zucchini and onions. Use it generously in a Greek salad or moussaka. Texas "caviar" is made from cooked black-eyed peas, diced green pepper, onion, finely chopped jalapeño peppers, diced pimento, finely minced garlic, and a vinaigrette dressing made with a substantial amount of finely chopped fresh oregano.

Try flavorful black beans as a sidekick to grilled steak with a generous addition of chopped fresh oregano and coriander (cilantro). Marinate small fresh mushrooms and chunks of yellow summer squash in olive oil, lemon juice, and chopped fresh oregano.

Tex-Mex cooks use oregano in *chiles rellenos,* enchilada sauce, and fresh tomato salsa. In Argentina there's a grilled cheese called *provoleta* offered at the barbecue restaurants: thick slices of firm provolone cheese placed directly on the grill with a generous sprinkling of dried oregano, the cheese grilled until it begins to melt. This is eaten with a knife and fork, or spread onto thick slices of bread. Try it with fresh oregano; it's marvelous.

Stir chopped fresh oregano into steamed cabbage with some fresh lemon juice and unsalted butter. It elevates this lowly vegetable to the sublime. Add oregano to meat loaf; sprinkle it generously over beef, lamb, or pork before roasting.

As a salt replacement, oregano ranks high. Use it in place of salt for vegetables, chicken, eggplant, summer squash, or peas. Sliced ripe tomatoes still warm from the garden taste marvelous with a sprinkling of chopped fresh oregano and a grinding of fresh black pepper; forget the salt. In Italy, the same sliced tomatoes would have the addition of chopped fresh basil. Try fresh oregano in a baked russet potato or sweet potato. You won't miss the salt or butter.

You can dry oregano leaves with excellent results; they'll increase somewhat in flavor. Dried oregano has the aroma that's identified with pizza and spaghetti sauce. The chopped leaves can also be frozen in ice trays, covered with water. Store the cubes in plastic bags, defrost in a strainer, and use as fresh.

Country Herb Bread Twist

This spectacular loaf, redolent with fresh herbs, is well worth the effort and makes wonderful eating straight from the oven spread with lots of sweet butter. If any of the bread lasts long enough to make it to the next morning, it makes excellent French toast or bread crumbs to top a supper casserole.

1   envelope active dry yeast
1   teaspoon sugar
¼   cup warm water (110°)
2   tablespoons (¼ stick) unsalted butter, melted
2½–3 cups all-purpose flour
1½   teaspoons salt
2   tablespoons minced fresh oregano
2   tablespoons minced fresh thyme
2   tablespoons minced fresh rosemary

Sprinkle yeast and sugar over ¼ cup warm water in a large bowl; stir to dissolve. Let stand until foamy.

Blend 1 cup water and 1 tablespoon melted butter into yeast mixture. Combine 2½ cups flour and salt. Stir into yeast mixture, ½ cup at a time, to form a slightly sticky dough, adding up to ½ cup additional flour if necessary.

Turn dough out onto a lightly floured surface and knead until smooth and elastic, about 5 minutes. Place dough in a large bowl that has been lightly buttered. Turn dough to coat entire surface. Cover with a clean cloth and let rise in a warm draft-free area until dough is doubled in volume, about 1½ hours.

Punch dough down. Divide dough into thirds. Turn out ⅓ onto a lightly floured surface and knead in fresh oregano. Shape dough by rolling dough between the palms of the hands into a rope 20 inches long, tapering the ends of the rope. Set aside.

Repeat process with ⅓ of dough, kneading in thyme. Repeat process with remaining ⅓ dough, kneading in rosemary.

Arrange ropes side by side close together. Starting at the middle and working toward one of the ends, braid the 3 ropes together, pressing them into a point at the tapered ends.

Turn the bread around and braid the ropes from the middle to the other end, pressing the ropes at the end in the same manner. Transfer the bread to a buttered baking sheet and let rise, covered loosely with a clean cloth, in a warm place for 45 to 50 minutes or until doubled in volume.

Preheat oven to 375°.

Brush loaf with remaining 1 tablespoon melted butter and bake for 20 to 30 minutes, or until golden and loaf sounds hollow when the bottom is tapped. Let cool on a rack for 30 minutes before serving.

MAKES 1 LARGE LOAF

Vegetable Chili

A Texan would never refer to this as chili, but its flavor is much the same. It's perfect when you're grilling steaks or chicken. Add a crusty loaf of herb bread, watermelon slices, and ice-cold beer to complete the meal.

½   cup dried kidney beans
2   teaspoons salt
2   tablespoons olive oil
1   large red onion, peeled and cubed
1   large yellow onion, peeled and cubed
4   garlic cloves, minced
2   celery ribs, cut into ½-inch dice
3   carrots, peeled and cut into ½-inch dice
2   tablespoons chili powder
1   tablespoon cumin
½   teaspoon cayenne pepper
2   tablespoons chopped fresh oregano
1   tablespoon chopped fresh basil
1   yellow squash, cut into ½-inch dice
1   zucchini, cut into ½-inch dice
1   sweet green pepper, seeds and ribs removed, cut into ½-inch dice
1   sweet red pepper, seeds and ribs removed, cut into ½-inch dice
1   sweet yellow pepper, seeds and ribs removed, cut into ½-inch dice
1   fresh jalapeño pepper, seeds and ribs removed, finely minced
1   cup coarsely chopped Italian plum tomatoes
½   cup tomato paste
¾   cup dry white wine
Salt and freshly ground black pepper, to taste
Sour cream
Sprigs of fresh oregano, for garnish

Soak beans in water to cover for 3 hours. Drain off water. Add 3 cups fresh water to beans and cook over medium heat until tender, about 45 minutes. Drain beans and reserve cooking liquid.

Heat olive oil in a large soup pot. Add red and yellow onions and garlic; sauté until tender but not browned, about 5 minutes. Add celery and carrots. Sauté for 4 minutes. Add chili powder, cumin, cayenne, oregano, and basil. Cook over low heat until the carrots are almost tender. Add the squash, zucchini, and peppers; cook for 5 minutes. Stir in tomatoes, tomato paste, kidney beans, reserved bean cooking liquid, and wine. Cook for 30 minutes, stirring often, until vegetables are tender. Season with salt and pepper, to taste. Serve with a dollop of sour cream and a sprig of fresh oregano.

SERVES 8 TO 10

Spicy Pork Bundles with Tomatillo Sauce

The herb wrapping is a crepe; the tie is spinach. Inside is pork, resplendent with oregano and other herbs. The result is a dramatic and spicy first course for a very special meal.

6   eggs
2   tablespoons minced fresh oregano
1   tablespoon minced fresh thyme
2   tablespoons minced fresh coriander (cilantro)
2½ tablespoons water
Vegetable oil
4   large spinach leaves with stems
½   pound lean ground pork
2   garlic cloves, minced
1   small onion, finely chopped
1   tablespoon minced fresh oregano
1   small tomato, peeled, seeded, and minced
1   teaspoon dried hot red pepper flakes
Tomatillo Sauce (recipe follows)

Beat together eggs, oregano, thyme, 1 tablespoon of the coriander (cilantro), and 2½ tablespoons water. Heat a 10-inch nonstick skillet over medium heat. Brush 1 teaspoon salad oil over bottom and sides of skillet. When pan is hot, pour ¼ cup of egg-herb mixture into skillet and quickly tilt pan to evenly cover pan bottom. Cook just until egg is set and dry to the touch. Do not cook the other side.

Turn out onto paper towels. Continue cooking wrappers until egg mixture is used. (You will have a couple of extra wrappers to allow for tearing as the wrappers tear easily unless handled very, very gently.)

In a large saucepan of boiling salted water, blanch spinach leaves until leaves are wilted and stems are

pliable, about 30 seconds. Refresh under running cold water and set aside.

In a heavy skillet over medium heat, cook pork, stirring, until browned and crumbly. Drain off excess fat. Add garlic, onion, and oregano. Cook, stirring, until garlic and onion are limp. Stir in tomato, remaining coriander, and red pepper flakes. Cook, stirring, for 1 minute. Remove from heat and cool to room temperature.

To assemble, divide pork mixture into 4 equal portions. Place a portion in the center of each wrapper. (At this point, a second set of hands comes in handy.) Gently gather edges of wrapper around filling. Wind wilted spinach around wrapper and tie a knot to secure. Cover and chill until ready to serve.

To reheat bundles, place them on a shallow pan that will fit on a rack of a steamer or on a rack inside a wok. Fill the bottom of the steamer or wok with 1 inch of water. Cover and bring the water to a boil. Steam just until bundles are hot, about 3 minutes. Serve on Tomatillo Sauce.

SERVES 4

Tomatillo sauce:
1	pound tomatillos, husked and pureed, or 1½ pounds canned tomatillos
½	pound tomatillos, husked and chopped
½	cup white wine vinegar
½	cup red wine vinegar
3	tomatoes, peeled, seeded, and chopped
3	tablespoons olive oil
2	tablespoons chopped fresh oregano
¼	teaspoon Tabasco sauce

Combine all ingredients. Chill for at least 3 hours.

MAKES ABOUT 3 CUPS

COOKING WITH OREGANO

Julienne of Carrots and Chayote with Fresh Oregano

Peel the chayote* only if the skin is tough and prickly. Use a mandoline to cut the carrots and chayote into thin julienne strips. Remember this nifty vegetable combination the next time you serve pork.

3   large carrots, peeled
2   tablespoons (¼ stick) unsalted butter
1½   pounds chayote, cut into matchstick-size
        julienne strips
2   garlic cloves, minced
3   tablespoons minced fresh oregano

Blanch carrots in boiling water for 3 minutes. Drain and cool with running cold water. Cut into matchstick-size julienne strips.

Melt butter in a large heavy skillet over medium heat. Add carrots, chayote, garlic, and oregano. Cook, stirring frequently, until vegetables are crisp-tender, about 10 minutes. Season with salt and pepper, to taste. Serve at once.

*Chayote is a light green tropical fruit with the size and shape of a papaya. Cooked chayote tastes something like summer squash; it has a firmer flesh that's juicy and crisp like a water chestnut.

SERVES 8

Cooking with Parsley

Parsley is no longer just that familiar bit of brilliant green garnish that we all grew up with. Parsley has also grown up—as an herb. Sophisticated chefs and cooks use generous amounts of flat-leaf parsley (also called Italian parsley and the best variety for cooking—use the curly variety for garnish, it's prettier) in marinades, pestos, coulis, sauces, and salads.

Parsley is used extensively for cooking in virtually every European and Middle Eastern country and is a necessary ingredient in bouquet garni and *fines herbes*. One bite of fresh parsley gives a peppery taste that adds a bright note to most dishes.

In elegant restaurants, sprigs of fresh parsley are deep-fried until crisp for a garnish. As a variation, dip parsley sprigs into tempura batter for a light, crunchy texture.

Italians stuff artichokes with a mixture of fresh bread crumbs, capers, garlic, and flat-leaf parsley, moistened with olive oil and lemon. In Venice, fillet of sole is frequently served with a sweet-sour sauce made from raisins, pine nuts, onion, olive oil, white wine vinegar, garlic, bay leaf, and flat-leaf parsley.

Parsley adds a pleasant nip to baby carrots that have been candied in unsalted butter, brown sugar, and fresh ginger. Make a parsley dip for crudités from chopped hard-cooked egg, sour cream, dry mustard, minced garlic, and finely chopped dill pickles.

Add parsley to pasta dough, biscuit dough, crepe batter, dumpling batter, or bread dough along with minced sun-dried tomatoes and chopped fresh dill. Stir chopped parsley into polenta; add it to soup,

ratatouille, and eggplant caviar to spread on hot triangles of pita bread. Add chopped parsley and chopped scallions to mashed potatoes; stir it into rice or orzo. Try a fish sauce made from parsley puree, a little heavy cream, and chicken stock; cook until thick but do not let it boil.

Add parsley to duck-liver mousse and country pâté. When making potato pancakes to serve with homemade applesauce and country ham, use a generous amount of chopped parsley. Like spinach, parsley can be creamed in a sauce and served as a vegetable. Add some shallots to the sauce for additional flavor.

When using parsley for long-cooking soups and stews, add the stems first and the chopped leaves at the last. If parsley is left in a sauce too long, the sauce will turn green.

Because grit and soil hide easily in the leaves, it is essential to wash parsley thoroughly. A quick method is to immerse parsley in bunches, holding the stem ends in cold water and shaking vigorously. If necessary, repeat with fresh water. Shake off the water and wrap in paper towels. Or, keep your bunch of parsley as a bouquet in water on the kitchen counter.

Puree parsley leaves with a little oil and freeze in small containers for later use. Or, wash and thoroughly dry the sprigs; place on a baking sheet and freeze. When frozen, store in plastic bags. Use straight from the freezer, chopping before it's defrosted.

Lobster Salad with Four Herbs and Tomato Coulis

A coulis is simply a reduced puree of vegetables, in this case ripe tomatoes, seasoned with herbs and spices. This is a lovely salad with wonderful shades of pinks, reds, greens, and yellows, garnished with fresh herbs. Buy some crusty peasant bread and a bottle of excellent white wine and serve this lunch to your best friend.

Make the Tomato Coulis the night before; it needs to chill.

Tomato coulis:

1   tablespoon unsalted butter
1   tablespoon olive oil
1   medium onion, finely chopped
2   garlic cloves, minced
4   large vine-ripened tomatoes, peeled, seeded, and coarsely chopped
Salt and freshly ground black pepper, to taste
2   tablespoons chopped flat-leaf parsley
1   teaspoon minced fresh rosemary
1   teaspoon minced fresh oregano
1   teaspoon minced fresh thyme

Heat butter and olive oil in a heavy saucepan. Add onion and garlic; sauté until tender and lightly colored, about 10 minutes. Stir in tomatoes and bring to a boil. Season with salt and pepper, to taste. Reduce heat and simmer, uncovered, for about 20 minutes, until coulis is reduced and thickened.

Transfer coulis to a food processor or blender; puree. Return coulis to saucepan; add parsley and other herbs. Simmer for 5 minutes. Chill. If coulis is too thick, thin it with a splash of tarragon vinegar.

1   pound cooked fresh lobster meat
1   large ripe avocado
Lemon juice
1   large red tomato, peeled, seeded, and coarsely chopped
1   large yellow tomato, peeled, seeded, and coarsely chopped
Tomato Coulis
Fresh oregano, coarsely chopped
Fresh thyme, coarsely chopped
Flat-leaf parsley, coarsely chopped
Fresh basil leaves, for garnish
Fresh rosemary sprigs, for garnish

Remove any cartilage from the lobster meat, leaving the pieces as large as possible. Chill.

Spoon Tomato Coulis on each plate. Peel and slice avocado and dip in lemon juice to prevent darkening. Arrange avocado slices, lobster pieces, and tomatoes on coulis. Scatter with chopped herbs and garnish with basil leaves and rosemary sprigs. Sprinkle with lemon juice.

SERVES 2

Roast Chicken with Gremolata

Gremolata, a mixture of flat-leaf parsley, lemon zest, and garlic, is used by Italian cooks for stuffing fish and stirring into soups and stews. Here it is tucked under the skin of a whole chicken to keep it moist and give it a piquant flavor. With the chicken, serve linguine tossed with chopped fresh spinach (wilted first in a small amount of olive oil), dried red pepper flakes, and shredded Parmesan cheese. Offer lemon wedges to squeeze over the chicken and pasta.

3–3½-pound whole frying chicken
Gremolata (recipe follows)
2   5-inch sprigs fresh rosemary

Preheat oven to 375°.

Loosen the skin over chicken breast with fingers, being careful not to puncture the skin. Pat a layer of Gremolata between skin and flesh of breast. Truss chicken but do not bend wings akimbo. Instead, place a rosemary sprig under each wing; tie wings to body with cotton string.

Place chicken, breast side up, on a rack in a shallow roasting pan. Roast, uncovered, for 1 hour or until meat near thighbone is no longer pink when slashed. Remove from oven and let stand for 10 minutes before carving.

Gremolata:
2   cups chopped flat-leaf parsley
2   tablespoons grated lemon zest
6   garlic cloves, minced

Combine all ingredients. Chill any remaining for another use.

SERVES 4

COOKING WITH PARSLEY

Cooking with Rosemary

In Sicily, rosemary grows profusely throughout the countryside to heights of five to six feet, its sweet fragrance permeating the air. The rosemary in Southern California herb gardens grows almost as tall, requiring a heavy hand with the pruning shears several times a year to keep it under control. Its delicate blue flowers and dark green long, narrow leaves with their silvery undersides are so lovely they beg passersby to break off a few sprigs and crush the leaves to release the heady aroma.

Rosemary has a bold, assertive flavor and is one of the most fragrant kitchen herbs. A long-standing natural with lamb, pork, and veal, rosemary has many other unexpected culinary uses. Its piney flavor is delicious with robust vegetables such as beets, cabbage, and beans. Rosemary is excellent in stuffings for poultry and fish. Add rosemary to bean, pea, or mushroom soup; stir it into stews. Butter flavored with chopped fresh rosemary is marvelous on vegetables such as new potatoes, beans, peas, spinach, and

zucchini. Add chopped fresh rosemary to a basic vinaigrette and pour over steamed beets, leeks, or green beans—sprinkle with toasted walnuts.

Try stirring a tablespoon of the finely chopped leaves into your usual plain scone, biscuit, muffin, or dumpling mixture before adding the liquid. Or add a tablespoon to a basic crepe batter along with two tablespoons freshly grated Parmesan cheese. Fold the crepes in quarters and serve with your best home-made tomato sauce for a simple but interesting side dish for roast beef, leg of lamb, pork, or game.

Sugar snaps are the sweetest of young peas. Sauté them in melted butter for about 3 minutes with a sprinkling of chopped fresh rosemary and a fine chiffonade of butter lettuce and they're dressed for company. Rosemary potato balls are a favorite with roasted meats. Cut russet potatoes into small balls (use a melon-ball cutter), cook in salted water for 5 to 6 minutes, drain on paper towels, and sauté until golden over moderately high heat in butter, olive oil, and lots of fresh rosemary.

Rosemary introduces a particularly interesting flavor when used as a coating for creamy dessert cheeses such as Boursin or Boursault. For 6 ounces of cheese, use 3 tablespoons rosemary leaves, patting them onto all surfaces. Wrap in foil or clear plastic wrap and refrigerate for one or two days. Let stand at room temperature for 30 minutes before serving. Serve with unsalted crackers.

One of the easiest ways to extract flavor from fresh rosemary is to lay the sprigs on top of roasts and vegetables while they cook, removing the sprigs before serving. Stuff a chicken or Cornish game hen with sprigs of rosemary and garlic before roasting.

Throw a handful of the sprigs onto hot coals to impart a wonderful flavor and aroma when grilling. Tie the sprigs together and use them as a basting brush.

To make a very pretty rosemary vinegar, place several sprigs in a glass jar and fill with red wine vinegar. Cover tightly and set on a sunny windowsill for several weeks. Sprinkle some of this rosemary vinegar over sliced oranges, paper-thin slices of red onion, tiny *Niçoise* olives, and bocconcini (little balls of fresh mozzarella, found in Italian markets and some supermarkets—if not available, substitute small pieces of other mozzarella). Drizzle with your best olive oil and grind on black pepper. Garnish with a sprig of fresh rosemary.

Rosemary is easy to dry, retaining much of its flavor. Crush dried rosemary before using to release the oils and to avoid the sensation of chewing on pine needles.

Leg of Lamb Roasted on a Bed of Rosemary

In northern Italy, it's common to receive a sprig of fresh rosemary when you purchase a leg of lamb at the butcher shop. Tender young lamb has an affinity with rosemary, and this method of roasting, on a bed of fresh rosemary sprigs, Italian plum tomatoes, whole bulbs of garlic, and lemon, produces a robust sauce to spoon over the slices (left).

Before the lamb, serve a salad of radicchio and roasted yellow peppers. With the lamb, serve roasted new potatoes coated with lots of garlic, mint, and olive oil. Offer crusty Italian bread for spreading with the roasted garlic and mopping up the sauces. Keep the dessert simple—grapes and a selection of cheeses.

6   whole unpeeled garlic bulbs
1   small leg of lamb (about 5 pounds)
2   garlic cloves, peeled and cut into slivers
¼   cup olive oil
Salt and freshly ground black pepper, to taste
12 large sprigs fresh rosemary
6   Italian plum tomatoes, sliced crosswise
Juice of 1 fresh lemon

Preheat oven to 400°.

In a saucepan, parboil garlic bulbs in water to cover for 5 minutes. Drain. Make slits in the lamb with the point of a knife. Insert garlic slivers. Rub lamb and garlic bulbs with olive oil. Sprinkle lamb with salt and pepper, to taste. Place rosemary sprigs and tomatoes in a shallow roasting pan.

Lay lamb on bed of rosemary and tomatoes and surround with garlic bulbs. Squeeze lemon juice over lamb. Roast for 1 hour (meat will be rare), or to desired doneness. Remove from oven; remove lamb to a carving board and let set for 10 minutes. Return roasting pan to oven to keep vegetables warm. Remove rosemary sprigs.

Carve lamb into thin slices. Arrange on heated serving plates with a garlic bulb on each plate. Spoon pan sauce over slices and serve warm.

SERVES 6

Marie's Rabbit with Fresh Rosemary

This is a lusty main dish that Marie Gilbertie often makes, based on a recipe from her Aunt Jean. Sal grows rabbits to insure a steady supply; the herbs and wine vary according to whim. This Italian rabbit dish is great over linguine or rice.

1   3-pound rabbit, cut into serving pieces
2   bay leaves
2   garlic cloves, minced
2   tablespoons chopped fresh rosemary
Salt and freshly ground black pepper, to taste
1½ tablespoons olive oil
1   teaspoon dried hot red pepper flakes
1   large tomato, peeled, seeded, and chopped
1   cup dry white wine
8   large basil leaves, chopped

In a large bowl, combine rabbit pieces, bay leaves, garlic, rosemary, and salt and pepper, to taste. Turn to coat evenly. Heat oil in a large heavy skillet over medium heat. Brown rabbit pieces in batches (do not crowd). Sprinkle with red chili flakes. Add tomato and white wine. Cover partially and simmer gently until rabbit meat is tender, about 1 hour. During last 5 minutes of cooking time, add basil leaves.

SERVES 4

Apricot Rosemary Chicken Baked in Parchment

This chicken is easy to make and so pretty—a large puffy package of parchment paper enclosing boned chicken breasts seasoned with rosemary, butter, and the delicate flavor of fresh apricots. Parchment paper is available in bakery supply stores and gourmet cooking shops.

Add a salad of radicchio leaves filled with warm baby vegetables tossed with a light vinaigrette, instead of butter, and a sprinkling of fresh herbs. The Mint Chocolate Mousse Cakes with Raspberry Puree (page 164) would make a luscious ending to this meal.

4	tablespoons (½ stick) unsalted butter
2	whole chicken breasts, boned, skin removed, and cut in half
4	fresh apricots, cut in half and pitted (if fresh apricots are not available, use 4 dried apricots that have been soaked in a little white wine for 30 minutes)
2	ounces prosciutto, finely minced
2	sprigs of fresh rosemary, lightly bruised
1	teaspoon chopped fresh sage
1	garlic clove, sliced paper-thin

Salt and freshly ground black pepper, to taste
Juice of 1 fresh lemon

Preheat oven to 350°.

Cut two circles of parchment paper 18 inches in diameter. Butter one side of each circle. Lay each chicken breast on one half of the buttered side of the parchment circles. Thinly slice apricots. Arrange apricots, prosciutto, rosemary, sage, and garlic over the chicken. Sprinkle with salt and pepper, to taste. Dot with remaining butter. Squeeze lemon juice over each breast.

Fold over parchment and crimp the edges to seal. Place on baking sheet and bake for 45 minutes. Place parchment packets on serving plates; break open and serve immediately.

SERVES 2

Stilton Cheese and Tomato Tart with Rosemary Pastry

A simply sensational appetizer or main course for a light lunch or supper, this tart should be served warm or at room temperature.

½	cup (1 stick) unsalted butter, well chilled and cut into 8 pieces
5	tablespoons ice water
1	egg yolk
1½	tablespoons chopped fresh rosemary
½	teaspoon salt
1½	cups all-purpose flour
2	shallots, finely minced
2	large tomatoes, peeled and thinly sliced
8	ounces Stilton cheese, crumbled
1	cup heavy cream
3	eggs

Salt and freshly ground black pepper, to taste

In a food processor using the steel blade, combine butter, water, egg yolk, 1 tablespoon rosemary, and salt. Process for 5 seconds using on/off turns. Add flour and blend just until dough holds together. Do not overprocess. Transfer dough to a plastic bag and press into a ball. Flatten into a disk and chill for 2 hours or overnight.

Butter a 10-inch tart pan. Roll dough out on lightly floured surface into a circle ⅛-inch thick. Transfer to prepared tart pan and gently press into place. Trim dough, leaving 1-inch overlap beyond edge of pan. Fold overlap inside to form double thickness and press firmly into place. Push dough about ¼ inch above edge of pan to allow for shrinkage during baking. Prick bottom and sides of pastry with a fork. Chill for 30 minutes.

Preheat oven to 400°.

Line pastry bottom with a circle of parchment paper and fill with dried beans or pie weights. Bake for 12 minutes. Remove paper and weights. Prick shell again and bake for another 5 minutes, or until lightly browned. Remove from oven.

Change oven temperature to 350°.

Sprinkle shallots in bottom of prepared tart shell. Arrange tomatoes in overlapping layers. In a large bowl, mix cheese, cream, and eggs. Add remaining ½ tablespoon rosemary and salt and pepper, to taste. Pour cheese custard over tomatoes.

Bake for 30 minutes or until puffed and lightly browned. Remove from oven and let stand for 5 minutes.

MAKES 12 APPETIZER OR 6 TO 8 MAIN-COURSE SERVINGS

Focaccia (Italian Flat Bread) with Rosemary

Heady with rosemary and olive oil, this flat Tuscan bread is topped with paper-thin slices of tomato, thinly sliced onion, coarse salt, and chunks of "Sun-dried" Tomatoes (page 236) steeped in rosemary oil. Serve this warm or at room temperature, cut into squares or triangles.

2   envelopes active dry yeast
1   teaspoon sugar
1¾ cups warm water (110°)
⅔   cup olive oil
1½ teaspoons salt
4–5 cups unbleached all-purpose flour
2   teaspoons dried hot red pepper flakes

Toppings:
2   tomatoes, sliced paper-thin
2   onions, sliced paper-thin
12   "Sun-dried" Tomatoes, preserved in
      rosemary oil (page 236), cut into chunks
Very small sprigs of fresh rosemary
Coarse salt

Dissolve yeast and sugar in 1 cup lukewarm water. Let sit until foamy. In another bowl, combine remaining ¾ cup water, ⅓ cup olive oil, and salt. Pour in yeast mixture. Blend in flour, 1 cup at a time, until dough comes together. Knead on a floured board for 10 minutes, adding flour as needed to make dough smooth and elastic.

Place dough in an oiled bowl, turn to coat well, cover with a cloth, and let rise in a warm, draft-free place for 1 hour, or until doubled in bulk.

In a small saucepan, heat remaining oil until very hot but not smoking. Add chili flakes and remove from heat. Let stand until cool.

Punch down dough and knead again on a floured board for about 5 minutes.

Preheat oven to 400°.

Divide dough in half and roll out on a floured board into two 8-inch squares about ½-inch thick. Place on a baking sheet and brush with prepared chili oil. Press toppings into the dough. Sprinkle with coarse salt. Bake until golden brown, about 20 minutes. Cut into squares and serve warm.

MAKES TWO 8-INCH SQUARE FLATBREADS

Cooking with Sage

Who doesn't remember the wonderful fragrance of sage, wafting from the kitchen on Thanksgiving morning? Sage is of course traditional in turkey stuffing. Used fresh, though, sage has a mild flavor unlike the strong flavor of dried sage. It's used extensively throughout Europe and the Mediterranean, where it grows wild with spiky lavender-blue flowers adding color to the arid hillsides.

In Italy, fresh sage leaves are fried whole and eaten with gnocchi, potatoes, and veal dishes. Focaccia, the flat bread of Italy, is frequently studded with fresh sage leaves. In England, fresh sage and onion stuffing is traditional with goose, and chopped fresh sage is mixed with cottage cheese to spread on dark bread. In Provence, sage is boiled with chestnuts and used to flavor watermelon preserves.

Beyond common sage, other varieties are also used in cooking: pineapple sage with its sweet pineapple fragrance is excellent in punch and tea. Pineapple sage often ends up in a jelly jar. Colorful sages such as scarlet and meadow sage are lovely in garden salads, and tricolor sage makes a beautiful garnish for cheese boards and crudités.

Bees are attracted to sage; sage honey is marvelous over homemade bread and muffins. Stir chopped fresh sage into biscuit dough; add it to cheese straws to pass around with wine or cocktails. Add sage to dumplings and scones. Sage does wonders for apple fritter batter.

Lay cut branches of sage on top of hot coals to impart a sage flavor to the cooking food and fill the air with sage aroma. Spread fresh sage leaves over a pork roast before cooking. Use it to cut the richness of fatty foods such as goose, duck, and oily fish. Stuff game hens with spinach, lemon, and fresh sage stuffing. Make a relish of tomatoes, garlic, onion, and chopped fresh sage to serve with hamburgers, hot dogs, or kielbasa. Marinate goat cheese in olive oil,

peppercorns, garlic, and small sage leaves. Add a generous amount of chopped fresh sage to your favorite recipe for barbecue sauce.

When your pasta machine is running nonstop for summer meals, try this version of a procedure made famous by Giuliano Bugialli. Stretch pasta dough very thin (about ⅛-inch thick) and place whole sage leaves on top of half the length of the pasta layer. Fold the other half over the leaves and press the layers together. Cut the pasta into squares and cook in boiling chicken stock for 1 to 3 minutes. The sage leaves will show through. Dress the pasta with a vinaigrette whirled in a food processor or blender with *niçoise* olives, sun-dried tomatoes, and fresh sage.

Cook clams in their shells (below) on the barbecue grill until they open (takes about 3 minutes per side). Pluck from their shell with a fork and dip into sage butter (3 tablespoons chopped fresh sage to ½ cup butter). Keep the sage butter warm in a small pan on the edge of the grill.

Fresh sage has a prominent lemon zest flavor that is lost when the herb is dried. If you must use it dried, leave the dried leaves whole and crush them just before you use them for best flavor. Fresh sage can be frozen; place small sprigs in plastic bags and freeze. Frozen sage will keep for up to two months. Pineapple sage doesn't keep its aroma or flavor dried. Use it fresh.

Calves' Liver with Fresh Sage and Grapefruit

In northern Italy, baby beef liver is traditionally cooked with fresh sage. The sautéed sage leaves become crisp and delicious. The tartness of the grapefruit contrasts beautifully with the sage.

Serve with risotto made with several Italian cheeses. For dessert, poach whole Bosc pears (peel, leaving the stems on, and slice off the bottom so they can stand upright) in white wine with lemon and orange zest. Serve pears standing, surrounded by a puddle of chocolate sauce.

¾	pound calves' liver, sliced thin
½	cup milk
3	tablespoons all-purpose flour

Salt and pepper, to taste

2	tablespoons (¼ stick) unsalted butter
1	tablespoon olive oil
1	shallot, minced
14	fresh sage leaves
1	grapefruit, peeled and sectioned
⅓	cup dry white wine

Cut the liver into strips about 1 inch wide. Soak liver strips in milk for 15 minutes. Drain and dredge strips in flour. Season with salt and pepper, to taste. In a heavy skillet, heat butter and oil. Add shallot and sauté for 2 minutes. Add liver strips and quickly sauté, turning frequently, until golden brown, about 5 minutes. With a slotted spoon, remove liver and arrange on a heated serving platter. Keep warm.

Add sage leaves to the drippings and sauté for 1 minute, stirring constantly. Arrange sage leaves on liver strips. Quickly sauté grapefruit sections in pan drippings and arrange on liver strips. Add wine to pan drippings and cook, stirring constantly, for 3 minutes, until slightly reduced. Spoon wine sauce over liver and grapefruit.

SERVES 2

Pan-sautéed Trout with Herbs Flamed in Gin

Fresh sage imparts a delicate flavor to the flesh of the trout and the flambéed gin makes this dish a knockout. The trout takes only a few minutes to cook, so have the rest of the meal prepared. Serve the trout with roasted new potatoes, dressed with butter and fresh rosemary, and steamed green beans. For dessert, squeeze fresh lime juice over sliced peaches and plums heaped in goblets.

4	fresh trout, 6 to 8 ounces each, boned and cleaned, heads and tails left on
20	small sprigs fresh sage

Salt and pepper, to taste

2	tablespoons (¼ stick) unsalted butter
4	tablespoons safflower oil

Juice of ½ lemon

4	large bay leaves
4	sprigs fresh flat-leaf parsley
4	large fresh basil leaves
4	small sprigs fresh rosemary
4	sprigs fresh mint
½	cup gin

Stuff each trout with 4 sprigs of sage. Sprinkle with salt and pepper, to taste. Tie trout with a bit of butcher string to hold closed. In a large sauté pan, heat the butter and oil. Sauté the trout over medium-high heat for 5 minutes. Turn and cook for another 5 minutes or until done when flaked with a fork. Squeeze on lemon juice.

Place trout on a flameproof platter; pour the juices over the fish. Arrange the remaining sage and the other herbs over the fish. Heat the gin in a small pan over low heat. Pour the gin over the fish and herbs; flame with a match. Serve the trout with the flamed herbs immediately.

SERVES 4

Veal Chops on a Bed of Vegetables and Herbs

Fresh sage, parsley, rosemary, and thyme add the sweet aromatic flavor that is perfect with veal, grilled to perfection and served on a bed of vegetables that have been sautéed with the fresh herbs (left). Follow with an arugula (roquette) and watercress salad served with baked goat cheese.

4   loin veal chops, 1 inch thick
1   garlic clove, cut in half
Salt and freshly ground black pepper, to taste
8   fresh sage sprigs
About 2 tablespoons olive oil
2   tablespoons (¼ stick) unsalted butter
1   shallot, minced
2   tablespoons chopped fresh sage
2   tablespoons chopped fresh parsley
2   tablespoons chopped fresh rosemary
2   tablespoons chopped fresh thyme
4   large sweet red peppers, seeded and sliced into thin strips
2   large red onions, cut into eighths

Rub both sides of the veal chops with cut sides of garlic; season with salt and pepper, to taste. Press one sage sprig on each side of each chop. Brush chops lightly with oil on both sides.

Grill chops over hot coals or under a preheated broiler, turning once, for 5 to 7 minutes per side, or until just cooked through.

While chops are grilling, melt butter in a large, heavy skillet. Add shallot and sauté for 2 minutes. Add chopped herbs, peppers, and onions; cook over low heat for 4 to 5 minutes, stirring frequently. Season with salt and pepper, to taste. Keep warm over low heat.

To serve, distribute vegetables evenly among 4 heated serving plates. Top with chops.

SERVES 4

Roast Turkey with Two Sage Stuffings

Roast turkey with savory stuffing is traditional on Thanksgiving. The surprise of two sage stuffings makes the tradition even more special (next page).

Prepare a bounty of vegetables to grace the table: braised carrots, onions, parsnips, and Brussels sprouts. Offer vegetable purees: squash, chestnut, and sweet potato. Use fresh herbs for cooking and garnishing throughout.

1   18–20-pound turkey
2   onions, peeled and sliced
1   carrot, peeled and sliced
2   celery ribs with leaves, chopped
3   sprigs fresh parsley
1   bay leaf
1   quart water
Corn Bread Stuffing with Parsley, Sage, Rosemary, and Thyme (recipe follows)
Chestnut and Sausage Stuffing with Sage (recipe follows)
¼   cup (½ stick) unsalted butter, softened to room temperature
2   tablespoons chopped fresh sage
2   tablespoons chopped fresh rosemary
2   tablespoons chopped fresh thyme
1   cup dry white wine
2   tablespoons unsalted butter mixed with 2 tablespoons all-purpose flour
Salt and freshly ground black pepper, to taste

Preheat oven to 325°.

Make giblet broth: remove neck and giblets from the turkey. Place in heavy saucepan with onions, carrot, celery, parsley, bay leaf, and water. Simmer, partially covered, over very low heat for 3 to 3½ hours, checking occasionally to add water as necessary.

Rinse turkey and pat dry with paper towels. Loosely stuff neck cavity with about 2 cups Corn

Bread Stuffing. Pull the neck skin over the cavity and fasten closed with skewers. Tuck wings akimbo.

Lightly stuff the body cavity with 6 to 7 cups Chestnut and Sausage Stuffing. Place a piece of crumpled foil over the exposed stuffing to prevent burning as the turkey roasts. Truss the turkey, or if the turkey has a metal clamp, arrange the drumsticks so that the clamp holds the drumsticks in place. Rub the turkey with the softened butter.

Place turkey, breast side up, on a rack in a roasting pan. Roast for 2½ hours. Add herbs and white wine to roasting pan. Continue to roast for 1 to 1½ hours, basting occasionally with pan drippings. If turkey browns too quickly, cover loosely with foil. Check for doneness by pricking the fleshy part of the thigh; juices should run clear. Or use a meat thermometer inserted in the fleshy part of the thigh. Turkey is done when the thermometer registers 185°.

Remove the turkey from the roasting pan and let turkey rest, loosely covered with foil, for 20 minutes before carving.

To make gravy, skim off fat in pan. Strain giblet broth into pan drippings. Stir over high heat, adding salt and pepper to taste and butter-flour mixture as needed to thicken gravy to desired consistency.

Corn bread stuffing with parsley, sage, rosemary, and thyme:
Make corn bread a day in advance.

CORN BREAD:
1¼ cups yellow cornmeal
¾ cup all-purpose flour
3   tablespoons sugar
1   teaspoon salt
1   tablespoon baking powder
1   cup milk
2   eggs, lightly beaten
¼ cup (1 stick) unsalted butter, melted and
    cooled

Preheat oven to 450°.

In a large bowl, sift together cornmeal, flour, sugar, salt, and baking powder. In a small bowl, combine milk, eggs, and half of the melted butter. Pour into the dry ingredients and mix briefly until just blended. Do not overmix. Pour the batter into a well-oiled 8-inch square baking pan.

Place pan in oven; reduce heat to 400°. Bake for 20 to 25 minutes, until the corn bread is golden and crusty around the edges. Remove from oven and cool on a rack.

STUFFING:
¼ cup (½ stick) unsalted butter
2   celery ribs, chopped
1   small onion, chopped
2   shallots, chopped
1   Granny Smith apple, chopped
¼ cup currants
Corn bread, cut into cubes
½ cup coarsely chopped pecans
2   tablespoons minced fresh parsley
2   tablespoons minced fresh sage
1   tablespoon minced fresh rosemary
1   tablespoon minced fresh thyme
2   eggs, beaten
Salt and freshly ground black pepper, to taste

In a large skillet, melt butter; add celery, onion, and shallots. Sauté until soft, about 5 minutes. Stir in apples and currants. Continue to cook for 5 minutes.

Combine corn bread cubes, celery mixture, pecans, sage, rosemary, and thyme. Stir in eggs. Season with salt and pepper, to taste. Stuff turkey neck cavity as directed. Place any remaining stuffing in a small buttered casserole; cover with foil and refrigerate until ready to bake alongside the turkey for 1 hour. Uncover during the last 20 minutes of baking time.

Chestnut and sausage stuffing with sage:

1   1-pound loaf white bread, homemade style, crusts removed
2   large onions, minced
2   tablespoons olive oil
2   tablespoons (¼ stick) unsalted butter
1   cup minced celery
1   pound sausage meat, cooked until crumbly
3   tablespoons chopped fresh sage
1½ pounds chestnuts, peeled and diced
2   tablespoons chopped fresh parsley
½–¾ cup chicken stock (preferably homemade)

Cut bread into 1-inch cubes. Place on an ungreased baking sheet and toast in a 275° oven for 30 minutes, or until lightly browned. Transfer bread cubes to a large mixing bowl.

In a large skillet, sauté onions in olive oil and butter until onions are soft but not browned. Stir in celery, cooked sausage, and sage. Cook, stirring for 5 minutes. Add the sage mixture to the bread cubes and stir in chestnuts, parsley, and enough chicken stock to moisten the stuffing to desired consistency.

Pack the turkey body cavity as directed. Place remaining stuffing in a buttered casserole; cover with foil and refrigerate until ready to bake separately alongside the turkey for 1 hour, uncovering during the last 20 minutes of baking time.

NOTE: To peel chestnuts, preheat oven to 375°. Using a sharp knife, cut a small x into the flat side of each chestnut, cutting through the woody shell. Arrange the chestnuts on a greased baking sheet and roast for about 10 minutes, until the x opens slightly. Peel and cool.

SERVES 12 TO 14

Pineapple-Sage Tropical Cooler

A tall, cool glass of punch made with herb tea is a good way to unwind on a hot summer day, a warm evening, or just about any time and any place—a stone bench in the herb garden, the gazebo, around the pool, or on the deck overlooking the hillside. Plenty of ice and chilled glasses are a must. From there, let your imagination soar as you experiment with different herb teas. Here pineapple sage tea is mixed with tropical juices for a most refreshing result.

1¼ cups water
3   tablespoons chopped fresh pineapple sage
     leaves
1½ cups fresh orange juice, chilled
¼   cup fresh lime juice, chilled
1   cup papaya nectar, chilled
1   cup guava nectar, chilled
1   7-ounce bottle sparkling mineral water
Sprigs of pineapple sage, for garnish

In a small saucepan, bring water to a boil. Remove from heat; add sage leaves and steep for 10 minutes. Strain tea, discarding sage leaves.

In a 2-quart pitcher, combine sage tea and fruit juices. (This can be done ahead and chilled for several hours or overnight.) Just before serving, add sparkling water and pour into six ice-filled tall glasses. Garnish with sage sprigs.

MAKES 6 8-OUNCE SERVINGS

Cooking with Savory

Savory is the traditional herb to use in black bean soup full of hot and garlicky sausages, baked lima beans with brown sugar and mustard, or marinated garbanzo bean salad—it's so closely associated with the cooking of beans that it has been nicknamed the "bean herb." Both summer and winter savory are used the same way in cooking, the summer variety being more subtle in flavor.

Summer savory is a favorite blending herb in the kitchen, with a taste similar to that of thyme, only milder. Winter savory has a heartier character with a sharp hot taste that makes it an excellent substitute for black pepper when a mild peppery flavor is wanted. The summer variety is usually preferred for cooking because of its milder flavor and nicer leaf texture.

Both varieties are slightly salty, making them an excellent substitute for salt. Mix either with fresh breadcrumbs for coating fish, pork, or veal. If your garden has produced an overabundance of zucchini, cut the zucchini lengthwise in ¼-inch-thick slices. Dip in beaten egg and savory bread crumbs. Sauté until golden in unsalted butter.

Savory is excellent with cabbage and Brussels sprouts. It's wonderful with fresh corn. Soak fresh unhusked corn in lightly salted water for about 1 hour. Peel back the husks. Place a tablespoon of unsalted butter, cut into small pieces, around the corn kernels along with small sprigs of summer savory. Re-cover the corn kernels with the husks and grill over medium-hot coals, turning frequently, for 10 to 15 minutes.

Sprinkle chopped fresh savory onto sliced toma-

toes, a broiled tomato, or into a baked potato. Use it over new potatoes instead of parsley or mint. Add savory to meatballs and meat loaves. Add a sprig to chilled tomato juice, vegetable juice, or a Bloody Mary.

The French use savory in terrines and the English like it with roast duck and game. In Switzerland, savory is used with most green vegetables. Steam fresh green beans or *haricots verts*, seasoning with chopped fresh summer savory and dotting with unsalted butter.

Bees love savory; savory honey is delicious on hot biscuits and muffins. Stir savory honey into baked beans, instead of brown sugar. Sprinkle chopped fresh savory over salads; add sprigs to warm vinegar and steep for a week. Use chopped fresh savory in vegetable soups or stews.

Summer savory dries very well, keeping much of the essential oils. If you grow both varieties, don't bother to dry it. In warm climates, winter savory will produce plenty and in colder regions, it comes inside for the winter, like rosemary, still producing more savory than you're likely to use.

Lemon Chicken in Savory Champagne Sauce

This is a rich and intensely flavored version of lemon chicken; chopped fresh savory and Italian plum tomatoes are the unexpected ingredients. Easy to prepare, this dish is ideal for entertaining and can be doubled or tripled for larger dinner parties. Serve with braised Florence fennel (finocchio) with crumbled goat cheese and wild rice tossed with sliced scallions and toasted pecans.

4   whole chicken breasts, boned and skin removed
½   cup dry white wine
1   cup fresh lemon juice
Grated zest of 2 lemons
2   tablespoons vegetable oil
5   tablespoons chopped fresh savory
3 to 4 Italian plum tomatoes, quartered
2   tablespoons Cognac or brandy
2   tablespoons (¼ stick) unsalted butter
4 to 6 lemon slices
1   cup nonvintage champagne (leftover champagne is fine)
½   cup heavy cream
½   cup crème fraîche

With a sharp knife, cut chicken breasts in quarters, lengthwise. Arrange in a single layer in a large glass baking dish. In a small bowl, combine wine, lemon juice, lemon zest, oil, and 3 tablespoons savory. Pour over chicken breasts. Cover and refrigerate for 6 hours or overnight.

Preheat oven to 375°.

Bake for 20 to 25 minutes or until chicken is tender, adding tomato quarters to baking dish during last 10 minutes.

Meanwhile, pour Cognac in a small saucepan. Warm it and flame with a match. When the flames subside, add butter and sauté lemon slices for 2 minutes per side. Remove lemon slices and set aside.

Add champagne to saucepan and cook over high heat until reduced by half. Whisk in cream and crème fraîche. Boil to the consistency of thick cream. Add remaining 2 tablespoons chopped savory.

Arrange chicken and tomatoes on individual serving plates. Spoon sauce over, then garnish with reserved lemon slices.

SERVES 4 TO 6

Baby Lima Beans and Lettuce in Savory Broth

Soup or salad? This dish is both—salad ingredients in a light broth infused with lemon and fresh savory. Offer as a first course, or make it the star of a light lunch with bread and cheese.

2	cups chicken stock (preferably homemade)
3	sprigs fresh savory

Grated zest of 1 lemon

1	cup shelled fresh baby lima beans (frozen can be substituted)
2	tablespoons chopped fresh summer savory
2	large whole radicchio leaves
2	small butter lettuce leaves, cut into a fine chiffonade
2	chicory leaves, torn

In a heavy saucepan, bring chicken stock to a boil; add savory sprigs and lemon zest. Remove from heat, cover, and let stand for 15 minutes to allow savory to flavor broth. With a slotted spoon, remove savory sprigs.

Bring broth to a boil. Add lima beans; cook until just tender, about 1 to 2 minutes. With a slotted spoon, remove beans and mix with chopped savory. Lay a radicchio leaf in each bowl. Fill with lima beans and arrange lettuce chiffonade and chicory to one side. Carefully add hot chicken broth. Serve at once, with a knife, fork, and spoon.

SERVES 2

Cooking with Shallots

Queenly shallots—they're undeniably addictive once you start using them. The grace note of fine cooking, shallots are one of the most important staples in the kitchen.

The flavor of fresh shallots falls somewhere between that of garlic and onions, but it is sweeter and more subtle. Shallots have a changeable personality. Minced raw shallots in a vinaigrette dressing, a mignonette sauce, or a red-skinned potato salad have a robust flavor and aroma. When cooked, shallots are delicate yet aromatic with a hint of sweetness. The method used in cooking shallots affects the flavor. In a poaching liquid, shallots are very mild. Sautéed shallots are more concentrated in flavor than poached ones, but not as robust as when used raw. Since their flavor marries particularly well with wine, shallots are essential in many sauces and fish dishes where a subtle but emphatic onion touch is needed. A béarnaise sauce or a beurre blanc without shallots? Inconceivable!

Shallots also have an affinity for mustard, and a marvelous tarragon mustard can be made by blanching 1 tablespoon minced shallots in boiling water for 1 minute. Drain and stir in 1 cup Dijon mustard, 1 tablespoon minced fresh tarragon, and a dash of pepper. Spread the mustard on black bread with paper-thin sliced chicken breast and sprigs of fresh watercress; whisk some into olive oil and vinegar for a zippy vinaigrette; or stir it into heavy cream or crème fraîche to pour over steamed leeks or Brussels sprouts. If any mustard is left over, store it in the refrigerator.

Like garlic, shallots can be baked alongside a chicken (or stuffed into the cavity by the handful) and eaten as a vegetable. Shallots that have been peeled, sliced, and deep-fried in peanut oil for a minute until golden brown are served as a condiment with many Indian dishes. Thai cooks use generous amounts of shallots in the blend of seasonings that makes their cuisine such a delight. Vendors in the open-air markets of Bangkok sell cool green lettuce leaves to fill with small cooked shrimp, sliced raw shallots, slivered fresh ginger, roasted peanuts, toasted coconut, coconut syrup, and a squeeze of fresh lime.

Look for shallots that are plump and firm with no sprouts or bruises. Under their brownish red skin is a clove of delicate ivory color tinged with purple. Store shallots like onions and garlic, in a net bag in an airy, cool spot. Shallots can't be dried but they can be frozen quite successfully and stored in an airtight container. Still frozen, they mince quite nicely.

One large shallot equals about 1 tablespoon chopped.

Sal's Spaghettini with Mediterranean Sauce

Pasta is one of Sal's favorite meals for Friday night, when he takes over the cooking; he combines it with whatever he has on hand, either fresh or in the freezer. Herbs in some form are always present—in this zesty dish, shallots are the magic ingredient. Serve it with broccoli rabe (another of Sal's favorites) braised in light olive oil with lemon and garlic, and Italian bread with herb butter. Invite the family or your food-loving friends; pour an earthy red wine and enjoy!

⅓ cup olive oil
8 shallots, minced
2 large Belgian endives, trimmed and coarsely chopped
2 2-ounce cans anchovy fillets, drained and chopped
16 large pitted ripe olives, quartered
2 cups water
1 pound spaghettini
Freshly grated Parmesan cheese, if desired

In a heavy skillet, sauté shallots in oil over medium heat until shallots are soft but not browned. Add endive, anchovy fillets, olives, and water. Cook for 5 to 8 minutes until endive is tender and sauce has thickened.

Meanwhile cook spaghettini in boiling salted water until tender but still firm to the bite. Drain; transfer to a large pasta bowl. Pour sauce over spaghettini and toss. Pass cheese separately, if desired.

SERVES 8

Mussels with Shallots

Mussels can become a passion. Thrown into huge kettles with white wine and herbs or steamed atop an herb-rich sauce, mussels provide an almost instantaneous meal, needing only the addition of a salad made of available greens and a fresh fruit tart of the season.

32 large fresh mussels
2 tablespoons olive oil
8 shallots, minced
1 garlic clove, minced
2 large fresh tomatoes, peeled, seeded, and chopped
1 tablespoon minced fresh thyme
1 tablespoon minced fresh basil
1 tablespoon minced fresh oregano
Freshly ground black pepper, to taste
3 tablespoons Cognac or brandy
2 tablespoons (¼ stick) unsalted butter, cut into 2 pieces
2 tablespoons chopped flat-leaf parsley

Wash mussels under cold running water, discarding any that are open. Place in a large bowl and cover with cold water. Let stand for 30 minutes. Drain and scrub mussels with stiff wire brush to remove beards.

Meanwhile, make sauce by heating olive oil in a large heavy skillet with cover. Sauté shallots and garlic in oil over medium heat until shallots are soft but not browned. Add tomatoes, thyme, basil, oregano, and pepper, to taste.

Arrange mussels on tomatoes; cover and cook until mussels have opened, about 4 minutes. Discard any mussels that do not open. Remove mussels from pan and keep warm. Add Cognac to tomato mixture and cook over high heat until reduced by one-half. Whisk in butter, one piece at a time. Place 8 mussels in each of 4 shallow serving bowls. Pour sauce over mussels and sprinkle with chopped parsley.

SERVES 4

Grilled Breast of Duck with Fresh Raspberry Shallot Sauce

Fresh or frozen duck breasts are available in many supermarkets and are wonderful to have on hand for summer grilling. The rich duck is marinated in red wine and thyme; the tart sauce is a blend of raspberry vinegar, shallots, and crème fraîche. A handful of fresh raspberries added at the end makes a beautiful garnish. Duck served this way should be the star of the meal, accompanied only by wild rice and a salad of summer greens.

1   cup red wine
4   sprigs fresh thyme
1   whole duck breast, boned with skin on
2   tablespoons (¼ stick) unsalted butter
8   shallots, finely minced
⅓   cup raspberry vinegar
1   tablespoon honey
¼   cup rich chicken stock (preferably homemade)
¼   cup crème fraîche
1   tablespoon chopped fresh parsley
1   cup fresh raspberries

In a glass bowl, combine wine and thyme. Marinate the duck breast in this mixture for 30 minutes. Remove duck breast, discarding marinade, and grill over a hot charcoal fire or under a preheated broiler for 7 to 9 minutes per side. (Be careful as the duck fat might cause the fire to flame up.) When the duck is done, remove it to a carving platter and keep warm.

In a heavy saucepan, melt butter over medium heat. Add shallots and sauté until wilted. Add the vinegar and cook over high heat until mixture is reduced to a syrup. Whisk in honey and chicken stock. Simmer for 1 minute.

Whisk in crème fraîche and parsley; simmer until sauce has been reduced and thickened slightly, about 5 minutes. Add raspberries and cook for 1 minute, stirring very gently. Season with salt and pepper, to taste.

Carve the duck in thin slices and spoon the sauce over the meat.

SERVES 2

Fresh Artichoke Soup with Shallots

This is a very pretty soup, subtle in color and flavor. The shallots and other herbs complement the sweet flavor of the artichokes and the toasted filberts (hazelnuts) add interest. Center your meal around this warming soup, following with a sprightly salad and several kinds of good bread and interesting cheese. For dessert, pour champagne or a fruity white wine over fresh strawberries in your prettiest goblet and garnish with a sprig of fresh mint.

5	large artichokes
1	quart chicken stock (preferably homemade)
2	cups beef stock (preferably homemade)
2	cups water
½	cup dry white wine
1	small boiling potato, peeled and diced
1	large onion, chopped
4	celery ribs, thinly sliced
6	shallots, chopped
2	tablespoons fresh lemon juice
1	teaspoon chopped fresh oregano
1	teaspoon chopped fresh marjoram
1	teaspoon chopped fresh thyme

Salt and freshly ground black pepper, to taste

½	cup heavy cream or crème fraîche
¼	cup toasted filberts, coarsely chopped

Cut off the stem and top of each artichoke. Trim the points with kitchen shears and remove the tough bottom leaves. Quarter the artichokes and remove and discard the chokes. In a large nonaluminum soup pot, combine remaining ingredients except cream and filberts.

Add artichoke quarters and bring to a boil. Reduce heat to simmer, cover, and cook for 1 hour or until artichokes are very tender.

Puree in batches in a food processor or blender. Strain the puree through a medium sieve. Return strained puree to the pot and add salt and pepper, to taste. Reheat and whisk in heavy cream. Stir until warmed through. Ladle into heated soup bowls and sprinkle with filberts.

SERVES 8

Crudité Shallots

The British devour gallons of spicy pickled onions with drafts of English beer. Pickled shallots are milder than onions, because the traditional malt vinegar is replaced by cider vinegar, resulting in a most unusual crudité. Store in a cool place for at least a week before serving.

2	pounds fresh shallots, peeled
1	tablespoon salt
2	cups cider vinegar
1½	cups water
⅓	cup sugar
1	tablespoon pickling spices
1	tablespoon whole mustard seeds
1	whole dried hot red chili pepper
6	whole black peppercorns
2	bay leaves

In a large bowl, combine shallots and salt. Cover and let stand overnight or for at least 8 hours. Rinse shallots repeatedly with cold water; drain on a cloth towel. In a saucepan, combine vinegar, water, sugar, pickling spices, mustard seeds, dried red chili pepper, and black peppercorns. Bring to a boil; reduce heat and simmer for 20 minutes.

Add shallots to pan and simmer for about 5 minutes until they are about half-cooked. Remove shallots with a slotted spoon and place in a sterilized quart jar along with the bay leaves. Pour the hot liquid over them, leaving ¼ inch of headspace; seal.

MAKES ABOUT 1 QUART

Cooking with Sorrel

For those who love sorrel, it's the star of the kitchen herb garden in the spring, evoking childhood memories of nibbling on sour grass. Sorrel is much like garlic, either loved with a passion or disdained with an equal passion. A staple in the French kitchen, sorrel tastes like sharp, sprightly spinach with a sour, lemony tang.

Sorrel can be overwhelming until you've acquired a taste for its sharp flavor; add it slowly, tasting as you go. A bit of chopped sorrel will hide the fact that you've omitted salt.

Keep a chiffonade of fresh sorrel, cooked in a skillet with a little unsalted butter until it literally melts, in the refrigerator to blend into soups, sauces, dips, and dressings; for filling an omelet; and for topping a baked potato or poached fish. Serve poached eggs on a bed of sorrel chiffonade that has been wilted with finely minced shallots for a summer brunch.

When whole large sorrel leaves are used as a wrapping for cooking, they impart a tenderizing effect as well as lending their subtle tartness for flavoring. Wrap jumbo sea scallops in large sorrel leaves. Steam-cook for 3 to 4 minutes and serve with a lime butter sauce. Use the tender leaves in place of lettuce in hot or cold sandwiches and hamburgers. Offer finely shredded sorrel for tacos and tostadas.

Tear the young leaves for salads of greens, cabbage, or potatoes, discarding the stems and center ribs of larger leaves. When using sorrel for a green or cabbage salad, wrap the washed leaves in paper towels and store in refrigerator to crisp before adding.

Cut back somewhat on the vinegar or lemon juice in the dressing. Shred fresh sorrel into radicchio leaves. Top with sliced fresh mushrooms and chopped fresh tomato that have been warmed in a little olive oil. Sprinkle lightly with red wine vinegar. Add salt and freshly ground black pepper, to taste.

Stir chopped fresh sorrel into your favorite gazpacho before chilling. Add shredded sorrel to a fish soup. Stir chopped sorrel into a beurre blanc to spoon over broiled salmon fillets. Additional fresh sorrel as a garnish will reinforce the clean flavor.

Try spinach and sorrel together for a subtle, flavorful combination. Add sorrel to creamed spinach, a spinach soufflé, or spinach soup or just wilt sorrel and spinach together and toss with unsalted butter and a few grains of grated nutmeg.

Sorrel is widely used in Russia; it's virtually unused in England, Italy, and other Mediterranean countries. The French use sorrel primarily in two ways: in soups and sauces. Their sorrel soup is a world classic, loved for its delicate sour taste. The soup is served hot or cold, enriched with a spoonful of crème fraîche or sour cream and chopped fresh sorrel.

To keep the bright green color of sorrel, quick cooking is essential. Heat will cause the color to fade quickly so add sorrel at the last minute.

Sorrel does not dry well. If your herb garden is prolific, you can freeze sorrel by pureeing the leaves; pack into freezer containers for a taste of summer during the dead of winter. Stir the puree into soups or mayonnaise to use as a sauce for poached fish or as a spread for sandwiches.

Red Snapper with Fresh Sorrel Sauce

A specialty of country inns and fine restaurants, grilled red snapper with a light sorrel sauce is easy to prepare and makes a lovely special dinner for two. If you own a fish grill, by all means use it. It makes turning the fish simple. Surround the fish with steamed baby vegetables for a colorful presentation; pour a fruity white wine.

1   2-pound red snapper
Vegetable oil, for brushing
Salt and freshly ground black pepper, to taste
Sorrel Sauce (recipe follows)

Brush fish well with oil and sprinkle with salt and pepper, to taste. Grill over hot coals or under a hot broiler for 10 to 12 minutes, turning once. Do not overcook. Transfer to heated serving platter and keep warm. Prepare sauce; spoon around fish and serve at once.

Sorrel sauce:
1   tablespoon butter
4   shallots, minced
¾   cup dry white wine
½   cup dry vermouth
16 young sorrel leaves, cut in chiffonade
¾   cup crème fraîche

Melt butter in a skillet. Sauté shallots. Add wine to deglaze pan. Add vermouth, sorrel, and crème fraîche. Cook until sauce thickens slightly.

SERVES 2

Scallop Salad with Sorrel Dressing

Ideal for salads, the tender leaves of raw sorrel impart their natural tartness to poached sea scallops in this colorful salad. The tangy, sour leaves are also in the dressing. Serve with crusty rolls and glasses of white wine for a casual summer luncheon on the patio.

1   pound sea scallops
½   cup dry white wine
½   cup water
2   shallots, finely minced
3   cups loosely packed small sorrel leaves
2   tablespoons white wine vinegar
2   teaspoons dry mustard
1   teaspoon sugar
½   cup olive oil
2   ripe avocados
2   large sweet red peppers, peeled and sliced in thin julienne strips
2   tablespoons chopped fresh chervil

Rinse scallops. In a large heavy skillet, combine wine, water, and shallots; bring to a boil. Add scallops; cover and poach for 5 minutes, or until scallops are just opaque in center when cut. Drain and chill until cold.

Rinse sorrel; trim off and discard any coarse stems. Chop enough leaves to make 2 tablespoons. Set aside. Wrap remaining sorrel leaves in paper towels, enclose in a plastic bag, and chill in the refrigerator to crisp.

In a food processor or blender, combine reserved 2 tablespoons chopped sorrel leaves, vinegar, dry mustard, and sugar. Process until mixture is a puree. With motor running, slowly add oil through the feed tube and process until well blended.

To assemble salads, place the sorrel on 4 chilled serving plates. Peel, pit, and slice avocados; fan out on the greens. Arrange the scallops and red peppers on plates. Drizzle each salad with prepared sorrel dressing and garnish with chopped chervil.

SERVES 4

Cooking with Tarragon

Tarragon, justifiably called the king of culinary herbs by the French, has earned its reputation as an incredibly sophisticated herb. Its mild licorice flavor is both mysterious and addictive. Think of a grilled salmon fillet cloaked with a classic béarnaise or tomato-tinged *sauce Choron*, a warm vegetable salad of green beans, baby corn, new potatoes, and cherry tomatoes with tarragon dressing, a simple omelet with fresh tarragon—all made memorable with lots and lots of fresh tarragon!

One of the four herbs of the blend of fresh or dried herbs known as *fines herbes* used in classic French cooking, tarragon's sweet, clean flavor is bold and full-bodied. Unlike many fresh herbs, tarragon stands up well to cooking; use it with some caution.

Chopped fresh tarragon adds just the right touch to tartar sauce, a pot of fresh tomato soup, or eggs scrambled with Brie. It has a natural ability to enhance strong-flavored foods such as duck, lamb, or seafood. Tarragon can also be used to enliven the flavor of earthy foods like beets, greens, and mushrooms. Add a sprig of fresh tarragon to a glass of tomato juice or use as a garnish for a Bloody Mary.

Tarragon vinegar is easily made by steeping whole sprigs of fresh tarragon and white vinegar in a covered glass jar for several weeks. Use the vinegar in salad dressings and sauces; the preserved tarragon can also be used and will keep indefinitely, submerged in the vinegar.

Add chopped tarragon to a fresh plum sauce to serve with roast lamb or pork. Include tarragon in the seasonings for salmon mousse or duck pâté. Quickly sauté julienned carrots, chayote, and yellow summer squash in unsalted butter and chopped fresh tarragon. Wrap salmon fillets in blanched lettuce leaves, grill over hot coals, and serve with a mustard-tarragon butter sauce. Stir-fry strips of boneless chicken breast, thinly sliced zucchini, and shredded carrot with fresh tarragon, garlic, and sliced onion. Serve over fluffy hot rice and drizzle with fresh lemon juice.

Drying tarragon emphasizes the licorice taste and haylike aroma at the expense of the more volatile oils; it's better to freeze your excess harvest. Tarragon sprigs can be frozen in airtight plastic bags with good results. The color will darken some, but the flavor will stay fresh for about four months. Snip it as needed for dishes that call for the fresh herb.

Beet Salad with Tarragon Crème Fraîche

Tarragon enhances the earthy flavor of fresh beets just plucked from the garden or the roadside vegetable stand. Since the beets are cooked only long enough to slip off their skins, this is essentially a raw beet salad—a simple idea that goes perfectly with the crème fraîche and tarragon dressing. Make this colorful salad part of a summer lunch with corn salad, thin herb bread and butter sandwiches, a soft cheese, black olives, and scallions.

1   pound fresh raw beets, tops removed
2   cups fresh salad greens, such as Boston
      lettuce, mâche, curly endive, etc., torn
      into bite-size pieces
⅓   cup crème fraîche
2   tablespoons chopped fresh tarragon
1   tablespoon raspberry or red wine vinegar
Salt and freshly ground pepper, to taste
¼   cup broken walnut pieces

Cover beets with boiling water and let stand for 1 minute. Peel and coarsely grate beets. Divide the torn greens among 4 salad plates. Arrange grated beets over the lettuce.

Meanwhile, in a small bowl, combine crème fraîche, tarragon, vinegar, and salt and pepper to taste. Drizzle the tarragon dressing over the salad and sprinkle with walnuts.

SERVES 4

Pear Appetizers with Fresh Tarragon Pesto

Pears and cheese are always a favorite combination but the unlikely addition of a fresh tarragon pesto and a loaf of crusty French bread results in the ultimate grilled cheese sandwich. Cut into triangles for an appetizer or serve in thick slices for a light supper or lunch.

3	large ripe pears
⅓	cup fresh lemon juice
1	20-inch-long loaf of French bread such as a baguette
½	cup chopped fresh tarragon
1½	cups chopped fresh parsley
2	garlic cloves, minced
½	cup freshly grated Parmesan cheese
½	cup olive oil
1	cup shredded Gruyère cheese
1	cup shredded Italian Fontina cheese

Coarsely ground black pepper, to taste

Peel, core, and slice pears. Place in bowl with lemon juice and turn to coat pears to prevent darkening. Slice bread in half lengthwise. Place on baking sheet and broil under preheated broiler about 6 inches from source of heat until toasted golden brown. Remove from oven and set aside.

In a food processor or blender, process tarragon, parsley, garlic, and Parmesan cheese. With the processor running, slowly add olive oil to form a smooth pesto. Spread pesto generously on toasted bread halves. Drain pears and arrange diagonally across bread.

Combine Gruyère and Fontina cheeses and sprinkle over pears. Generously sprinkle cheese with black pepper. Broil 8 inches from source of heat until cheese begins to melt. Cut into triangles and serve. Makes about 12 appetizer servings.

SERVES 4 TO 6 AS AN APPETIZER

Rhubarb Tarragon Ice

So many good cooks are rediscovering this red, sweet-sour fruit. Teamed here with pungent fresh tarragon, rhubarb provides a cleansing palate refresher as a midcourse sorbet or a light dessert. If fresh rhubarb is unavailable, you can substitute 3 10-ounce packages of frozen sliced rhubarb, thawed.

2	pounds fresh rhubarb
2	cups sweet dessert wine, such as a good quality port or sherry
⅔	cup superfine sugar
2	tablespoons fresh lemon juice
2	teaspoons minced fresh tarragon

Preheat oven to 350°.

Wash and trim rhubarb; cut into small pieces. Place in glass baking dish with cover; bake, covered, for about 25 minutes or until soft.

Process rhubarb and any juice in a food processor or blender until smooth. In a large bowl, combine processed rhubarb, wine, sugar, lemon juice, and tarragon. Mix well. Pour into a shallow, freezer-proof nonaluminum pan and freeze for 1 hour. With a mixer or wooden spoon, break up rhubarb puree and beat until frothy. Refreeze for 30 minutes. Beat again and freeze for 2 to 3 hours or until firm.

SERVES 6 TO 8

Steamed Seafood with Foamy Tarragon Sauce

Perfect for dieters and those who just prefer intense flavor without additional calories, this light version of béarnaise sauce enhances the flavor, aroma, and color of fresh seafood. Vegetables cooked in this manner emerge crisp, bright, and full of natural vitamins. A green salad and fresh fruit are all you need to complete this meal.

2   cups dry white wine
3   carrots, peeled and cut in fine julienne strips
2   white turnips, peeled and cut in fine julienne strips
3   celery ribs, cut in fine julienne strips
4   scallions, cut in fine julienne strips
Salt and freshly ground pepper, to taste
4   sprigs fresh tarragon
½   pound sea scallops
½   pound medium shrimp, shelled and deveined
12 hard-shell clams, well scrubbed
12 mussels, well scrubbed
3   egg yolks
1   tablespoon fresh lemon juice
2   tablespoons unsalted butter, cut into 3 pieces

Pour wine into the bottom of a steamer. Bring to a boil over medium-high heat. Place vegetables on steamer rack. Sprinkle with salt and pepper to taste and lay on tarragon sprigs. Cover and steam for 4–5 minutes.

Arrange seafood over vegetables; cover and steam for about 5 minutes or until scallops and shrimp are opaque and clams and mussels are open. Remove rack from steamer and keep vegetables and seafood warm. Cook steaming liquid over high heat until reduced to about ⅓ cup.

Transfer liquid to the top of a double boiler. Whisking rapidly, add egg yolks and lemon juice. Place over simmering water and cook, whisking constantly, until thickened. Add butter, one piece at a time, whisking constantly.

Arrange seafood on individual serving plates. Nap with sauce and garnish with steamed vegetables.

SERVES 4

Broiled Salmon Steaks with Sauce Choron

A tomato-tinged béarnaise sauce with lots of fresh tarragon served over salmon steaks, cut from the center of a fresh 6- to 7-pound salmon, makes both a visual and gustatory delight (right). Be sure to preheat the broiler— that way the salmon cooks quickly and evenly with the sweet meat remaining tender and moist.

Serve with cucumbers that have been quickly sautéed in unsalted butter and fresh chives. Offer a garden salad of radicchio and arugula (roquette) with baked goat cheese. For dessert, make a tangerine ice sprinkled with threads of candied tangerine peel.

Juice of 1½ lemons
2   center-cut salmon steaks, cut 1¼ inches thick
Salt and pepper, to taste
¼   cup white wine vinegar
2   tablespoons finely chopped shallots
2   tablespoons finely chopped fresh tarragon
2   egg yolks
2   tablespoons water
½   cup (1 stick) unsalted butter
1   small ripe tomato, peeled, seeded, and finely chopped
1   tablespoon finely chopped flat-leaf parsley

Preheat the broiler. Put salmon steaks on a broiler pan and squeeze on juice of ½ lemon. Season with salt and pepper, to taste.

To prepare sauce: Combine vinegar, shallots, and 1 tablespoon chopped tarragon in the top of a double boiler. Bring to a boil over medium heat and cook until liquid evaporates but shallots and tarragon are still moist. Remove from heat and cool. Add egg yolks and water to saucepan and cook over simmering water, whisking constantly.

Whisk in butter, juice of ½ lemon, and chopped tomato. Continue to cook over low heat, whisking constantly, for about 5 minutes or until sauce is thickened. Add salt and pepper, to taste. Stir in remaining 1 tablespoon tarragon and chopped parsley. Keep sauce warm while preparing salmon.

Broil the salmon steaks 4 inches from the source of heat for about 5 minutes. Turn the salmon, squeeze on juice of remaining ½ lemon, and cook 5 minutes more, or until fish is done.

To serve, nap sauce onto heated serving plate and top with broiled salmon. Serve at once.

SERVES 2

Orange Tarragon Chicken Breasts Stuffed with Wild Rice

Tarragon has a legendary affinity for chicken. Here, the accompanying sauce is lightened and the customary heavy cream found in recipes for chicken with tarragon sauce is replaced by fresh orange juice, which provides a sweet fresh taste perfectly accentuated by the fresh tarragon. Serve with whole roasted onions sprinkled with chopped red onion and steamed broccoli rabe. For dessert, offer a compote, such as Three Mint, Three Melon Balls (page 166).

3   tablespoons unsalted butter
2   garlic cloves, minced
½   cup wild rice
Water
¼   cup raisins
4   large chicken breasts, boned, with skin intact
Salt and freshly ground pepper, to taste
4   sprigs fresh tarragon
2   large shallots, finely chopped
1   cup dry white wine
1   cup fresh orange juice
1   tablespoon chopped fresh tarragon
1   teaspoon grated orange zest
Salt and pepper, to taste

In a heavy saucepan, sauté garlic in 1 tablespoon butter until soft but not browned. Cook rice in water to cover until tender; drain. Add rice and raisins to garlic mixture and stir to glaze. Set aside.

Preheat oven to 350°.

Lay chicken breasts skin side down on plastic wrap. Pound with a mallet to flatten. Arrange ¼ of rice mixture near one edge of a chicken breast. Lay a sprig of tarragon on rice and roll chicken up tightly to enclose rice and tarragon. Secure with toothpicks. Repeat with remaining breasts. In a heavy skillet, brown chicken rolls in 1 tablespoon butter, turning carefully to brown all sides. Remove toothpicks, transfer chicken to a shallow baking dish, and bake for 30 minutes, or until done.

Meanwhile, prepare sauce by melting the remaining 1 tablespoon butter in a large heavy saucepan over medium heat. Add shallots and stir until soft but not browned. Add wine and increase heat to high. Boil until reduced to a glaze, about 2 tablespoons. Add orange juice and boil until reduced to ½ cup. Add tarragon and orange zest. Continue cooking until sauce is thickened to desired consistency. Season with salt and pepper, to taste.

To serve, nap chicken breasts with orange sauce and garnish with additional fresh tarragon.

SERVES 4

Cooking with the Thymes

Fields of thyme dot the hillsides of Provence, the tiny flowers a target of eager bees from nearby hives, providing a never-ending supply of fresh thyme and marvelous thyme honey for chefs and Provençal cooks. Lemon thyme nestles in the rock garden near the kitchen door of a New England farmhouse, its pale lilac flowers attracting bees from a neighbor's hive, sending forth its lemony scent every time it's brushed. No matter where it's grown or what its variety, thyme is a favorite herb of good cooks—and bees—everywhere.

Nobody seems to agree on the flavor of thyme: some call it clovelike, others say the flavor is mintlike. All do agree that fresh thyme is pungent. Regarded as

a mandatory herb in French cooking, thyme is most often used as a background flavor, but more and more, cooks are discovering that it's wonderful alone when preparing soups, stews, roasts, or vegetables—especially yams, squash, onions, carrots, dried beans, and tomatoes.

An excellent choice for butters, dips, and vinegar, for meat, fish, and poultry, common thyme (most often used for cooking) has reached far beyond its Mediterranean origin and has become one of the most valuable kitchen herbs. Thyme is used extensively in Creole and Mexican dishes and is an essential ingredient in West Indian cuisine. Early American pioneers frequently used thyme. Cookbooks published back in the 1800s call for its use in corn fritters and clam chowder. They also suggest frying thyme in butter to pour over vegetables and boiled potatoes. In the first American cookbook, *American Cookery* by Amelia Simmons, published in 1796, thyme is regarded as "most useful . . . good in soups and stuffings."

Citrusy lemon thyme gives two flavors at once and is particularly nice for seasoning veal and poultry. Mixed with butter and a little Dijon mustard, it imparts a wonderful flavor to fish. It can also be used in desserts, poached fruits, and glazes where a lemon flavor would be acceptable. Another thyme variety often used in cooking is nutmeg thyme, with a faint flavor and fragrance of nutmeg. It is best used in sauces or desserts such as fruit tarts and custards. Oregano thyme is a favorite for marinara sauces and other tomato-based foods.

Add fresh thyme to New England or Boston clam chowder; use lemon thyme in a Provençal bouillabaisse full of mussels, clams, sea bass, and shrimp. Combine a generous tablespoon of chopped fresh thyme with milk for soaking soft-shell crabs before sautéeing them in unsalted butter—a simple, marvelous way of preparing this springtime delicacy from the Maryland shore.

In the Mediterranean and throughout the Caribbean, every market stall has bunches of fresh thyme tucked between colorful displays of vegetables. Combine fresh thyme and olive oil for basting grilled vegetables such as radicchio, peppers, eggplant, and tomatoes. Toss fresh thyme into pasta primavera for a light summer dinner on the terrace. Add fresh thyme to a chestnut and potato puree or a parsnip and pear puree, both dazzling complements to roast pork or game.

Quickly sauté veal scallops in unsalted butter with small sprigs of fresh thyme, deglaze the pan with white wine, and prepare a sauce with crème fraîche, chopped tomato, and a bit of Dijon mustard.

Stuff sweet red and yellow peppers with diced chicken that has been poached in thyme-infused chicken stock, then mixed with chopped fresh jalapeño peppers, minced garlic, chopped onion, chopped tomatoes, and shredded Monterey Jack cheese. Mix in chopped fresh thyme and oregano; bake at 350° for 45 minutes until peppers are soft.

Teamed with parsley, marjoram, and bay leaves, thyme is an essential herb of the classic bouquet garni. The tiny leaves have a warm, earthy smell and dry extremely well, losing only a little of their flavor intensity. Dried thyme is excellent on fish and shellfish, pork, and lamb. Crumble dried thyme leaves over a duck before roasting; stir the dried leaves into brioche batter for an interesting accompaniment to poultry or game.

Roasted Sea Bass with Lemon Thyme and Parsley Crust

Exploding with the flavors of Provence, this perfectly roasted fish arrives at the table with a savory crust of bread crumbs, lemon thyme, and parsley. Cooked this way, the sea bass stays moist and the herbs impart a delicate flavor to the flesh of the fish. The accompanying Tomato Sauce with Niçoise Olives (recipe follows) is very easy to make and is intensely flavored with sun-dried tomatoes.

Serve the sea bass with roasted new potatoes coated with olive oil, lots and lots of garlic, and chopped fresh rosemary. Offer a salad full of garden arugula (roquette) and a dessert of fresh blueberry pie, and you have the perfect menu for a summer meal, especially when accompanied by a chilled Chardonnay and lively table talk with good friends.

1   3–4-pound whole sea bass
Salt and pepper, to taste
1   tablespoon olive oil
½   cup chopped fresh parsley
2   tablespoons chopped fresh lemon thyme
1   cup coarse dry breadcrumbs

Tomato sauce with Niçoise *olives:*
⅓   cup olive oil
2   cups peeled and chopped fresh tomatoes
1   garlic clove, minced
6   ounces sun-dried tomatoes packed in oil, drained and cut into fine julienne strips
1   sprig fresh thyme
1   bay leaf
½   cup *Niçoise* olives, pitted and chopped

Sprinkle inside of fish with salt and pepper, to taste. Brush outside generously with oil. Combine parsley, garlic, and lemon thyme. Press herbs firmly into all sides of fish. Drizzle with additional oil and press on breadcrumbs.

Preheat oven to 400°.

Place fish in a lightly oiled baking pan and roast for 8 to 10 minutes, depending upon thickness. Then brown under the broiler about 6 inches from source of heat until crumbs are crusty and golden brown.

Meanwhile, in a large heavy skillet, heat the ⅓ cup olive oil. Add tomatoes, garlic, sun-dried tomatoes, thyme, and bay leaf. Cook for a few minutes, until the garlic has lost its raw taste. Add the olives and serve alongside each portion of grilled fish.

SERVES 4

Seafood and Sausage Gumbo

Every Cajun cook has a favorite recipe for gumbo. This version relies on the pungent flavor of thyme to stand up to the spiciness of the other ingredients. The addition of vinegar keeps the okra from becoming stringy. Start with oysters on the half shell, follow with a crisp green salad, and serve the gumbo over bowls of rice with plenty of crusty bread for mopping up the sauce.

6	tablespoons (¾ stick) butter
¼	cup all-purpose flour
1	large onion, chopped
3	celery ribs, chopped
1	large sweet green pepper, seeded and chopped
2	garlic cloves, minced
4	cups chicken stock (preferably homemade)
1	large tomato, peeled and chopped
½	tablespoon Tabasco
1	teaspoon paprika
¼	teaspoon cayenne pepper
1	tablespoon minced fresh thyme
½	teaspoon minced fresh oregano
¼	teaspoon dried hot red pepper flakes
1	bay leaf
2	tablespoons safflower oil
2	cups sliced fresh okra
1	teaspoon white vinegar
1	pound spicy sausage (such as andouille or kielbasa), cut into rounds
1	pound medium shrimp, peeled and deveined
½	pound cooked crabmeat, flaked

Salt and freshly ground black pepper, to taste
1 teaspoon gumbo filé powder
Hot cooked white rice

In a large, heavy soup pot, melt the butter over medium heat. Add the flour and stir until flour browns and forms a roux. Add the onion, celery, green pepper, and garlic. Stir and cook until onion is soft. Stir in the chicken stock and cook for 5 minutes, scraping the bottom of the pan for any browned bits. Add tomato, Tabasco, paprika, cayenne, thyme, oregano, dried red pepper, and bay leaf. Reduce heat and simmer for 5 minutes.

Meanwhile, in a large, heavy skillet, heat oil over medium heat. Add the okra and vinegar and cook for 5 to 6 minutes. Add cooked okra and any liquid to the soup pot.

Add the sausage to the soup pot; cover and cook over low heat for 45 to 60 minutes. Meanwhile, poach shrimp in boiling water to cover until just pink. Drain and add shrimp to soup pot along with flaked crabmeat. Taste and adjust seasoning, adding salt and pepper, to taste. Remove gumbo from heat and stir in filé powder. Let sit, covered, for 5 minutes. Spoon hot rice into individual soup bowls and ladle gumbo over.

SERVES 4 TO 6

Grilled Scallops with Light Thyme Sauce

Scallops are particularly suited for grilling; the fast cooking over hot coals seals in the juices, imparting a rich flavor. The aggressiveness of thyme adds the right flavor to the sauce.

Grill yellow crookneck squash and small heads of radicchio and serve with a loaf of herb bread and a soft white wine. End this summery meal with a fresh fruit tart.

½   cup dry white wine
½   cup chicken broth (preferably homemade)
2   shallots, minced
2   tablespoons minced fresh thyme
½   cup whipping cream or crème fraîche
¼   cup (½ stick) cold unsalted butter, cut into
    4 pieces
1½ pounds fresh sea scallops
¼   cup olive oil
2   tablespoons fresh lemon juice

In a large skillet, combine wine, broth, shallots, and thyme. Bring to a boil over high heat; continue to boil, uncovered, until reduced by half. Stir in cream and boil, uncovered, until reduced to about ¾ cup. Reduce heat to medium and whisk in butter, one piece at a time, stirring constantly after each addition until butter is melted. Keep warm by pouring into a glass measuring cup and setting in hot water.

Rinse scallops to remove any bits of shell or sand; pat dry with paper towels. Thread scallops onto metal skewers. Place on a well-oiled grill 4 to 6 inches above a solid bed of hot coals.

Combine olive oil and lemon juice. Baste scallops with lemon olive oil and cook, turning once, until scallops are opaque throughout. Cut to test for doneness after 5 to 7 minutes. Do not overcook. Pour prepared thyme sauce onto 4 warm serving plates. Lay scallops on sauce.

SERVES 4

Spinach and Strawberry Salad with Thyme Vinaigrette

The unlikely combination of spinach and fresh strawberries offers a wonderful flavor surprise for spring dinners when fresh strawberries are at their peak. The sweetness of the berry is a delightful contrast to the fresh flavor of spinach; fresh thyme adds an interesting accent.

It's a perfect light salad for a picnic in a meadow bursting with wildflowers. Pack thermos containers with duck curry and hot cooked rice. Accompany with little bowls of cashews, chopped scallions, fresh pineapple chunks, raisins, and grated fresh coconut. Offer a pretty basket of homemade cookies for dessert.

2   bunches fresh spinach, washed and torn
    into bite-size pieces
1   pint ripe fresh strawberries, washed, hulled,
    and halved lengthwise
½   cup olive oil
¼   cup white wine vinegar
½   teaspoon Dijon mustard
1   tablespoon chopped fresh thyme
1   small red onion, minced
Salt and pepper, to taste

In chilled individual salad plates, arrange well-drained spinach leaves and strawberries. In a small bowl, whisk together oil, vinegar, mustard, thyme, and red onion. Season with salt and pepper, to taste. Drizzle some of the vinaigrette over each salad and serve.

SERVES 4 TO 6

Puffed Apple Thyme Big Dutch Babies

This spectacular pancake is a variation of the Dutch Babies oven pancake, a recipe that originated at a family-run restaurant called Manca's in Seattle during the first half of this century. The batter puffs up dramatically in the oven and the addition of apples and thyme adds an interesting grace note.

Begin with sliced oranges topped with whole berry cranberry sauce and slice some country ham to go with the pancake.

¼   cup (½ stick) unsalted butter
3   eggs
¾   cup all-purpose flour
¾   cup milk
2   tart green apples (such as Granny Smith), thinly sliced and sprinkled with fresh lemon juice
¼   cup packed light brown sugar
2   tablespoons chopped fresh thyme
Warm maple syrup

Preheat oven to 425°.

Place butter in a 3-quart ovenproof pan such as a paella pan, iron frying pan, or shallow flat-bottomed baking dish. Set in oven until butter melts. Meanwhile, mix batter by combining eggs, flour, and milk in a bowl until just blended (batter will be lumpy).

Toss apple slices with brown sugar and thyme. Remove pan from the oven and pour in batter. Arrange apples in the center of the batter and bake the pancake for 20 to 25 minutes, depending on pan size, until puffed and golden brown. Cut into wedges and serve with warm maple syrup.

SERVES 4

Fresh Figs Poached in White Wine and Fresh Thyme

When in season, luscious fresh purple figs with rosy centers and soft green figs can be transformed into this marvelous, light dessert. Serve them cold with a dollop of softly whipped cream or crème fraîche.

¼   cup honey (preferably thyme honey)
1   bottle dry white wine
Continuous spiral of zest from 1 fresh lemon
2   tablespoons fresh lemon juice
6   sprigs fresh thyme
2   bay leaves
4   white peppercorns
2–2½ pounds fresh figs
Lightly whipped cream or crème fraîche

In a large, nonaluminum saucepan, combine honey and wine; bring to a boil. Lower heat and cook, stirring constantly, until honey is completely dissolved. Add lemon peel, lemon juice, thyme, bay leaves, and peppercorns.

Place figs in wine syrup and poach over low heat, uncovered, for 4 minutes, turning figs every minute. Remove figs with a slotted spoon and place in a ceramic bowl.

Reduce poaching liquid to about 1½ cups. Spoon over figs and chill. Serve figs with some of the poaching syrup in individual bowls, topped with whipped cream or crème fraîche.

SERVES 6 TO 8

Apples and Pears Sautéed with Fresh Nutmeg Thyme

Try this combination when red Bartlett pears from Oregon are in season for a fresh and chunky compote that's delicious when served still warm. Nutmeg thyme adds an interesting tone to the sweetness of the fruit, although lemon or common thyme could be used. Ready in minutes, this fruit sauté goes well with pork, country ham, game, or turkey. It's also delicious folded into crepes or omelets.

2   tablespoons butter
2   large Golden Delicious apples, cored and cut into thick slices
3   medium-size red pears, cored and cut into thick slices
1   tablespoon fresh lemon juice
4   teaspoons minced fresh nutmeg thyme

Melt butter in a heavy skillet over medium heat. Add apple slices and cook for 2 minutes. Stir in pears and lemon juice. Cook for another 2 minutes. Sprinkle with nutmeg thyme and cook for 1 minute. Serve warm.

SERVES 4

Oregano-Thyme Tomato Bread

Still warm from the oven, this fragrant herb bread is delicious served with sweet parsley butter. Any leftovers can be toasted the next day, spread with cream cheese, and sprinkled with chopped Greek olives for a quick hors d'oeuvre.

2   tablespoons olive oil
2   garlic cloves, minced
3   tablespoons minced fresh oregano thyme
1   tablespoon sugar
1   envelope active dry yeast
½   cup warm water (110°)
¾   pound ripe tomatoes, peeled, seeded, and pureed (about 1½ cups of puree)
2   teaspoons salt
3½–4½ cups all-purpose flour
Yellow cornmeal
1   egg, beaten with 1 tablespoon water, to glaze

Heat olive oil in a heavy skillet over medium heat. Add garlic and stir, cooking until garlic is soft but not browned. Stir in oregano thyme and set aside to cool.

In a large bowl, sprinkle ½ teaspoon sugar and yeast over warm water. Stir until yeast dissolves. Cover with a clean cloth and let stand until yeast foams, about 10 minutes. Stir in garlic-thyme mixture, tomato puree, and remaining sugar.

Combine salt and flour. Add flour, 1 cup at a time, and blend until dough is smooth and cleans the sides of the bowl. Turn out onto floured breadboard and knead until soft and elastic, about 10 minutes, adding more flour as necessary to keep dough from sticking to the board. Lightly oil a large bowl with olive oil and place dough in prepared bowl. Turn to coat all sides with oil. Cover with a clean cloth and let stand in a warm, draft-free area until dough doubles in volume, about 1½ to 2 hours.

Punch dough down and turn out onto floured board. Knead for 3 minutes. Shape dough into a large smooth round and flatten slightly. Sprinkle an ungreased baking sheet with cornmeal and place dough on cornmeal. Cover with a clean cloth and return to the warm, draft-free area until the loaf has almost doubled in size, about 45 minutes.

Preheat oven to 400°, positioning rack in the center of the oven.

Brush loaf with egg glaze and bake for 15 minutes. Reduce oven temperature to 350° and continue baking for about 30 minutes, or until the loaf sounds hollow when tapped and has a deep orange color. If loaf browns too quickly, cover loosely with a sheet of aluminum foil. Cool on a rack and serve slightly warm.

MAKES 1 LARGE ROUND LOAF

Cooking with Other Herbs and Edible Flowers

Borage: Best loved by cooks (the bees love it too!) for its pinkish buds that explode into vivid blue star blossoms and the gloriously scented vinegar that it makes, borage has little further use in the kitchen other than for tea or salads.

Tea made from fresh borage is mildly spicy; add a sprig of mint for better flavor. The leaves have a faint taste of cucumber and can be added to salads or vegetables. But it's the borage flowers that star. Scatter them onto salads, puddings, and ice cream.

Chili Peppers: Hot red peppers are becoming increasingly important in the kitchen with the growing interest in the hot, spicy foods of Mexico, the American Southwest, Thailand, and India.

Sprinkle the dried flakes into the pot when you're preparing shrimp for a salad or shrimp cocktail. Use the flakes on pizza and grilled rabbit. Add to eggs when making an omelet or stir into apricot preserves for dipping batter-fried oysters and shrimp. Use fresh chilies in stir-fry dishes, tomato salsa, and sauces.

Festoons of shining red chilies are a part of many cooking cultures, belonging to the scenes of early California missions or Indian pueblos of the Southwest. The drying process is simple: tie the stems of the fresh chilies close together to create a massed effect (16 to 18 per strand). Loop one end of the twine over a hook in an area that is dry with air circulating freely around the strand (photo on page 221). Let hang for several weeks until the chilies darken to a glistening red-black hue and feel smooth and dry. The chilies will keep indefinitely. Cut off what you need.

Hyssop: Widely used in the Middle East and parts of Europe, hyssop is good with lamb and rabbit. In England, it's a traditional herb to use with cranberries. Add hyssop to fruit cups, pies, and drinks. It's one of the fresh herbs that get stronger as it cooks, so add it late in the cooking of stews and soup.

Lemongrass:
Lemongrass is the herb cook's discovery: stalks of tropical grass with an elusive lemon fragrance and flavor. It's more and more featured in herb gardens in tropical climates and more easily available in Oriental produce markets, supermarkets, and natural food stores.

Next time you're serving pork, try this Southeast Asian method: whirl together a mixture of fresh lemongrass, olive oil, onion, garlic, roasted peanuts, black pepper, and a little Chinese five-spice powder. Marinate pieces of boneless pork in this mixture for several hours; thread onto metal skewers with small white onions and cherry tomatoes. Grill for 15 minutes, basting with the marinade. Serve over hot rice with a sauce made from equal parts of soy sauce and lime juice, minced garlic, and finely shredded carrot.

Lavender:
Fresh lavender has offbeat culinary uses, mainly in salads and vinegar.

Sprinkle the chopped flowers over fruit compotes or fresh cooked peas or onto roast beef or lamb before roasting. Many great cooks in Provence blend lavender with rosemary and fennel seeds for roasting meat and fish.

Fresh blackberry ice cream with lavender flowers:
¾   cup superfine sugar
2   cups heavy cream or half and half
4   cups fresh blackberries
Fresh lavender flowers, for garnish

Stir the sugar into cream or half and half until sugar dissolves. Puree blackberries in a blender or food processor. Strain through a fine sieve.

Add puree to cream mixture. Freeze in an ice-cream machine according to the manufacturer's directions. Serve in small bowls, sprinkled with lavender flowers.

MAKES ABOUT 1 QUART

Noodle salad with lemongrass peanut dressing:
1   pound linguine noodles
2   tablespoons peanut oil
1   cup shredded carrots
1   cup bean sprouts
1   cup thinly sliced radishes
1   cucumber, cut lengthwise into paper-thin strips (use a vegetable peeler)
1   bunch scallions, cut in fine julienne strips
1   sweet red pepper, cut in fine julienne strips
Pickled ginger (sold in Oriental sections of supermarkets and gourmet shops)
Lemongrass Peanut Dressing (recipe next page)

Cook noodles in boiling salted water until just tender. Drain and toss with peanut oil. Arrange noodles at one side of each of 4 large serving plates. Arrange the vegetables and a small amount of pickled ginger in mounds around the edge. Serve at room temperature with Lemongrass Peanut Dressing.

RECIPE FOR DRESSING FOLLOWS

Lemongrass Peanut Dressing:

2   garlic cloves, minced
4   shallots, minced
6   tablespoons creamy peanut butter
2   tablespoons soy sauce
3   tablespoons red wine vinegar
1   small fresh jalapeño pepper, minced
2   6-inch fresh lemongrass stalks
1   teaspoon sesame oil
2   tablespoons peanut oil
2   tablespoons dry sherry
1   teaspoon powdered wasabi (Japanese horseradish) mixed with 1 teaspoon water
½   cup chicken stock (preferably homemade)

Combine all ingredients in a food processor or blender until smooth. Cover and set aside. Do not refrigerate. Blend again before using.

SERVES 4

Purslane:

An herb that is often considered a weed by cooks, purslane actually has much culinary potential and has long been used by French and Mexican cooks in green salads and simple vegetable dishes. Expect a crisp texture and a sharp, almost hot, vinegary flavor.

Best just raw or very lightly cooked, purslane adds a tasty flavor to soups, scrambled eggs, or Mexican tomato sauce. Long cooking causes it to develop a slippery texture and change of color, so add the chopped leaves no sooner than the last minute of cooking time. Combine purslane with fresh sorrel for the French *potage bonne-femme*. Use the small, pretty yellow flowers for a garnish.

Nasturtiums:

Brilliant nasturtium blossoms in colors ranging from creamy white through various yellows and oranges to deep crimson are well established as a salad ingredient, scattered with abandon for a colorful, edible garnish. But nasturtiums also adapt to a variety of other culinary uses.

The beautiful leaves of the nasturtium carry the mild peppery bite of watercress while the flowers add a mellow flavor of honey sweetness. The tender young leaves can be used in sandwiches and the large leaves (nasturtium plants often produce leaves up to 8 inches in diameter) are well suited to the centuries-old practice of cooking food, such as rice or seafood, in leaves. Be sure both leaves and blossoms are unsprayed.

Include some nasturtium leaves when making mayonnaise and use as a sauce for salmon or trout, over green vegetables, or as a dip for seafood or crudités.

Sprinkle the blossoms and small leaves over butter-sautéed fillets for a nippy garnish. Combined with cucumbers (cut in half lengthwise, with seeds removed, and thinly sliced) and a simple vinaigrette, shredded nasturtium leaves add a pleasing peppery taste. Garnish with the blossoms for color and snap.

Fill an omelet with nasturtium blossoms before folding. Garnish with a dollop of sour cream and nasturtium leaves and blossoms.

Violets:

Young violet leaves and flowers have a flavor similar to that of white pepper; both can be added to spring salads for a tasty garnish. The flowers can be candied to decorate ice cream, cakes, and puddings.

Candied violets:

Wash and dry violets thoroughly. With a soft camel's hair brush, paint egg white over each flower. Sprinkle with superfine sugar. Set on wax paper to dry. Store between layers of wax paper in a covered tin until ready to use.

Combining Fresh Herbs
in the Kitchen

Gourmet shops are full of bottles and jars of dried herb blends—*fines herbes, bouquet garni,* herbs for poultry stuffing, Tex-Mex blends, Cajun mixes, *herbes de Provence*—the list goes on and on. During the fresh season and after the harvest, herb blends can be easily made using the bounty of your kitchen herb garden.

Some pointers to keep in mind:

When experimenting with herb blends, remember to be a little stingy; it's easier to add more of a particular herb than to take some out.

Herb blends made with fresh herbs must be used within 1 week. Dried herb blends, stored in airtight containers away from strong sunlight, will keep for six months to a year.

Experiment with herb blends, combining herbs that you like best and think will taste good together. Usually, combinations of two or three herbs provide sufficient balance without the herb flavors clashing.

If you're replacing fresh herbs with dried herbs, use ⅓ of the amount called for with fresh herbs. The basic rule is 1 tablespoon fresh herbs for each teaspoon dried herbs, or 3 to 1.

Some favorite blends:

Sonoran Seasoning

This herb blend is excellent on grilled seafood, meats, poultry, and fresh vegetables. For a delicious potato topping, brush slices of partially cooked (simmered 10 minutes) potatoes with melted unsalted butter and sprinkle generously with Sonoran Seasoning. Bake in 425° oven until crisp, about 25 minutes.

1	tablespoon pure chili powder
1	tablespoon freshly ground black pepper
1	tablespoon cumin
3	tablespoons chopped fresh oregano
2	tablespoons chopped fresh thyme
5	tablespoons chopped fresh coriander (cilantro)
1	small fresh jalapeño chili pepper
2	garlic cloves, minced

Combine all ingredients in a blender or food processor. Grind finely. Store in a glass jar, tightly covered. Use within 1 week.

MAKES ABOUT 1 CUP

Bajan Seasoning

It seems that almost every island in the West Indies has its own special seasoning mix or hot sauce that adds character to its cuisine. The beautiful island of Barbados is no exception with this sensational combination of fresh herbs and hot peppers. Mix into mayonnaise for fish sauces or salad dressing; add to butter for basting meats, seafood, and poultry. There are hundreds of variations of Bajan seasonings—the one given here is more of a guide than an exact recipe. Thyme and parsley seem to be the key herbs; other herbs can be added or deleted, according to taste.

2	bunches scallions, coarsely chopped
¼	cup strained fresh lime juice
¼	cup minced fresh parsley
2	tablespoons minced fresh thyme
1	tablespoon minced fresh rosemary
1	garlic clove, minced
2	small fresh jalapeño chili peppers, seeded and minced
2	teaspoons paprika
¼	teaspoon Tabasco

Salt and freshly ground black pepper, to taste

In a food processor or blender, combine all ingredients until finely chopped. Store in a covered container in the refrigerator. Use within 1 week.

MAKES ABOUT 1 CUP

Country Blend

Use this fresh herb blend for salads, soups, and butter sauces for steamed fresh vegetables. Spoon into hot baked potatoes and forget the butter and salt.

4   tablespoons chopped fresh basil
4   tablespoons chopped fresh tarragon
4   tablespoons chopped fresh chervil
5   tablespoons chopped fresh thyme

Combine all herbs and refrigerate in an airtight container. Use within 1 week.

MAKES ABOUT 1 CUP

Fish Herbs

Add this herb blend to fish soup and sauces, use for court bouillon, and sprinkle onto fish or seafood before baking or grilling.

5   tablespoons chopped fresh basil
5   tablespoons chopped fresh fennel leaves
4   tablespoons chopped fresh flat-leaf parsley

Combine all herbs and refrigerate in an airtight container. Use within 1 week.

MAKES ABOUT 1 CUP

Stuffing Blend

This savory blend is good in soup as well as a basic herb mixture for stuffings to go with any poultry or fish. Sauté some of the mixture in unsalted butter and use as a sauce for grilled trout or swordfish.

6   tablespoons chopped fresh sage
1   tablespoon chopped fresh thyme
3   tablespoons chopped fresh sweet marjoram
2   tablespoons chopped fresh lovage
2   tablespoons chopped fresh flat-leaf parsley

Combine all herbs and refrigerate in an airtight container. Use within 1 week.

MAKES ABOUT 1 CUP

Pasta Perfect

Excellent for pasta sauces and fresh tomato sauce, this blend can be mixed with chopped carrots, garlic, and tomatoes for an excellent stuffing for fish or flank steak.

5   tablespoons chopped fresh basil
2   tablespoons chopped fresh thyme
3   tablespoons chopped fresh oregano
4   garlic cloves, minced
2   tablespoons chopped fresh flat-leaf parsley

Combine all ingredients. Refrigerate in an airtight container. Use within 1 week.

MAKES ABOUT 1 CUP

Herb Butters

Fresh herbs from the garden and unsalted butter—a savory combination that has thousands of possible uses. Once you've tried making herb butter, you'll serve it not only with bread, but with meats, fish, poultry, eggs, and vegetables. As a general rule, use ½ cup roughly chopped fresh herbs to ½ cup unsalted butter. Some herbs are easily creamed into softened butter; others require a few seconds in the food processor or blender. Some you'll want to infuse into melted butter. Experiment with fresh herb butters—that's part of the fun!

Fresh herb butters freeze exceptionally well for several weeks. If stored in the refrigerator, use within a day or two. Chill fresh herb butter before using to allow the flavors to mix.

Some favorites:

Basil Butter

Use this marvelous butter in vegetables and soups, and for sautéeing chicken or fish. Melt a teaspoon over poached eggs; use for scrambled or fried eggs.

½   cup (1 stick) unsalted butter, softened to room temperature
½   cup shredded fresh basil leaves

Combine butter and basil. Refrigerate for 3 hours before using.

MAKES ABOUT ½ CUP

Sage Butter

Zesty on seafood or chicken, this butter is also wonderful with hot biscuits or on pancakes and waffles.

½   cup (1 stick) unsalted butter, softened to room temperature
6   large fresh sage leaves, minced

Cream together butter and sage. Refrigerate for 3 hours before using.

MAKES ABOUT ½ CUP

Green Herb Butter

Fresh herbs, whirled with unsalted butter to make a delicate green spread for open-faced or tea sandwiches, provide a touch of freshness in flavor and appearance. Vary the herb according to the harvest. Here, mint is the herb to spread on thin-sliced rye bread for rare roast lamb sandwiches.

½   cup (1 stick) unsalted butter, softened to room temperature
½   cup lightly packed fresh mint leaves
1   teaspoon fresh lemon juice

Combine butter and mint in a blender or food processor until thoroughly mixed. Refrigerate for 3 hours before using.

MAKES ABOUT ¾ CUP

Tarragon Butter

Spread this butter on thin-sliced French bread and top with thinly sliced smoked turkey. Or, spread on whole wheat bread and top with thinly sliced tomatoes, sliced hard-cooked eggs, and chopped anchovies. It's equally delicious over grilled fish or chicken.

1   tablespoon minced shallot
2   tablespoons white wine vinegar
5   tablespoons minced fresh tarragon
½   cup (1 stick) unsalted butter, softened to room temperature

In a small saucepan, combine shallot and vinegar. Bring to a boil and cook until vinegar is absorbed. Let mixture cool. Stir tarragon and cream mixture into butter. Blend well. Pack into a small, covered container and refrigerate until ready to use.

MAKES ABOUT ½ CUP

Coriander (Cilantro) Butter

Huevos rancheros or scrambled eggs are worthy of this marvelous butter. Or, for a perfect lunch, spread on French bread and top with thinly sliced red onion and shredded Monterey Jack cheese. Broil until the cheese melts.

2   garlic cloves, unpeeled
½   cup (1 stick) unsalted butter, softened to room temperature
½   cup minced fresh coriander (cilantro) leaves
1   teaspoon fresh lemon juice

In a small saucepan, blanch garlic in boiling water for 10 minutes. Remove from water; cool and peel. Finely mince garlic. In a small bowl, cream butter. Add minced garlic, coriander, and lemon juice. Pack butter into a small, covered container and refrigerate until ready to use.

MAKES ABOUT ¾ CUP

Fines Herbes *Butter*

A heavenly mixture of fines herbes and unsalted butter— use this in the French tradition with fish, poached eggs, vegetables, meats, and of course, French bread.

½   cup salted butter, softened to room temperature
1   tablespoon chopped fresh chives
1   tablespoon chopped fresh parsley
1   tablespoon chopped fresh tarragon
1   tablespoon chopped fresh chervil

Combine butter and fresh herbs. Refrigerate for 3 hours before using.

MAKES ABOUT ½ CUP